PASS KEY TO THE GRE TEST

GRADUATE RECORD EXAMINATION

Third Edition

W9-AWG-215

Sharon Weiner Green
Former Instructor of English

Ira K. Wolf, Ph.D.
President, PowerPrep, Inc.
Former Professor of Mathematics
Former Director of University
  Teacher Preparation Program

**BARRON'S
EDUCATIONAL
SERIES, INC.**

All inquiries should be addressed to:
Barron's Educational Series, Inc.
250 Wireless Boulevard
Hauppauge, New York 11788
www.barronseduc.com

Library of Congress Catalog Card No.: 00-064177

International Standard Book No. 0-7641-0782-8

Library of Congress Cataloging-in-Publication Data

Green, Sharon.
    Pass key to the GRE, Graduate Record Examination / Sharon Weiner Green, Ira K. Wolf. — 3rd ed.
      p. cm.
    ISBN 0-7641-0782-8
    1. Graduate Record Examination—Study guides. I. Title: Barron's pass key to the GRE, Graduate Record Examination. II. Wolf, Ira K. III. Title.
LB2367.4.G75   2000
378.1'662—dc21   00-064177

PRINTED IN THE UNITED STATES OF AMERICA
9 8 7 6

CONTENTS

Preface   v
Acknowledgments   vi
Timetable for a Typical Computer-Based
   Graduate Record Examination   vii

1 / What You Need to Know About the GRE   1

An Overview of the Computer-Based
   GRE General Test   1
Commonly Asked Questions About the
   Computer-Based GRE   2
GRE Test Format   4
   Verbal Ability   4
   Quantitative Ability   6
   Analytical Ability   11

2 / Testing Tactics for the Computer-Based GRE   15

Before the Test   15
On the Day of the Test   16
Once the Test Has Started   17

3 / Verbal Ability: Tips and Practice   21

The Antonym Question   22
The Analogy Question   28
The Sentence Completion Question   34
The Reading Comprehension Question   39
Practice Questions   47

4 / Building Your Vocabulary	52
The GRE High-Frequency Word List	54

5 / Analytical Ability: Tactics and Practice	80
Analytical Reasoning	81
Logical Reasoning	97
Practice Questions	110

6 / Quantitative Ability: Tactics and Practice	119
Facts and Formulas	119
General Math Tactics	129
Discrete Quantitative Questions	143
Quantitative Comparison Questions	153
Data Interpretation Questions	169

7 / Test Yourself: Three Practice Tests	182
Model Test 1	185
Answer Key	217
Answer Explanations	217
Model Test 2	243
Answer Key	273
Answer Explanations	273
Model Test 3	295
Answer Key	324
Answer Explanations	324

PREFACE

Welcome to the brand-new third edition of Barron's *Pass Key to the GRE,* the compact version of Barron's *How to Prepare for the GRE.* Designed to give you access to up-to-the-minute information about the Graduate Record Examination, *Pass Key to the GRE* provides you with a short course in GRE preparation to meet your immediate needs.

It gives you an overview of the GRE General Test, answers key questions commonly asked by undergraduates, and explains everything you need to know about the computer-adaptive GRE.

It takes you step by step through dozens of verbal, mathematical, and analytical questions that simulate actual GRE questions, showing you how to solve them and how to avoid going wrong.

It provides you with dozens of proven, highlighted testing tactics that will help you attack the different types of questions on the GRE.

It offers you the newly revised, up-to-date, 333-word High Frequency Word List—333 words from *abate* to *zealot* that have been shown by computer analysis to occur and recur on actual published GREs.

It offers you an extensive mathematical review that provides a refresher course for students primarily involved in nonscientific disciplines.

Best of all, it offers you the opportunity to take three complete practice GREs so you can test yourself, answering questions that correspond to actual GRE questions in content, format, and level of difficulty.

Do not vacillate. As you prepare to vie for a place in a leading graduate school program, show your resolution to succeed by applying yourself sedulously to the contents of this book. Let Barron's *Pass Key to the GRE* open the door to graduate education for you.

ACKNOWLEDGMENTS

TIMETABLE FOR A TYPICAL COMPUTER-BASED GRADUATE RECORD EXAMINATION

Total Testing Time: 2 hours and 45 minutes,
3 hours, or 3 hours and 15 minutes

Section	Time Allowed	Description
	variable	*Tutorial*
1	30 minutes	*Verbal Ability* 6 sentence completion questions 7 analogy questions 8 reading comprehension questions 9 antonym questions
2	45 minutes	*Quantitative Ability* 14 quantitative comparison questions 10 discrete quantitative (standard multiple-choice) questions 4 data interpretation questions (tables/graphs)
		10-minute break
3	60 minutes	*Analytical Ability* 26 analytical reasoning questions 9 logical reasoning questions
4	30, 45, or 60 minutes	*Verbal, Quantitative, or Analytical Ability*

NOTE: On the actual GRE, these sections may appear in any order.

1

WHAT YOU NEED TO KNOW ABOUT THE GRE

AN OVERVIEW OF THE COMPUTER-BASED GRE GENERAL TEST

The computer-based GRE General Test is a multiple-choice examination designed to measure your verbal, quantitative, and analytical skills. High GRE scores strongly correlate with the probability of success in graduate school: the higher you score, the more likely you are to complete your graduate degree. For this reason, many graduate and professional schools require applicants to take the GRE General Test, a test now given only on computer. (They may also require you to take the new computer-based GRE Writing Test and/or a pencil-and-paper GRE Subject Test in your particular field. Subject Tests currently are available in 14 fields.)

The computer-based GRE General Test you take will have three, four, or five sections. There will always be

- a 30-question verbal section (30 minutes)
- a 28-question quantitative section (45 minutes)
- a 35-question analytical section (60 minutes)

In addition, there may be

- an unidentified experimental section, which would be a second verbal, quantitative, or analytical section
- an identified optional research section

The verbal section measures your ability to use words as tools in reasoning; you are tested not only on the extent of your vocabulary but on your ability to discern the relationships that exist both within written passages and among individual groups of words. The quantitative section measures your ability to use and reason with numbers or mathematical concepts; you are tested not on advanced mathematical theory but on general concepts expected to be part of everyone's academic background. The analytical section measures your ability to make rational assessments about unfamiliar, fictitious relationships and to think through arguments logically.

There are five very important points you should be aware of:

1. This is a computer-adaptive test; the test adapts to your skill level. It is customized. If you answer one or two questions correctly, the computer starts to select harder ones for you; if you get several questions wrong, the computer provides easier ones for you.

2. In each section, before you can move from one question to the next, you *must* answer the question currently on screen.

3. Once you have clicked on an answer and confirmed your choice, you *cannot* go back to that question and change your answer choice.

4. Not every question is worth the same number of points; harder questions are worth more than easy ones.

5. The GRE General Test does *not* penalize you for incorrect answers. Therefore, you should leave no question unanswered. When you don't know an answer, try to make an educated guess; if you can't, make a wild guess, and move on.

Keep these points in mind as you learn more about what's on the computer-based test, and, in the next chapter, about the tactics and strategies that will help you maximize your test score.

COMMONLY ASKED QUESTIONS ABOUT THE COMPUTER-BASED GRE

How Can I Learn to Handle the Mechanics of Taking a Computer-Based Test?

If you're unfamiliar with computerized testing, have no fear. Before you get to the actual computer-based GRE, you have to work through four tutorials that train you in the mechanics of taking this particular test. They are:

- How to Use a Mouse
- How to Select an Answer
- How to Use the Testing Tools
- How to Scroll

You can't skip these tutorials: They're mandatory, even for computer majors. They're also important: Every computer program has its idiosyncrasies, and you need to familiarize yourself with how to handle this particular computer setup.

Plan to take your time on these tutorials, and don't worry about how much time you're taking. The 20 to 30 minutes you spend working through the tutorials *before* you begin testing don't count against your time for taking the test.

Can I Tell How Well I'm Doing on the Test from the Sorts of Questions the Computer Is Assigning Me?

Don't even try. It never pays to try to second-guess a computer. There's no point in wasting time and energy wondering whether it's feeding you harder questions or easier ones. Let the computer keep track of how well you're doing: You concentrate on answering questions and pacing yourself.

Should I Guess?

Often you *must* guess. On the CBT, the screen displays only one question at a time. To get to the next question, you must answer the question currently on screen, even if you haven't a clue as to what the correct answer might be. So if the question on screen has you stumped, guess and don't worry whether you've guessed right or wrong. Your job is to get to the next question you *can* answer.

How Can I Determine the Unidentified Experimental Section?

You can't. Do not waste time in the exam room trying to identify the experimental section. If you are presented with four sections, do your best on all four.

When Can I Take the Computer-Based GRE?

You can take the computer-based GRE General Test almost any Monday through Saturday all year round. Telephone the Sylvan Candidate Services Call Center at 1-800-GRE-CALL (1-800-473-2255).

You can also register by mail to take the GRE. Simply complete the Computer-Based Test Authorization Voucher request located in the center of the *Registration and Information Bulletin* or download a registration form on-line at *www.gre.org*. Then mail the completed form and a check or money order for the appropriate fee (currently $99; $125 for test locations outside the United States and U.S. territories) to Graduate Record Examinations, Educational Testing Service, P.O. Box 6020, Princeton, NJ 08541-6020. You will receive your authorization voucher in two to three weeks and can then call Sylvan Candidate Services to schedule your test date.

How and When Are GRE Scores Reported?

The General Test raw score, the number of correct answers, is converted to a score on a scale of 200 to 800. With no correct answers at all, a student would still have a score of 200. With one or two incorrectly answered questions, a student could still have a score of 800. You receive separate scores (from 200 to 800) on the verbal, quantitative, and analytical reasoning sections. Your score report will include both your scaled scores and your percentile rank indicating the percent of examinees scoring below your scaled scores on the General Test.

As soon as you have finished taking the test, the computer will calculate your three scaled scores (verbal, quantitative, and analytical reasoning) and display them to you on screen. You should receive your official report confirming these scores in the mail approximately six weeks after the test date.

GRE TEST FORMAT

Verbal Ability

The verbal section consists of 30 questions. These fall into four types: antonyms, analogies, sentence completions, and reading comprehension questions. Your academic success will depend on your verbal abilities, especially your ability to understand scholarly prose and to work with specialized and technical vocabulary.

Here is how the 30-question verbal section generally breaks down:

- 8 – 10 antonym questions
- 6 – 8 analogy questions
- 5 – 7 sentence completion questions
- 6 – 10 reading comprehension questions (based on two to four passages)

Although the amount of time spent on each type of question varies from person to person, in general, antonyms take the least time, then analogies, then sentence completions, and, finally, reading comprehension questions.

Antonym Questions

The antonym questions are the most straightforward vocabulary questions on the test. You are given a word and must choose, from the five choices that follow it, the best antonym (opposite). Some of these words may be totally unfamiliar to you.

Analogy Questions

Like antonyms, analogy questions are vocabulary questions. They test your understanding of the relationships among words and ideas. You are given one pair of words and must choose another pair that is related in the same way. Many relationships are possible. The two terms in the pair can be synonyms; one term can be a cause, the other the effect; one can be a tool, the other the worker who uses the tool.

Sentence Completion Questions

The sentence completion questions ask you to choose the best way to complete a sentence from which one or two words have been omitted. These questions test a combination of reading comprehension skills and vocabulary. You must be able to recognize the logic, style, and tone of the sentence so that you will be able to choose the answer that makes sense in context. You must also be able to recognize differences in usage. The sentences cover a wide variety of topics from a number of academic fields. They do not, however, test specific academic knowledge. You may feel more comfortable if you are familiar with the topic the sentence is discussing, but you should be able to handle any of the sentences using your knowledge of the English language.

Reading Comprehension Questions

Reading comprehension questions test your ability to understand and interpret what you read. This is probably the most important ability you will need in graduate school and afterward.

Although the passages may encompass any subject matter, you do not need to know anything about the subject discussed in the passage in order to answer the questions on that passage. The purpose of the questions is to test your reading ability, not your knowledge of history, science, literature, or art.

Quantitative Ability

The quantitative section consists of 28 questions:

- 14 quantitative comparison questions
- 10 discrete quantitative questions (another name for standard multiple-choice questions)
- 4 data interpretation questions

In order to answer these questions, you need to know arithmetic, some very elementary algebra, and a little geometry. Most of this material you learned in elementary and middle school. You do not need to know any advanced mathematics. The questions are intended to determine if you have a basic knowledge of elementary mathematics, and if you have the ability to reason clearly.

Quantitative Comparison Questions

Of the 28 mathematics questions on the GRE, half of them (14) are what is known as quantitative comparisons. It is very likely that you have not seen such a question since you were in high school preparing for the SAT I; if you didn't have to take the SAT I, it is possible that you have never even seen a quantitative comparison. Therefore, read these instructions *very* carefully.

In these questions there are two quantities, one in Column A and one in Column B, and it is your job to compare them. For these problems there are *only four possible answers:*

> The quantity in Column A is greater;
> The quantity in Column B is greater;
> The two quantities are equal; and
> The relationship cannot be determined from the information given.

In this book, these four answer choices will be referred to as A, B, C, and D, respectively. In some of the questions, information about the quantities being compared is centered above the columns. This information *must* be taken into consideration when comparing the two quantities.

Column A	Column B
$(3 + 4)^2$	$3^2 + 4^2$

$(7)^2 = 49$ $9 + 16 = 25$

- Evaluate each column: $(3 + 4)^2 = 7^2 = 49$, whereas $3^2 + 4^2 = 9 + 16 = 25$.
- Since $49 > 25$, the quantity in Column A is greater. The answer is A.

Average = Mean

Column A	Column B
$a + b = 16$	
The average (arithmetic mean) of a and b	8

The quantity in Column A is the average of a and b: $\frac{a + b}{2}$. Since we are told that $a + b = 16$, the quantity in Column A is $\frac{a + b}{2} = \frac{16}{2} = 8$.

So, the quantities in Columns A and B are equal. The answer is C.

    NOTE: We cannot determine the value of either a or b; all we know is that their sum is 16. Perhaps $a = 10$ and $b = 6$, or $a = 0$ and

$b = 16$, or $a = -4$ and $b = 20$. *It doesn't matter.* The average of 10 and 6 is 8; the average of 0 and 16 is 8; and the average of -4 and 20 is 8. Since $a + b$ is 16, the average of a and b is 8, *all the time, no matter what.* The answer, therefore, is C.

Column A	Column B

- If $a = 1$, $a^3 = 1$ and $a^2 = 1$. *In this case,* the quantities in the two columns are equal.
- This means that the answer to this problem *cannot* be A or B. Why?
- The answer can be A (or B) only if the quantity in Column A (or B) is greater *all the time.* But it isn't — not when $a = 1$.
- So, is the answer C? *Maybe.* But for the answer to be C, the quantities would have to be equal *all the time.* Are they?
- No. If $a = 2$, $a^3 = 8$ and $a^2 = 4$, and *in this case* the two quantities are *not equal.*
- The answer, therefore, is D.

Discrete Quantitative Questions

Of the 28 mathematics questions on the GRE, 10 are standard multiple-choice questions, what the ETS calls discrete quantitative questions. The way to answer such a question is to do the necessary work, get the solution, and then look at the five choices to find your answer.

> Edison High School has 840 students, and the ratio of the number of students taking Spanish to the number not taking Spanish is 4:3. How many of the students take Spanish?
>
> (A) 280   (B) 360   (C) 480   (D) 560   (E) 630

To solve this problem requires only that you understand what a ratio is. Ignore the fact that this is a multiple-choice question. *Don't even look at the choices.*

- Let $4x$ and $3x$ be the number of students taking and not taking Spanish, respectively.
- Then $4x + 3x = 840 \Rightarrow 7x = 840 \Rightarrow x = 120$.

- The number of students taking Spanish is $4 \times 120 = 480$.
- Having found the answer to be 480, *now look at the five choices,* see 480 listed as Choice C, click on that choice, and confirm your answer.

Another type of multiple-choice question that appears on the GRE is the Roman numeral-type question. These questions consist of three statements labeled I, II, and III. The five answer choices give various possibilities for which of the statements are true. Here is a typical example.

If x is negative, which of the following must be true?

    I. $x^3 < x^2$

    II. $x + \dfrac{1}{x} < 0$

    III. $x = \sqrt{x^2}$

(A) I only   (B) II only   (C) I and II only
(D) II and III only   (E) I, II, and III

To solve this problem, examine each statement independently, and think of it as a true-false question.

- If x is negative, x^3 is negative, and so *must* be less than x^2, which is positive. Statement I is true.
- If x is negative, so is $\dfrac{1}{x}$, and the sum of two negative numbers is negative. Statement II is true.
- The square root of a number is *never* negative, and so could *not possibly* equal x. Statement III is false.
- Only I and II are true. The answer is C.

Data Interpretation Questions

Four of the questions in the quantitative section are data interpretation questions. There are always two questions based on one set of data, and later in the section, two more questions based on a second set of data. As you might guess from their name, these questions are based on information provided in graphs, tables, or charts. The questions test your ability to interpret the data that have been provided. You will either have to do a calculation or make an inference from the given data.

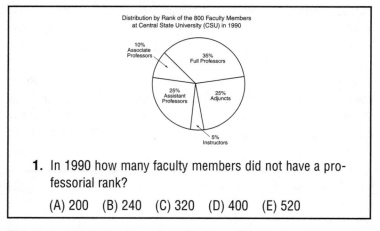

Distribution by Rank of the 800 Faculty Members
at Central State University (CSU) in 1990

10% Associate Professors

35% Full Professors

25% Assistant Professors

25% Adjuncts

5% Instructors

1. In 1990 how many faculty members did not have a professorial rank?

(A) 200   (B) 240   (C) 320   (D) 400   (E) 520

This is a straightforward question that can easily be answered by looking at the chart and doing a small calculation.

• In 1990, 30% of the faculty were not professors (5% were instructors and 25% were adjunct faculty).
• 30% of 800 = .30 × 800 = 240.

2. From 1990 to 2000 the number of faculty members at CSU increased by 20%. If the total number of assistant, associate, and full professors remained the same, and the number of instructors increased by 50%, how many adjunct faculty were there in 2000?

(A) 240   (B) 340   (C) 384   (D) 480   (E) 516

This question is more complicated and requires several calculations.

• Since the number of faculty members increased by 20%, in 2000 there were 960 people on the faculty (20% of 800 = 160, and 800 + 160 = 960).
• In 1990, there were 560 professors (70% of 800 = 560). So in 2000, there were also 560 professors.
• In 1990, there were 40 instructors (5% of 800 = 40); since that number increased by 50%, there were 60 instructors in 2000.
• Of the 960 faculty members in 2000, 560 were professors and 60 were instructors. The remaining 340 were adjuncts (960 − 560 − 60 = 340).

Analytical Ability

The analytical ability section consists of 35 questions:

- 26 analytical reasoning questions
- 9 logical reasoning questions

The analytical reasoning questions are always presented in sets of four or five questions based on a single set of conditions that remains on the screen as you answer each of the questions in that set. The logical reasoning questions are usually scattered throughout the section — one or two (occasionally three) separating the sets of analytical reasoning questions.

Analytical Reasoning Questions

Answering the four or five analytical reasoning questions based on a set of conditions is similar to trying to solve a logical puzzle. Because few students have ever seen questions such as these, and even fewer have ever tried to solve them, most students find the analytical reasoning questions to be the most difficult part of the GRE. Fortunately, there are many tactics available to help you solve these puzzles. To gain mastery and confidence, try the many sample problems in this book, and carefully study the explanations.

To illustrate what analytical reasoning questions are like, here is a typical set of conditions, followed by two questions. Remember, on the GRE there will always be four or five questions based on each set of conditions.

Michel Lubetzki, the personnel director of Computers.com has to interview six applicants — Burns, Cohen, Davis, Eckel, Fox, and Gavalas — for an opening in the data processing department. Each interview will take place on the same day. The interviews will be scheduled at 9:00, 10:00, 11:00, 1:00, 2:00, and 3:00, with a lunch break at noon. In making up the interview schedule, Mr. Lubetzki will be bound by the following conditions:

Fox will have the first interview in the afternoon.

Davis must be interviewed earlier in the day than Eckel.

> Burns must be interviewed earlier in the day than either Eckel or Fox.
>
> Cohen and Gavalas must be interviewed consecutively, and in that order.
>
> **1.** If Burns is only available at 10:00, in how many ways can the interviews be scheduled?
>
>   (A) 1   (B) 2   (C) 3   (D) 4   (E) 6

In order to keep them straight, write down the conditions on your scratch paper, but to save time, abbreviate as much as possible. For example, write only the first letter of each name, and use symbols, such as D < E to mean that D is interviewed before E.

In conjunction with the given, the added requirement that Burns be interviewed at 10:00 completely determines the schedule. Since Cohen and Gavalas need to be interviewed consecutively, their interviews must be at 2:00 and 3:00, respectively, the only two-hour slot available once Burns is scheduled at 10:00 and Fox at 1:00. Since Burns must interview before Eckel, Eckel has to be scheduled for 11:00, and the first interview of the day will go to Davis. There is only 1 possible schedule:

<u>D</u>	<u>B</u>	<u>E</u>	<u>F</u>	<u>C</u>	<u>G</u>
9	10	11	1	2	3

The answer is Choice A.

> **2.** If Gavalas has the last interview of the day, each of the following could be true EXCEPT
>
>   (A) Burns has the first interview of the day.
>   (B) Davis has the first interview of the day.
>   (C) Davis has his interview at 10:00.
>   (D) Eckel has her interview at 10:00.
>   (E) Cohen has his interview at 2:00.

If Gavalas has the last interview (at 3:00), then Cohen has his interview at 2:00. Since both Burns and Davis have their interviews before Eckel has hers, they must have their interviews at 9:00 and 10:00 (in either order), and Eckel must have hers at 11:00.

_	B/D	_	E	F	C	G
9		10	11	1	2	3

This shows that Choice E must be true, and that Choices A, B, and C could be true. Only Choice D cannot be true.

Logical Reasoning Questions

Logical reasoning questions are intended to test your ability to "understand, analyze, and evaluate arguments." This is usually accomplished by having you read a short passage, and answer a question that requires you to analyze the argument in that passage. As a result, logical reasoning questions look a lot like short reading comprehension questions, but they are really quite different. Occasionally, there are two questions that are based on the same passage, but, as in the following example, usually there is just one.

It has long been apparent that the nation's violent crime problem is disproportionately a juvenile crime problem. Those under age 18 constitute a fifth of the population, but account for nearly half of the arrests for the seven major crimes on which the FBI maintains national statistics. The statistical trend lines suggest the problem is growing; the number of juveniles arrested for murder and aggravated assault rose 82 percent and 91 percent respectively from 1967 to 1976. Yet, under the laws of most states, courts are obliged to treat these young hard-core hoodlums as if they were little worse than wayward delinquents.

Each of the following statements is an assumption made by the author EXCEPT

(A) Statistical trend lines are accurate predictors.
(B) 1967 to 1976 were not abnormal years.
(C) The laws of most states are consistent involving juveniles.
(D) The laws governing juvenile criminals are lenient in most states.
(E) The nation's nonviolent crime problem does not involve juveniles.

All of the statements except (E) are assumed by the author. He would not rely on statistical trend lines if they were not accurate predictors (A). If the years from 1967 to 1976 were abnormal years, his statistics would be suspect (B). The final sentence of his argument states that the laws in most states handle juveniles in the same manner and leniently (C) and (D). He does not address juveniles and nonviolent crime (E).

2

TESTING TACTICS FOR THE COMPUTER-BASED GRE

Before studying the specific tips that will enable you to do your best on this computer-based test or CBT, briefly review the key features of the exam:

- A typical CBT consists of 93 questions in three sections (plus an experimental section).
- The verbal section contains 30 questions: roughly 9 antonyms, 7 analogies, 6 sentence completions, 8 reading comprehension questions. These appear on screen in no set order: 2 sentence completions may be followed on screen by 2 antonyms.
- The mathematics section contains 28 questions: 14 are quantitative comparisons, 10 are standard multiple-choice questions, and 10 are data interpretation questions based on tables or graphs.
- The analytical section contains 35 questions: 26 analytical reasoning questions (puzzle-solving) and 9 logical reasoning questions (argument analysis).
- Because the CBT you take will be tailored to your skills, it may vary slightly from the typical test described above.
- You receive more credit for getting a hard question right than you do for answering an easy question correctly.
- You cannot skip questions; you must answer the question on screen and confirm that you are satisfied with your answer choice before you can proceed to the next question.
- Once you have confirmed an answer, you cannot go back and change it.

BEFORE THE TEST

Tactic 1

Schedule the Test for Your Best Time of Day
When you sign up to take the test on a specific date, you will be given a choice of time slots. Some people are morning people;

others work well in the midafternoon. Consider how your energy and alertness levels vary during the course of a day. Also, consider possible transportation problems, such as rush hour. With these and other relevant factors in mind, select the time slot that works best for you.

Tactic 2

Allow Yourself Enough Time for the Test
The GRE Bulletin recommends that you allow $4^1/2$ hours for the CBT. There are three scored sections on the test; there may also be one or two additional sections. These sections range in length from half an hour to a full hour each; you must also allow time for a ten-minute break midway through the session, as well as for the untimed tutorial on computer-based testing. You will also need up to half an hour for signing in, during which time you may be photographed and even fingerprinted! If you sign up to take the GRE at 8:00 a.m., do not make a dentist appointment for 12:00. You can't possibly get there on time, and you'll just spend the last hour of the test worrying about it.

Tactic 3

Get a Good Night's Sleep
The way to do your best on any test you ever take is to get a good night's sleep so you are well rested and alert.

Tactic 4

Memorize the Directions for Each Type of Question
These don't change. The test time you would spend reading the directions can be better spent answering the questions.

ON THE DAY OF THE TEST

Tactic 5

Take as Much Time as You Need to Work Through the Tutorials that Precede the Actual Test
The computerized GRE makes you work through four tutorials:

- How to Use a Mouse
- How to Select an Answer
- How to Use the Testing Tools
- How to Scroll

Remember you must complete these tutorials. They are mandatory, even if you are an expert in computer usage. And it can only be helpful to thoroughly familiarize yourself with these particular computer functions.

Tactic 6

Before You Move on from the Tutorial Section to the Actual Test, Take a Break

Raise your hand to let the proctor know you need assistance, and, when he or she comes up to your carrel, ask for a restroom break. Feel free to wash your face, nibble a quick snack, stretch, or do anything else that will relax you before you move into the test-taking mode. Any time out you take before the test actually starts is "free": it doesn't cost you any of that all important question-answering time.

ONCE THE TEST HAS STARTED

Tactic 7

Avoid Clicking on the Boxes at the Bottom Left of the Screen

As you will learn in the tutorial, there are six boxes at the bottom of the screen, three to the left and three to the right. They read, in order, from left to right: Quit, Exit, Time, Help, Confirm, Next. Avoid the ones to the left, especially the two leftmost ones. If you click on either of those boxes, you're abandoning ship, quitting either the particular section on which you're working or the whole test. There is no point in doing so. Even if you're dissatisfied with your performance and unwilling to have your scores sent to the graduate schools you selected, you still can use this test as a practice session. Don't bail out midway.

Tactic 8

Keep Track of the Time

Your job is to answer correctly as many questions as you can within the time allowed for that particular section of the test. Because of the computer-adaptive nature of the test, you can't simply skip time-consuming questions or questions that stump you, and hope to return to them if you have time left over. To move on to the next question, you must enter and confirm an answer for the question currently on your screen. Therefore, whenever you decide it's worth your while to spend time working through a complicated question, you've got to keep one eye on the clock to make sure getting this one answer correct isn't costing you too much time.

Tactic 9

Don't Get Bogged Down by Any One Question

Now more than ever it is important for you to avoid getting so caught up in figuring out one question that you lose track of the time. Remember, you can't move on to the next question until you've answered the one on screen. If a question is taking too long, guess at the answer and go on to the next question. This is not the time to prove that you can stick to a job no matter how long it takes.

Tactic 10

On the Other Hand, Don't Rush

Since your score will depend on how many *correct* answers you give *within a definite period* of time, speed and accuracy both count. Don't fall into the common errors born of haste. Read *all the answer choices,* not just some. Make sure you are answering *the question asked* and not one it may have reminded you of or one you thought was going to be asked. Write down key words like NOT and EXCEPT to make sure that you do not end up trying to answer the exact opposite of the question asked.

Tactic 11

Don't Be Trigger-Happy: Think Before You Click

Once you get into the swing of things, clicking "Next" to indicate you're ready to go on to the next question and "Confirm" to indicate that you're sure of your answer, watch out that you don't start double-clicking automatically. Take a moment to consider each answer choice.

Tactic 12

Be Especially Careful Answering Questions That Resemble Questions You've Seen Before

In the GRE, the test-makers test and retest the same concepts. They follow basic patterns, modifying questions subtly or substantially. Thus, in your CBT, you may come across questions that look very much like ones you have previously seen in published GREs or on *www.gre.org,* the GRE web site. You may even come across some that resemble questions you've just seen on an earlier section of your test. Don't assume that you know the answer to a question because it looks like one you've seen before. Read the question closely. Don't let subtle shifts in wording catch you unaware.

Tactic 13

Never Rush Through the First Questions of a Section

Remember, your answers to these initial questions have a greater impact on your score than your answers to the last few questions of the section do.

Tactic 14

Always Eliminate as Many Wrong Answers as You Can

Deciding between two choices is easier than deciding among five. Even if you have to guess, every answer you eliminate improves your chances of guessing correctly.

Tactic 15

Don't Waste Time Second-Guessing Yourself

Once you confirm an answer, that's it; you no longer have a chance to change that answer. If, later on in a section, you suddenly realize you got an earlier question wrong, don't sit there kicking yourself. Self-reproach is a waste of time. Remember, the only question you have to worry about is the one now on screen, so concentrate on it.

Similarly, don't try to second-guess the computer. There's no point in wasting time and energy wondering whether it's feeding you harder questions or easier ones. Let the computer keep track of how well you're doing. You concentrate on answering questions and pacing yourself.

Tactic 16

Be Alert for the Five-Minute Warning

Toward the end of each section, a brief flash of the clock will indicate that you have only five minutes left. Even if you have clicked "Time" to hide the remaining time display, the time display will come on automatically at this point. Also, instead of showing just the hours and minutes remaining, the display will change to show seconds as well.

Don't miss your five-minute warning signal. As you work through each section, be aware of the clock. When you are running out of time, eliminate any answer choices you can and then guess. At that point, even random guessing those last questions is better than leaving them unanswered.

3

VERBAL ABILITY: TIPS AND PRACTICE

In this chapter you'll learn how best to handle each type of verbal question, using strategies and tips that have helped thousands of GRE-takers before you. You'll feel confident taking the exam because you'll be familiar with the types of questions on it; your mind will switch easily into GRE gear.

Long-Range Strategy

The best way to have prepared for the verbal sections of the GRE is to have analyzed a great deal of good writing over the past five or ten years. As a lower division college student, you were exposed to a variety of fields, in the process increasing your vocabulary and growing accustomed to the way words are used in context. As an upper division student, however, you probably had to concentrate on your individual major. *Don't* limit your reading to your own field. Continue to expand your horizons, and, as you do, make a conscious effort to pay attention to the new words you encounter.

GENERAL TIPS FOR ANSWERING VERBAL QUESTIONS

1. An important point to remember when you are answering the verbal questions is that the test is looking for the best answer, the most likely answer. This is an inappropriate time for you to demonstrate your ingenuity by imagining exotic situations that would justify different answers. If you can imagine a bizarre situation that would make one of the sentence completion answers correct—forget it! This test is scored by a machine, and a machine has

absolutely no imagination or sense of humor. To a machine, an imaginative answer is a wrong answer. Stick to the most likely answer.

2. Remember also that correct answers to questions early in the section affect your score more than correct answers to questions towards the end. Take your time and get these initial answers right!

3. The reading comprehension questions take by far the most time. To make sure that you get to all the other questions, observe the following strategy:

 Consider random-guessing the answers to a pair of reading questions **without reading the passage** on which the questions are based. The time you save by doing so may allow you to come up with the correct answers to five or ten short-answer questions later in the section.

THE ANTONYM QUESTION

In the antonym question, you are looking for a word or phrase most nearly *opposite* in meaning to the capitalized word. You have five possible choices. Look at each one of them.

Long-Range Strategy

The key strategy for learning antonyms is (once again) READ. However, it is possible to fine-tune your vocabulary by exploring unabridged dictionaries, in which usage notes make clear the fine distinctions between related words, and by studying high-level vocabulary lists such as our High-Frequency Word List, more than 300 words that have occurred and reoccurred on GREs published in the 1980s and 1990s.

Use the High-Frequency Word List as a guide in making flash cards. Scan the list looking for words you recognize but cannot use in a sentence or define. You have a feel for these words—you are on the brink of knowing them. Effort you put into mastering such "borderline" words will pay off soon.

Pay particular attention to words you thought you knew—but didn't. See whether any of them are defined in an unexpected way. If they are, make a special note of them. As you know from the preceding chapters, the GRE often stumps students with questions based on unfamiliar meanings of familiar-looking words.

To improve the effectiveness of your flash-card sessions, try following these suggestions:

Writing the Flash Card
Be brief—but include all the information you need. On one side write the word. On the other side write a *concise* definition—two or three words at most—for each major meaning of the word you want to learn. Include an antonym, too: the synonym-antonym associations can help you remember both words. To fix the word in your mind, use it in a short phrase. Then write that phrase down.

Memorizing the Flash Card
Carry a few of your flash cards with you every day. Look them over whenever you have a spare moment or two. Work in short bursts. Try going through five flash cards at a time, shuffling through them rapidly so that you can build up your rapid sight recognition of the words for the test. You want these words and their antonyms to spring to your mind instantaneously, so that you can speed through the antonym questions on the GRE.

Test your memory: don't look at the back of the card unless you must. Go through your five cards several times a day. Then, when you have mastered two or three of the cards and have them down pat, set those cards aside and add a couple of new ones to your working pile. That way you will always be working with a limited group, but you won't be wasting time reviewing words you already recognize on sight.

Never try to master a whole stack of flash cards in one long cram session. It won't work.

TIPS TO HELP YOU COPE

1. Think of a context for the capitalized word. Take a quick look at the word in capital letters. If you don't recollect its meaning right away, try to think of a phrase or sentence in which you have heard it used. The context may help you come up with the word's meaning.
2. Before you look at the choices, think of antonyms for the capitalized word. If the question word is a word you

know, try quickly to think of opposites for it before you look at the answer choices. Even if you don't find those very words in the answers, you may find it easier to look for similar words (and to eliminate inappropriate ones).

3. Read all the choices before you decide which is best. A possible answer is not always the *best* answer. Words have shades of meaning. In matching a word with its opposite, you must pay attention to these shades of meaning. Check to see whether the connotations of the capitalized word are *directly contrary* to those of your answer choice. Suppose that the question word is *inchoate* and the answer choices include *fully in operation* and *inherently sensible*. Loosely, *inchoate* means lacking order or lacking full development. However, the salient feature of something inchoate is that it is *not yet* fully perfected or developed. Thus, *inchoate* is directly contrary in meaning to *fully in operation*.

4. Look at the answer choices to determine the main word's part of speech. Words may have more than one part of speech. If you don't know whether you're dealing with the common noun *harbor* or the less common verb *harbor* (give refuge to), look at the answer choices. They will all have the same part of speech.

5. Consider secondary meanings of the capitalized word as well as its primary meaning. If none of the answer choices seems right to you, take another look at the capitalized word. It may have more than one meaning. The GRE often constructs questions that make use of secondary, less well-known meanings of deceptively familiar words.

6. Break down unfamiliar words into recognizable parts. When you come upon a totally unfamiliar word, don't give up. Break it down and see if you recognize any of its parts. Pay particular attention to prefixes—word parts added to the beginning of a word—and to roots, the building blocks of the language. For example, if you know the root *ver*, truth, in the word *verify*, you can figure out that *veracity*, *veritable*, and *verisimilitude* must all have something to do with truth.

7. In eliminating answer choices, test words for their positive or negative connotations. When you are dealing with a partially unfamiliar word, a word that you cannot define

or use in a sentence but that you know you have seen previously, try to remember in what sort of context you have
seen that word. Did it have positive connotations, or did it
have a negative feel? If you are certain the capitalized
word has positive connotations, then, since you are looking for its antonym, you *know* the correct answer must
have negative ones. Thus, you can eliminate any answer
choices that have positive connotations and guess among
the answer choices that are negative in tone.

8. As always, watch out for eye-catchers, answer choices that
are designed to tempt the unwary into guessing wrong. Eye-
catchers are words that somehow remind you of the capitalized word. They're related in a way; they feel as if they
belong in the same set of words, the same *semantic field.*

Examples to Get You Started

Example 1

MAGNIFY:

(A) forgive
(B) comprehend
(C) extract
(D) diminish
(E) electrify

You need a context for *magnify.* The term "magnifying glass"
should immediately come to mind. A magnifying glass enlarges
things. The opposite of enlarging something is to make it smaller or
diminish it. The answer is Choice D.

Example 2

Suppose your word is *industrious,* hard-working. What opposites
come to your mind? You might come up with *lazy, idle, slothful,
inactive*—all words that mean lacking industry and energy.

Now look at the choices:

INDUSTRIOUS:

(A) stupid
(B) harsh
(C) indolent
(D) complex
(E) inexpensive

Lazy, idle, and slothful all are synonyms for *indolent.* Your correct answer is Choice C.

This tactic will help you even when you have to deal with unfamiliar words among your answer choices. Suppose you do not know the meaning of the word *indolent.* You know that one antonym for your key word *industrious* is *lazy.* Therefore, you know that you are looking for a word that means the same as *lazy.* At this point you can go through the answer choices eliminating answers that don't work.

Example 3

TRACTABLE: *docile, mild, easily guided*

(A) overwrought   (D) unruly
(B) mischievous   (E) indolent
(C) merciless

Suppose you have only a vague sense of the meaning of *tractable.* You associate it with such vaguely positive terms as *gentle, docile, amiable.* For this reason, you stop short when you come to Choice C. Reasoning that someone gentle and docile is *not* pitiless or *merciless*, you look no further and mark down Choice C.

Choice C, however, is incorrect. True, a tractable person is docile and easily guided, even mild. Someone who lacks docility, however, is not necessarily merciless. Such a person is difficult to guide, obstinate, in fact *unruly.* The correct answer is Choice D.

Example 4

APPROPRIATE:

(A) correct a flaw   (D) verify a statement
(B) endorse   (E) relinquish
(C) divert

Is the word in capitals the adjective *appropriate* (suitable, proper) or the verb *appropriate* (to set aside, acquire)?

A quick look at the answer choices reveals that it is a verb. (The *-ate* and *-ify* word endings are common verb endings.) One definition of the verb *appropriate* is to take something or make it particularly one's own, as in *appropriating money* or *appropriating land.* Thus, its opposite is to yield or *relinquish* something, Choice E.

Example 5 *lean to one side*

LIST:

(A) overturn
(B) be upright
(C) lie flat

(D) fall forward
(E) veer from side to side

List here has nothing to do with making lists or enumerating. It has to do with moving. When it *lists* to starboard, a ship simply leans to one side or tilts. The best antonym for this meaning of *list* is Choice B, *be upright.*

Example 6

SYNCHRONOUS:

(A) not in working order
(B) without problems
(C) out of position

(D) not in phase
(E) without permission

Syn- means together. *Chron-* means time. Something *synchronous* must have to do with occurring together in time, like the *synchronous* movements of swimmers keeping time with one another. The antonym for *synchronous* thus is Choice D, *not in phase.*

The word part approach can help you interpret new words you encounter. However, apply it cautiously. In many words the roots, prefixes, and suffixes have lost their original meanings. In others, the same root occurs, but with markedly differing effects. It would not do to call a *philanthropist* a *philanderer*, for instance, though both words contain the root for love.

Example 7

REDOUBTABLE: *awesome & imposing*

(A) unanticipated
(B) unambiguous
(C) unimposing

(D) inescapable
(E) immutable

Few test-takers attempting this question would answer it correctly. Why? Once more an early answer choice has been set up to tempt you. In this case, the presence of the familiar word *doubt* in the unfamiliar word *redoubtable* suggests that the word *redoubtable* has something to do with uncertainty. You know that *ambiguous* means uncertain in meaning. Thus, Choice B, *unambiguous*, is particularly appealing here. It is particularly appealing, and it is wrong.

Doubt in *redoubtable* is used in the sense not of uncertainty but of fear. A *redoubtable* foe causes fear; such a person is awesome or imposing. Someone *unimposing* causes no such fear. The correct answer is Choice C.

THE ANALOGY QUESTION

Analogy questions ask you to determine the relationship between a pair of words and then recognize a similar or parallel relationship between a different pair of words.

Some analogy questions are clear-cut. Others are quite complex. To answer them correctly involves far more than knowing single meanings of individual words: it involves knowing the usual contexts in which these words are found, and their connotations as well.

Long-Range Strategy

Continue to build up your vocabulary and to study the connotations as well as the literal meanings of words. Also, learn the common types of relationships that may exist between words.

1. Definition
   REFUGE : SHELTER
   A *refuge* (place of asylum) by definition *shelters*.
2. Defining Characteristic
   TIGER : CARNIVOROUS
   A *tiger* is defined as a *carnivorous* or meat-eating animal.
3. Class and Member
   AMPHIBIAN : SALAMANDER
   A *salamander* is an example of an *amphibian*.
4. Group and Member
   HOUND : PACK
   A *hound* is a member of a *pack*.
5. Antonyms
   WAX : WANE
   Wax, to grow larger, and *wane*, to dwindle, are opposites.

6. Antonym Variants
   NERVOUS : POISE
   Nervous means lacking in *poise*.

7. Synonyms
   MAGNIFICENT : GRANDIOSE
   Magnificent and *grandiose* are synonyms; they have the same meaning.

8. Synonym Variants
   VERBOSE : WORDINESS
   Someone *verbose* is wordy; he or she exhibits *wordiness*.

9. Degree of Intensity
   FLURRY : BLIZZARD
   A *flurry* or shower of snow is less extreme than a *blizzard*.

10. Part to Whole
    ISLAND : ARCHIPELAGO
    Many *islands* make up an *archipelago*.   *archipelago*

11. Function
    BALLAST : STABILITY
    Ballast provides *stability*.

12. Manner
    STRUT : WALK
    To *strut* is to *walk* proudly.

13. Action and Its Significance
    WINCE : PAIN
    A *wince* is a sign that one feels *pain*.

14. Worker and Article Created
    POET : SONNET
    A *poet* creates a *sonnet*.

15. Worker and Tool
    PAINTER : BRUSH
    A *painter* uses a *brush*.

16. Worker and Action
    ACROBAT : CARTWHEEL
    An *acrobat* performs a *cartwheel*.

17. Worker and Workplace
    MINER : QUARRY
    A *miner* works in a *quarry* or pit.

18. Tool and Its Action
    CROWBAR : PRY
    A *crowbar* is a tool used to *pry* things apart.
19. Cause and Effect
    SOPORIFIC : SLEEPINESS
    A *soporific* causes *sleepiness.*
20. Sex
    DOE : STAG
    A *doe* is a female deer; a *stag,* a male deer.
21. Age
    COLT : STALLION
    A *colt* is a young *stallion.*
22. Time Sequence
    CORONATION : REIGN
    The *coronation* precedes the *reign.*
23. Spatial Sequence
    ROOF : FOUNDATION
    The *roof* is the highest point of a house; the *foundation,* the lowest point.
24. Symbol and Quality It Represents
    DOVE : PEACE
    A *dove* is the symbol of *peace.*

TIPS TO HELP YOU COPE

1. Before you look at the choices, try to state the relationship between the capitalized words in a clear sentence. Then test the possible answers by seeing how well they fit in your sentence. Frequently, only one will make sense, and you will have the correct answer.
2. If more than one answer fits the relationship in your sentence, look for a narrower approach. Pay special attention to how a dictionary would define the words involved. Do not settle for what "may be" a good relationship. Precision is important in analogies: a *shard* is not merely a piece of pottery; it is a *broken-off* piece or fragment of pottery. Specify the relationship that exists "by definition."

3. Consider secondary meanings of words as well as their primary meanings. Frequently, the test-makers attempt to mislead you by using familiar words in relatively uncommon ways. When an apparently familiar word seems incongruous in a particular analogy, consider other definitions of that word.

4. Watch out for eye-catchers among your answer choices. When you look at answer choices, do you find that certain ones seem to leap right off the page? For example, if you're faced with the analogy ARMOR : BODY, does your eye jump straight to the answer choice *helmet : steel*? This is an eye-catcher, an answer choice that tempts you because it reminds you in some way of the original capitalized pair.

5. Look at the answer choices to determine a word's part of speech. In GRE analogy questions, the relationship between the parts of speech of the capitalized words and the parts of speech of the answer choices is identical. If your capitalized words are a noun and a verb, each of your answer pairs will be a noun and a verb. If they are an adjective and a noun, each of your answer pairs will be an adjective and a noun. If you can recognize the parts of speech in a single answer pair, you know the parts of speech of every other answer pair and of the original pair as well. The grammatical information built into the question can help you recognize analogy types and spot the use of unfamiliar or secondary meanings of words.

6. Eliminate answer choices whose terms are only casually linked. One of your basic GRE strategies is to eliminate as many wrong answer choices as you can. In the case of analogy questions, look for answer pairs whose terms lack a clear, defined relationship. In your capitalized pairs, the words are always clearly linked:

An island *is part of* an archipelago.
Something perfunctory *is lacking in* enthusiasm.
To gibe or sneer *is to exhibit* scorn.

In the answer pairs, the relationship between the words may sometimes seem casual at best. Discard such choices.

Examples to Get You Started

Example 1

TORRENT : DROPLET ::

(A) water : eddy
(B) swamp : desert
(C) downpour : puddle

(D) avalanche : pebble
(E) hurricane : wreckage

A *torrent* (violent downpour or rushing stream) is made up of *droplets*. An *avalanche* or sudden fall of rocks, snow or earth is made up of *pebbles*. Choice D is correct.

Don't let Choice C fool you: while a downpour, like a torrent, is a violent rain, it is not made up of puddles; rather, it leaves puddles in its aftermath.

Example 2

PSEUDOPOD : AMOEBA ::

(A) branch : tree
(B) minnow : fish
(C) bristle : hedgehog

(D) tentacle : octopus
(E) shell : snail

"A pseudopod is part of an amoeba." You have stated a relationship between the capitalized words in a sentence, but you have not stated a relationship that is precise enough. After all, branches are parts of trees, bristles are parts of hedgehogs, tentacles are parts of octopuses, and shells are parts of snails. Go back to the original pair of words for more details. How does an amoeba use a pseudopod? What function does it serve? "An amoeba uses a pseudopod for grasping." Try the answer choices in this new test sentence. "A tree uses a branch for grasping." False. "A hedgehog uses a bristle for grasping." False. "A snail uses its shell for grasping." False. "An octopus uses a tentacle for grasping." Choice D clearly is best.

Example 3

NEBULOUSNESS : DEFINITION ::

(A) apathy : zeal
(B) impetuosity : intuition
(C) penetration : depth

(D) rectitude : somberness
(E) rigidity : homogeneity

What relationship exists between *nebulousness* and *definition*? *Nebulousness* means haziness or indistinctness; a nebulous idea lacks clarity or sharpness. But what does haziness have to do with *definition*? After all, a definition is a statement of the meaning of a word or phrase.

Definition in fact possesses a secondary meaning: "sharp demarcation of outlines or limits; distinctness of outline or detail." With this meaning in mind, you can state the essential relationship between the capitalized words: *nebulousness* is a lack of *definition*. Analogously, *apathy* (indifference, lethargy) is a lack of *zeal* or enthusiasm. The correct answer is Choice A.

fret → mark decoratively

Example 4

EMBROIDER : FABRIC ::

(A) fret : wood
(B) spin : yarn
(C) refine : ore

(D) sculpt : chisel
(E) glaze : glass

Ostensibly, this is a simple analogy. One embroiders fabric to ornament it, embellishing it with needlework. The relationship between the capitalized words is clear. However, the bulk of the examinees responding to this question would answer it incorrectly. The problem lies not in the original analogy but in the answer pairs.

The actual answer is, surprisingly, Choice A, *fret : wood*; fret, as used here, means to mark decoratively, ornamenting a surface with interlaced designs, as cabinet makers decorate wood with interlaced patterns; fretting wood, thus, is directly analogous to embroidering fabric.

Sappers → attack and try to destroy

Example 5

SAP : VITALITY ::

(A) persevere : fortitude
(B) bore : tedium
(C) examine : opinion

(D) drain : resolve
(E) enhance : allure

At first glance, you might think that both *sap* and *vitality* were nouns; *sap*, after all, is a common noun (maple syrup comes from the *sap* of the maple tree), and *vitality* ends in *-ity*, a common noun suffix. However, *persevere* is clearly a verb. Simply from looking at the first answer choice, you know *sap* is a verb, not a noun.

What occurs when someone's vitality is sapped? It decreases and becomes weak. When vitality is sapped, it is undermined. Think of a fortress being undermined by military engineers; "sappers," the British army called them. Only one answer choice conveys this sense of something strong weakening: Choice D. If one's resolve (resolution, determination) is drained, it is depleted or undermined.

THE SENTENCE COMPLETION QUESTION

The sentence completion questions ask you to choose the best way to complete a sentence from which one or two words have been omitted. You have five possible choices. One fits *best.*

Long-Range Strategy

When you encounter a new word, don't just memorize its meaning in rote fashion. Study the way it is used, and then use it correctly yourself in three or more sentences. Try to work the word into conversations and discussions, even if it startles your friends. The way to make a word your own is to use it.

TIPS TO HELP YOU COPE

1. Before you look at the choices, read the sentence and think of a word that makes sense. The word you think of may not be the exact word that appears in the answer choices, but it probably will be similar in meaning to the right answer.
2. Look at all the possible answers before you make your final choice. You are looking for the word that *best* fits the meaning of the sentence as a whole. In order to be sure you have not been hasty in making your decision, substitute all the answer choices for the missing word. That way you can satisfy yourself that you have come up with the answer that best fits.
3. In double-blank sentences, go through the answers, testing the *first* word in each choice (and eliminating those that

don't fit). Read through the entire sentence. Then insert the first word of each answer pair in the sentence's first blank. Ask yourself whether this particular word makes sense in this blank. If the initial word of an answer pair makes no sense in the sentence, you can eliminate that answer pair.

4. Look for signal words indicating that one thing causes or logically determines another—words like *because, since, consequently*, and *hence*.

5. Look for words indicating that the omitted part of the sentence supports or continues a thought developed elsewhere in the sentence—words like *furthermore, moreover, likewise*, and *as well*. In such cases, a synonym or near-synonym for another word in the sentence may provide the correct answer.

6. Look for words explicitly or implicitly indicating a contrast between one idea and another—words like *although, however, nonetheless*, and *notwithstanding*, which set up a reversal of a thought, or words like *anomaly, incongruity*, and *paradox*, whose meaning inherently indicates a contrast. In such cases, an antonym or near-antonym for another word in the sentence may provide the correct answer.

7. Use your knowledge of word parts and parts of speech to get at the meanings of unfamiliar words. If a word used by the author is unfamiliar, or if an answer choice is unknown to you, break the word down into its component parts—prefixes, suffixes, roots—to see whether they provide a clue to its meaning. Change the unfamiliar word from one part of speech to another to see whether it is more recognizable in an alternate form. You may not recognize the noun *inebriety;* you probably are familiar with the adjective *inebriated.*

8. Break down complex sentences into simpler components. By rephrasing dependent clauses and long participial phrases, you wind up with short, simple sentences whose logical connections are easy to understand.

9. If a sentence contains a metaphor, check to see whether that metaphor controls the writer's choice of words (and your answer choice).

Examples to Get You Started

Example 1

Try coming up with your own word to complete the following sentence.

Because experience had convinced her that he was both self-seeking and avaricious, she rejected the notion that his donation had been
– – – – .

   This sentence presents a simple case of cause and effect. The key phrase here is *self-seeking and avaricious*. The woman has found the man to be selfish and greedy. *Therefore,* she refuses to believe he can do something – – – – . What words immediately come to mind? *Selfless, generous, charitable?*
   Now look at the answer choices:

(A) redundant   (D) ephemeral
(B) frivolous   (E) altruistic — *Selfless*
(C) inexpensive

   The missing word is, of course, *altruistic.* The woman expects him to be selfish (*self-seeking*) and greedy (*avaricious*), not altruistic (magnanimous). The correct answer is Choice E.

Example 2

When you're racing the clock, you feel like marking down the first correct-sounding answer you come across. *Don't.* You may be going too fast. *Never* decide on an answer before you have read all the choices.
   See how this tactic helps you deal with another question patterned on examples from the GRE.

The evil of class and race hatred must be eliminated while it is still in an – – – – state; otherwise it may grow to dangerous proportions.

(A) amorphous   (D) embryonic
(B) overt   (E) independent
(C) uncultivated

   On the basis of a loose sense of this sentence's meaning, you might be tempted to select Choice A. After all, this sentence basically

tells you that you should wipe out hatred before it gets too dangerous. Clearly, if hatred is vague or *amorphous*, it is less formidable
than if it is well-defined. However, this reading of the sentence is
inadequate: it fails to take into account the sentence's key phrase.

The key phrase here is *grow to dangerous proportions*. The writer
fears that class and race hatred may grow large enough to endanger
society. He wants us to wipe out this hatred before it is fully grown.
Examine each answer choice, eliminating those answers that carry no
suggestion that something lacks its full growth. Does *overt* suggest
that something isn't fully grown? No, it suggests that something is
obvious or evident. Does *uncultivated* suggest that something isn't
fully grown? No, it suggests that something is unrefined or growing
without proper care or training. Does *independent* suggest that
something isn't fully grown? No, it suggests that something is free
and unconstrained. Only one word suggests a lack of full growth:
embryonic (at a rudimentary, early stage of development). The correct
answer is Choice D.

Example 3

Dealing with double-blank sentences can be tricky. Testing the first
word of each answer pair may help you narrow things down.

Critics of the movie version of *The Color Purple* – – – – its saccha-
rine, overoptimistic mood as out of keeping with the novel's more
– – – – tone.

(A) applauded...somber   (D) denounced...sanguine
(B) condemned...hopeful   (E) decried...acerbic
(C) acclaimed...positive

For a quick, general sense of the opening clause, break it down.
What does it say? *Critics* – – – – *the movie's sugary sweet mood*.
How would critics react to something sugary sweet and over-
hopeful? They would disapprove. Your first missing word must be a
synonym for *disapprove*.
Now eliminate the misfits. Choices A and C fail to meet the test:
applauded and *acclaimed* signify approval, not disapproval. Choice
B, *condemned*, Choice D, *denounced*, and Choice E, *decried*, however, all express disapprobation; they require a second look.

To decide among choices B, D, and E, consider the second blank. The movie's sugary, overly hopeful mood is out of keeping with the novel's tone: the two moods disagree. Therefore, the novel's tone is not hopeful or sickly sweet. It is instead on the bitter or sour side; in a word, *acerbic*. The correct answer is clearly Choice E.

Remember, in double-blank sentences, the right answer must correctly fill **both** blanks. A wrong answer choice often includes one correct and one incorrect answer. ALWAYS test both words.

Example 4

Note the function of the implicit contrast signal in the following GRE question.

Paradoxically, the more – – – – the details this artist chooses, the better able she is to depict her fantastic, other-worldly landscapes.

   (A) ethereal   (D) extravagant
   (B) realistic   (E) sublime
   (C) fanciful

The artist creates imaginary landscapes that do not seem to belong to this world. We normally would expect the details comprising these landscapes to be as fantastic and supernatural as the landscapes themselves. But the truth of the matter, however, is paradoxical: it contradicts what we expect. The details she chooses are realistic, and the more realistic they are, the more fantastic the paintings become. The correct answer is Choice B.

Example 5

A knowledge of related words can help you deal with unfamiliar vocabulary in the following question.

This island is a colony; however, in most matters, it is – – – – and receives no orders from the mother country.

   (A) synoptic   (D) autonomous
   (B) methodical   (E) disinterested
   (C) heretical

First, eliminate any answer choices that are obviously incorrect. If a colony receives no orders from its mother country, it is essentially self-governing. It is not necessarily *methodical* or systematic, nor is it by definition *heretical* (unorthodox) or *disinterested* (impartial). Thus, you may rule out choices B, C, and E.

The two answer choices remaining may be unfamiliar to you. Analyze them, using what you know of related words. Choice A, *synoptic*, is related to the noun *synopsis*, a summary or abridgment. This has nothing to do with how a colony might govern itself. Choice D, *autonomous*, comes from the prefix *auto-* (self) and the root *nom-* (law). An autonomous nation is independent; it rules itself. Thus, the correct answer is *autonomous*, Choice D.

THE READING COMPREHENSION QUESTION

The reading comprehension questions take more time than any other questions on the test because you have to read an entire passage before you can answer them. They test your ability to understand what you read—both content and technique.

Long-Range Strategy

Read, Read, Read! Just do it.

There is no substitute for extensive reading as a preparation for the GRE and for graduate school. The only way to obtain proficiency in reading is by reading books of all kinds. The GRE tends to take its reading passages from *Scientific American*, from prestigious university presses (Harvard, Princeton, Oxford), and from scholarly journals. If you want to turn yourself into the kind of reader graduate schools are looking for, you must develop the habit of reading complex material—every day.

TIPS TO HELP YOU COPE

1. First read the passage; then read the questions. Reading the questions before you read the passage will not save you time. It will cost you time. If you read the questions first, when you turn to the passage you will have a number of question words and phrases dancing around in your

head. You will be so involved in trying to spot the places they occur in the passage that you will not be able to concentrate on comprehending the passage as a whole.

2. Read as rapidly as you can with understanding, but do not force yourself. Do not worry about the time element. If you worry about not finishing the test, you will begin to take shortcuts and miss the correct answer in your haste.

3. As you read the opening sentences, try to anticipate what the passage will be about. Ask yourself who or what the author is talking about.

4. As you continue reading, try to identify what *kind* of writing this is, what *techniques* are being used, who its intended *audience* may be, and what *feeling* (if any) the author has toward his subject. Try to retain names, dates, and places for quick reference later. In particular, try to remember where in the passage the author makes *major points*. Then, when you start looking for the phrase or sentence that will justify your choice of answer, you will be able to save time by going back to that section of the passage immediately without having to reread the entire selection.

5. When you tackle the questions, *go back to the passage* to verify your choice of answer. Do not rely on your memory alone.

6. Watch out for words or phrases in the question that can alert you to the kind of question being asked.

Questions asking about the main idea of the passage:
The main point of the passage is to . . .
The passage is primarily concerned with . . .
The author's primary purpose in this passage is to . . .
The chief theme of the passage can best be described as . . .
Which of the following titles best states the central idea . . .

Questions asking for information stated in the passage:
According to the author . . .
The author states all of the following EXCEPT . . .

According to the passage, which of the following is true of the...

Which of the following is NOT cited in the passage as evidence of . . .

Questions asking you to draw a conclusion:
It can be inferred from the passage that . . .
The author implies that . . .
The passage suggests that . . .
Which of the following statements about . . . can be inferred from the passage?
It can be argued that . . .
The author would most likely . . .
The author probably considers . . .

Questions asking how the author's ideas apply to other situations:
With which of the following aphorisms would the author be in strongest agreement?
The author's argument would be most weakened by the discovery of which of the following?
The author's contention would be most clearly strengthened if which of the following were found to be true?
Which of the following examples could best be substituted for the author's example of . . .

Questions asking about the author's emotional state:
The author's attitude toward . . . is . . .
The author regards the idea that . . . with . . .
The author's tone in the passage . . .

Questions asking about the passage's method of organization:
Which of the following best describes the development of this passage?
In presenting the argument, the author does all of the following EXCEPT . . .
The relationship between the second paragraph and the first paragraph can best be described as . . .
In the passage, the author makes the central point primarily by . . .

Questions asking about contextual meaning:

As used in the passage, the term . . . can best be described as . . .

The phrase . . . is used in the passage to mean that . . .

As used by the author, the term . . . refers to . . .

The author uses the phrase . . . to describe . . .

7. When asked to find the main idea, be sure to check the opening and summary sentences of each paragraph. Authors typically provide readers with a sentence that expresses a paragraph's main idea succinctly. Although such *topic sentences* may appear anywhere in the paragraph, readers customarily look for them in the opening or closing sentences.

   Note that in GRE reading passages, topic sentences are sometimes implied rather than stated directly. If you cannot find a topic sentence, ask yourself these questions:

   Who or what is this passage about?

   What aspect of this subject is the author talking about?

   What is the author trying to get across about this aspect of the subject?

8. When asked to choose a title, watch out for choices that are too specific or too broad. A paragraph is a group of sentences revolving around a central theme. An appropriate title for a paragraph, therefore, must express this central theme. It should be neither too broad nor too narrow in scope; it should be specific and yet comprehensive enough to include all the essential ideas presented by the sentences. A good title for a passage of two or more paragraphs should express the thoughts of ALL the paragraphs.

9. When asked about specific details in the passage, spot key words in the question and scan the passage to find them (or their synonyms). To answer questions about supporting details, you *must* find a word or group of words in the passage supporting your choice of answer. Do not be misled into choosing an answer (even one that makes good sense) if you cannot find it supported by the text.

10. When asked to make inferences, take as your answer what the passage logically suggests, not what it states

directly. Look for clues in the passage; then choose as your answer a statement that is a logical development of the information the author has provided.

11. When asked to determine questions of attitude, mood, or tone, look for words that convey emotion, express values, or paint pictures. These images and descriptive phrases get the author's feelings across.

12. When asked to give the meaning of an unfamiliar word, look for nearby context clues. Often authors will use an unfamiliar word and then immediately define it within the same sentence. The two words or groups of words are juxtaposed—set beside one another—to make their relationship clear. Often an unfamiliar word in one clause of a sentence will be defined or clarified in the sentence's other clause.

Examples to Get You Started

Example 1

Read the following passage, which examines the nature of visual recognition.

What is involved in the process of visual recognition? First, like computer data, visual memories of an object must be stored; then, a mechanism must exist for them to
Line   be retrieved. But how does this process work? The eye trig-
(5)   gers the nerves into action. This neural activity constructs a picture in the brain's memory system, an internal image of the object observed. When the eye once again confronts that object, the object is compared with its internal image; if the two images match, recognition takes place.
(10)   Among psychologists, the question as to whether visual recognition is a parallel, single-step operation or a sequential, step-by-step one is the subject of much debate. Gestalt psychologists contend that objects are perceived as wholes in a parallel operation: the internal image is matched with
(15)   the retinal impression in one single step. Psychologists of other schools, however, suggest the opposite, maintaining

that the individual features of an object are matched serially with the features of its internal image. Some experiments have demonstrated that the more well-known an object is,
(20)   the more holistic its internal image becomes, and the more parallel the process of recognition tends to be. Nonetheless, the bulk of the evidence appears to uphold the serial hypothesis, at least for simple objects that are relatively unfamiliar to the viewer.

Now look at the following question on a specific detail in the passage.

According to the passage, psychologists of the Gestalt school assume which of the following about the process of visual recognition?

I. The image an object makes on the retina is exactly the same as its internal image.
II. The mind recognizes a given object as a whole; it has no need to analyze the object's constituent parts individually.
III. The process of matching an object with its internal image takes place in a single step.

(A) II only
(B) III only
(C) I and III only
(D) II and III only
(E) I, II, and III

You can arrive at the correct answer to this question by elimination.

First, quickly scan the passage looking for the key word *Gestalt*. The sentence mentioning Gestalt psychologists states they maintain that objects are recognized as wholes in a parallel procedure. The sentence immediately preceding defines a parallel procedure as one that takes only one step.

Now examine the statements. Do Gestalt psychologists maintain that an object's retinal image is exactly the same as its internal image? Statement I is unsupported by the passage. Therefore, you can eliminate choices C and E.

Statement II is supported by the passage: lines 12–14 indicate that Gestalt psychologists believe objects are recognized as wholes. Therefore, you can eliminate Choice B.

Statement III is supported by the passage: lines 14–15 indicate that Gestalt psychologists believe matching is a parallel process that occurs in one step. Therefore, you can eliminate Choice A.

Only Choice D is left. It is the correct answer.

Note how necessary it is to point to specific lines in the passage when you answer questions on specific details.

Example 2

Try this relatively easy inference question, based on the previous passage about visual recognition.

One can infer from the passage that, in visual recognition, the process of matching

(A) requires neural inactivity

(B) cannot take place if an attribute of a familiar object has been altered in some way

(C) cannot occur when the observer looks at an object for the very first time

(D) has now been proven to necessitate both serial and parallel processes

(E) can only occur when the brain receives a retinal image as a single unit

Go through the answer choices, eliminating any choices that obviously contradict what the passage states or implies. Remember that in answering inference questions you must go beyond the obvious, beyond what the authors explicitly state, to look for logical implications of what they say.

Choice A is incorrect. Nothing in the passage suggests that the matching process requires or demands neural inactivity. Rather, the entire process of visual recognition, including the matching of images, requires neural *activity*.

Choice D is incorrect. It is clear from the passage that the matching process is not fully understood; nothing yet has been absolutely *proven*. The weight of the evidence seems to support the serial hypothesis, but controversy still surrounds the entire question.

Choice E is incorrect. It can be eliminated because it directly contradicts information in the passage stating that recognition most likely is a serial or step-by-step process rather than a parallel one receiving an image as a single unit.

Choices B and C are left. Which is a possible inference? Choice C seems a possible inference. Although the author never says so, it seems logical that you could not match an object if you had never seen it before. After all, if you had never seen the object before, you would have no prior internal image of it and would have nothing with which to match it. What of Choice B? Nothing in the passage mentions altering any attributes or features of a familiar object. Therefore, *on the basis of the passage* you have no way to deduce whether matching would or would not be possible if such a change took place. There is not enough information in the passage to justify Choice B as an inference. The correct answer is Choice C.

Example 3

Refer once more to the passage on visual recognition on page 43 to answer the following question.

> Which of the following phrases could best replace "the more holistic its internal image becomes" (line 20) without significantly changing the sentence's meaning?
>
> (A) the more its internal image increases in detail
> (B) the more integrated its internal image grows
> (C) the more its internal image decreases in size
> (D) the more it reflects its internal image
> (E) the more indistinct its internal image appears

What words or phrases in the vicinity of "the more holistic its internal image becomes" give you a clue to the phrase's meaning? The phrase immediately following, "becomes more parallel." If the recognition process becomes more parallel as an object becomes more familiar, then matching takes place in one step in which all the object's features are simultaneously transformed into a single internal representation. Thus, to say that an object's internal image becomes more holistic is to say that it becomes more integrated or whole. The correct answer is Choice B.

Look at the words in the immediate vicinity of the word or phrase you are defining. They will give you a sense of the meaning of the unfamiliar word.

PRACTICE QUESTIONS

The purpose of this section is to familiarize you with the kinds of questions that appear on the GRE by presenting practice questions closely modeled on actual questions from recent GREs. Knowing what to expect when you take the examination is an important step in preparing for the test and succeeding in it.

ANTONYM QUESTIONS

<u>Directions:</u> Each question below consists of a word printed in capital letters, followed by five lettered words or phrases. Choose the lettered word or phrase that is most nearly *opposite* in meaning to the word in capital letters.

1. QUIXOTIC:
- (A) slow
- (B) abstemious
- (C) pragmatic
- (D) benevolent
- (E) grave

2. DISPARITY:
- (A) timidity
- (B) complacency
- (C) bigotry
- (D) likeness
- (E) influence

3. CRITICAL:
- (A) unimportant
- (B) uncertain
- (C) silent
- (D) coherent
- (E) destructive

4. SOBRIETY:
- (A) influence
- (B) nonchalance
- (C) holiness
- (D) civility
- (E) mirth

5. RESTIVENESS:
- (A) completeness
- (B) conviction
- (C) concern
- (D) docility
- (E) petulance

ANALOGY QUESTIONS

Directions: In each of the following questions, a related pair of words or phrases is followed by five lettered pairs of words or phrases. Select the lettered pair that best expresses a relationship similar to that expressed in the original pair.

6. PERFORATE : HOLES ::

(A) speckle : spots
(B) evaporate : perfume
(C) decorate : rooms

(D) filter : water
(E) repent : sins

7. PUGNACIOUS : BATTLE ::

(A) timorous : beg
(B) loquacious : drink
(C) tenacious : persist

(D) veracious : lie
(E) wicked : survive

8. CLEARSIGHTED : PERSPICACITY ::

(A) daring : temerity
(B) reserved : impulsiveness
(C) transparent : opacity

(D) severe : clemency
(E) lethargic : energy

9. PLEAD : SUPPLIANT ::

(A) disperse : rioter
(B) shun : outcast
(C) revere : elder

(D) beg : philanthropist
(E) translate : interpreter

10. EPIGRAM : PITHY ::

(A) allegory : lengthy
(B) saga : heroic
(C) anecdote : humorous

(D) elegy : satiric
(E) proverb : modern

SENTENCE COMPLETION QUESTIONS

Directions: Each sentence below has one or two blanks, each blank indicating that something has been omitted. Beneath the sentence are five lettered words or sets of words. Choose the word or set of words for each blank that *best* fits the meaning of the sentence as a whole.

11. Her novel published to universal acclaim, her literary gifts acknowledged by the chief figures of the Harlem Renaissance, her reputation as yet - - - - by envious slights, Hurston clearly was at the - - - - of her career.

(A) undamaged...ebb
(B) untarnished...zenith
(C) untainted...extremity
(D) blackened...mercy
(E) unmarred...brink

12. Unlike the gregarious Capote, who was never happier than when he was in the center of a crowd of celebrities, Faulkner, in later years, grew somewhat - - - - and shunned company.

(A) congenial
(B) decorous
(C) dispassionate
(D) reclusive
(E) ambivalent

13. She is a pragmatist, as - - - - to base her future on impractical dreams as she would be to build a castle on shifting sand.

(A) determined
(B) disinclined
(C) quick
(D) apt
(E) diligent

14. During the middle of the eighteenth century, the - - - - style in furniture and architecture, marked by scrollwork and excessive decoration, flourished.

(A) austere
(B) functional
(C) medieval
(D) rococo
(E) abstract

15. Although eighteenth-century English society as a whole did not encourage learning for its own sake in women, nonetheless it illogically - - - - women's sad lack of education.
   (A) palliated
   (B) postulated
   (C) decried
   (D) brooked
   (E) vaunted

READING COMPREHENSION QUESTIONS

<u>Directions:</u> The passage is followed by questions based on its content. After reading the passage, choose the best answer to each question. Answer all questions following the passage on the basis of what is *stated* or *implied* in the passage.

"The emancipation of women," James Joyce told one of his friends, "has caused the greatest revolution in our time in the most important relationship there is—that between
Line men and women." Other modernists agreed: Virginia
(5) Woolf, claiming that in about 1910 "human character changed"; and, illustrating the new balance between the sexes, urged, "Read the 'Agamemnon,' and see whether...your sympathies are not almost entirely with Clytemnestra." D.H. Lawrence wrote, "perhaps the deepest
(10) fight for 2000 years and more, has been the fight for women's independence."

But if modernist writers considered women's revolt against men's domination one of their "greatest" and "deepest" themes, only recently—in perhaps the past 15
(15) years—has literary criticism begun to catch up with it. Not that the images of sexual antagonism that abound in modern literature have gone unremarked; far from it. But what we are able to see in literary works depends on the perspectives we bring to them, and now that women—
(20) enough to make a difference—are reforming canons and interpreting literature, the landscapes of literary history and the features of individual books have begun to change.

16. According to the passage, women are changing literary criticism by
   (A) noting instances of hostility between men and women
   (B) seeing literature from fresh points of view
   (C) studying the works of early twentieth-century writers
   (D) reviewing books written by feminists
   (E) resisting masculine influence

17. The author quotes James Joyce, Virginia Woolf, and D.H. Lawrence primarily in order to show that
   (A) these were feminist writers
   (B) although well-meaning, they were ineffectual
   (C) before the twentieth century, there was little interest in women's literature
   (D) modern literature is dependent on the women's movement
   (E) the interest in feminist issues is not new

18. The author's attitude toward women's reformation of literary canons can best be described as one of
   (A) ambivalence   (D) endorsement
   (B) antagonism   (E) skepticism
   (C) indifference

19. Which of the following titles best describes the content of the passage?
   (A) Modernist Writers and the Search for Equality
   (B) The Meaning of Literary Works
   (C) Toward a New Criticism
   (D) Women in Literature, from 1910 On
   (E) Transforming Literature: What Women See

Answers

1. **C**	6. **A**	11. **B**	16. **B**
2. **D**	7. **C**	12. **D**	17. **E**
3. **A**	8. **A**	13. **B**	18. **D**
4. **E**	9. **E**	14. **D**	19. **E**
5. **D**	10. **B**	15. **C**	

4

BUILDING YOUR VOCABULARY

Now that you have mastered the appropriate strategies for dealing with the four basic types of questions on the Graduate Record Examination that test your verbal ability, you have the opportunity to spend some time refining your vocabulary and acquainting yourself with the fine shades of meaning that words possess. Studies show that whereas the average high school graduate recognizes about 50,000 words, the average college graduate recognizes around 70,000. That indicates that during your four years of college you have rapidly acquired about 20,000 new words (many of them technical terms from a variety of disciplines), some of which may have connotations and nuances that still escape you.

Graduate school will tax your vocabulary building skills even further. To succeed in your graduate program, you must be able to absorb new words and concepts rapidly. The time you devote now to learning vocabulary-building techniques for the GRE will pay off later, and not just on the GRE. In this chapter you'll find a fundamental tool that will help you enlarge your vocabulary: Barron's GRE High-Frequency Word List.

No matter how little time you have before you take the GRE, you can familiarize yourself with the level of vocabulary you will confront on the test. Look over the words on our GRE High-Frequency Word List. Study them well: these words, ranging from everyday words such as *ambiguous* and *partisan* to less commonly known ones such as *aberrant* and *panegyric*, have occurred and reoccurred (as answer choices or as question words) in GREs published in the 1980s and 1990s.

Long-Range Strategy

There is only one effective long-range strategy for vocabulary building: READ. Read widely and well. Sample different subjects—astrophysics, sociobiology, Arthurian romances, art history—and different styles. Extensive reading is the one sure way to make your vocabulary grow.

As you read, however, take some time to acquaint yourself specifically with the sorts of words you must know to do well on the GRE. To get an idea of the level of vocabulary you must master, look over the High-Frequency Word List on the following pages.

TIPS TO HELP YOU COPE

For those of you who wish to work your way through the word list and feel the need for a plan, we recommend that you follow the procedure described below in order to use the list most profitably:

1. Divide the list into groups of 30 words.
2. Allot a definite time each day for the study of a group.
3. Devote at least one hour to each group.
4. First go through the group looking at the short, simple-looking words (6 letters at most). Mark those you don't know. In studying, pay particular attention to them.
5. Go through the group again looking at the longer words. Pay particular attention to words with more than one meaning and familiar-looking words that have unusual definitions that come as a surprise to you. Study these secondary definitions.
6. List unusual words on index cards that you can shuffle and review from time to time. (Study no more than 5 cards at a time.)
7. Use the illustrative sentences as models and make up new sentences of your own.
8. In making up new sentences, use familiar examples and be concrete: the junior high school band tuning up sounds *discordant;* Ebenezer Scrooge, before he reforms, is *parsimonious.*

For each word, the following is provided:

1. The word (printed in heavy type).
2. Its part of speech (abbreviated).

3. A brief definition.
4. A sentence illustrating the word's use.
5. Whenever appropriate, related words are provided, together with their parts of speech.

The word list is arranged in strict alphabetical order.

THE GRE HIGH-FREQUENCY WORD LIST

abate v. subside or moderate. Rather than leaving immediately, they waited for the storm to *abate*.

aberrant ADJ. abnormal or deviant. Given the *aberrant* nature of the data, we came to doubt the validity of the entire experiment.

abeyance N. suspended action. The deal was held in *abeyance* until her arrival.

abscond v. depart secretly and hide. The teller who *absconded* with the bonds went uncaptured until someone recognized him from his photograph on *America's Most Wanted.*

abstemious ADJ. sparing in eating and drinking; temperate. Concerned whether her vegetarian son's *abstemious* diet provided him with sufficient protein, the worried mother pressed food on him.

admonish v. warn; reprove. He *admonished* his listeners to change their wicked ways. admonition, N.

adulterate v. make impure by adding inferior or tainted substances. It is a crime to *adulterate* foods without informing the buyer; when consumers learned that Beechnut had *adulterated* its apple juice by mixing the juice with water, they protested vigorously. adulteration, N.

aesthetic ADJ. artistic; dealing with or capable of appreciating the beautiful. The beauty of Tiffany's stained glass appealed to Alice's *aesthetic* sense. aesthete, N.

aggregate v. gather; accumulate. Before the Wall Street scandals, dealers in so-called junk bonds managed to *aggregate* great wealth in short periods of time. also ADJ. aggregation, N.

alacrity N. cheerful promptness; eagerness. Phil and Dave were raring to get off to the mountains; they packed up their ski gear and climbed into the van with *alacrity*.

Ambi

alleviate v. relieve. This should *alleviate* the pain; if it does not, we shall have to use stronger drugs.

amalgamate v. combine; unite in one body. The unions will attempt to *amalgamate* their groups into one national body.

ambiguous ADJ. unclear or doubtful in meaning. His *ambiguous* instruction misled us; we did not know which road to take. ambiguity, N.

ambivalence N. the state of having contradictory or conflicting emotional attitudes. Torn between loving her parents one minute and hating them the next, she was confused by the *ambivalence* of her feelings. ambivalent, ADJ.

ameliorate v. improve. Many social workers have attempted to *ameliorate* the conditions of people living in the slums.

anachronism N. something or someone misplaced in time. Shakespeare's reference to clocks in *Julius Caesar* is an *anachronism;* no clocks existed in Caesar's time. anachronistic, ADJ.

analogous ADJ. comparable. She called our attention to the things that had been done in an *analogous* situation and recommended that we do the same.

anarchy N. absence of governing body; state of disorder. The assassination of the leaders led to a period of *anarchy.*

anomalous ADJ. abnormal; irregular. She was placed in the *anomalous* position of seeming to approve procedures that she despised.

antipathy N. aversion; dislike. Tom's extreme *antipathy* for disputes keeps him from getting into arguments with his temperamental wife. Noise in any form is *antipathetic* to him. Among his other *antipathies* are honking cars, boom boxes, and heavy metal rock.

apathy N. lack of caring; indifference. A firm believer in democratic government, she could not understand the *apathy* of people who never bothered to vote. apathetic, ADJ.

appease v. pacify or soothe; relieve. Tom and Jody tried to *appease* the crying baby by offering him one toy after another. However, he would not calm down until they *appeased* his hunger by giving him a bottle, appeasement, N.

apprise v. inform. When she was *apprised* of the dangerous weather conditions, she decided to postpone her trip.

approbation N. approval. Wanting her parents' regard, she looked for some sign of their *approbation.*

appropriate V. acquire; take possession of for one's own use. The ranch owners *appropriated* the lands that had originally been set aide for the Indian's use.

arduous ADJ. hard; strenuous. Her *arduous* efforts had sapped her energy.

artless ADJ. without guile; open and honest. Red Riding Hood's *artless* comment, "Grandma, what big eyes you have!" indicates the child's innocent surprise at her "grandmother's" changed appearance.

ascetic ADJ. practicing self-denial; austere. The wealthy, self-indulgent young man felt oddly drawn to the strict, *ascetic* life led by members of some monastic orders. also N. asceticism, N.

assiduous ADJ. diligent. It took Rembrandt weeks of *assiduous* labor before he was satisfied with his portrait of his son.

assuage V. ease or lessen (pain); satisfy (hunger); soothe (anger). Jilted by Jane, Dick tried to *assuage* his heartache by indulging in ice cream. One gallon later, he had *assuaged* his appetite but not his grief. assuagement, N.

attenuate V. make thin; weaken. By withdrawing their forces, the generals hoped to *attenuate* the enemy lines.

audacious ADJ. daring; bold. Audiences cheered as Luke Skywalker and Princess Leia made their *audacious,* death-defying leap to freedom and escaped Darth Vader's troops. audacity, N.

austere ADJ. forbiddingly stern; severely simple and unornamented. The headmaster's *austere* demeanor tended to scare off the more timid students, who never visited his study willingly. The room reflected the man, *austere* and bare, like a monk's cell, with no touches of luxury to moderate its *austerity.*

autonomous ADJ. self-governing. Although the University of California at Berkeley is just one part of the state university system, in many ways Cal Berkeley is *autonomous,* for it runs several programs that are not subject to outside control. autonomy, N.

aver V. state confidently. I wish to *aver* that I am certain of success.

banal ADJ. hackneyed; commonplace; trite; lacking originality. The hack writer's worn-out clichés made his comic sketch seem *banal.* He even resorted to the *banality* of having someone slip on a banana peel!

belie v. contradict; give a false impression. His coarse, hard-bitten exterior *belied* his innate sensitivity.

beneficent ADJ. kindly; doing good. The overgenerous philanthropist had to curb his *beneficent* impulses before he gave away all his money and left himself with nothing.

bolster v. support; reinforce. The debaters amassed file boxes full of evidence to *bolster* their arguments.

bombastic ADJ. pompous; using inflated language. Puffed up with conceit, the orator spoke in such a *bombastic* manner that we longed to deflate him. bombast, N.

boorish ADJ. rude; insensitive. Though Mr. Potts constantly interrupted his wife, she ignored his *boorish* behavior, for she had lost hope of teaching him courtesy.

burgeon v. grow forth; send out buds. In the spring, the plants that *burgeon* are a promise of the beauty that is to come.

burnish v. make shiny by rubbing; polish. The maid *burnished* the brass fixtures until they reflected the lamplight.

buttress v. support; prop up. Just as architects *buttress* the walls of cathedrals with flying *buttresses,* debaters *buttress* their arguments with facts. also N.

cacophonous ADJ. discordant; inharmonious. Do the students in the orchestra enjoy the *cacaphonous* sounds they make when they're tuning up? I don't know how they can stand the racket. cacophony, N.

capricious ADJ. unpredictable; fickle. The storm was *capricious;* it changed course constantly. Jill was *capricious,* too; she changed boyfriends almost as often as she changed clothes.

castigation v. punishment; severe criticism. Sensitive even to mild criticism, Woolf could not bear the *castigation* that she found in certain reviews. castigate, v.

catalyst N. agent that brings about a chemical change while it remains unaffected and unchanged. Many chemical reactions cannot take place without the presence of a *catalyst.*

caustic ADJ. burning; sarcastically biting. The critic's *caustic* remarks angered the hapless actors who were the subjects of his sarcasm.

chicanery N. trickery; deception. Those sneaky lawyers misrepresented what occurred, made up all sorts of implausible alternative scenarios to confuse the jurors, and in general depended on *chicanery* to win the case.

coagulate V. thicken; congeal; clot. Even after you remove the pudding from the burner, it will continue to *coagulate* as it stands. coagulant, N.

coda N. concluding section of a musical or literary composition. The piece concluded with a distinctive *coda* that strikingly brought together various motifs.

cogent ADJ. convincing. It was inevitable that David chose to go to Harvard; he had several *cogent* reasons for doing so, including a full-tuition scholarship. Katya argued her case with such *cogency* that the jury had to decide in favor of her client.

commensurate ADJ. equal in extent. Your reward will be *commensurate* with your effort; what you earn will depend on how hard you work.

compendium V. brief, comprehensive summary. This text can serve as a *compendium* of the tremendous amount of new material being developed in this field.

complaisant ADJ. trying to please; obliging. Accustomed to VIP treatment, the star expected the hotel manager to be *complaisant*, if not totally obsequious. Imagine her shock when she was greeted curtly and then ignored.

compliant ADJ. yielding; conforming to requirements. Because Joel usually gave in and went along with whatever his friends desired, his mother worried that he might be too *compliant*.

conciliatory ADJ. reconciling; soothing. She was still angry despite his *conciliatory* words. conciliate, V.

condone V. overlook; forgive; give tacit approval; excuse. Unlike Widow Douglass, who *condoned* Huck's minor offenses, Miss Watson did nothing but scold.

confound V. confuse; puzzle. No mystery could *confound* Sherlock Holmes for long.

connoisseur N. person competent to act as a judge of art, etc.; a lover of an art. She had developed into a *connoisseur* of fine china.

contention N. claim; thesis. It is our *contention* that, if you follow our tactics, you will boost your score on the GRE. contend, V.

contentious ADJ. quarrelsome. Disagreeing violently with the referees' ruling, the coach became so *contentious* that the referees threw him out of the game.

contrite ADJ. penitent. Her *contrite* tears did not influence the judge when he imposed sentence. contrition, N.

conundrum N. riddle; difficult problem. During the long car ride, she invented *conundrums* to entertain the children.

converge V. approach; tend to meet; come together. African-American men from all over the United States *converged* on Washington to take part in the historic Million Man March. convergence, N.

convoluted ADJ. coiled around; involved; intricate. His argument was so *convoluted* that few of us could follow it intelligently.

craven ADJ. cowardly. Lillian's *craven* refusal to join the protest was criticized by her comrades, who had expected her to be brave enough to stand up for her beliefs.

daunt V. intimidate; frighten. "Boast all you like of your prowess. Mere words cannot *daunt* me," the hero answered the villain.

decorum N. propriety; orderliness and good taste in manners. Even the best-mannered students have trouble behaving with *decorum* on the last day of school. decorous, ADJ.

default N. failure to act. When the visiting team failed to show up for the big game, they lost the game by *default.* When Jack failed to make the payments on his Jaguar, the dealership took back the car because he had *defaulted* on his debt.

deference N. courteous regard for another's wish. In *deference* to the minister's request, please do not take photographs during the wedding service.

delineate V. portray; depict; sketch. Using only a few descriptive phrases, Austen *delineates* the character of Mr. Collins so well that we can predict his every move. delineation, N.

denigrate V. belittle or defame; blacken. All attempts to *denigrate* the character of our late President have failed; the people still love him and cherish his memory.

deride V. ridicule; make fun of. The critics *derided* his pretentious dialogue and refused to consider his play seriously. derision, N.

derivative ADJ. unoriginal; obtained from another source. Although her early poetry was clearly *derivative* in nature, the critics thought she had promise and eventually would find her own voice.

desiccate V. dry up. A tour of this smokehouse will give you an idea of how the pioneers used to *desiccate* food in order to preserve it.

desultory ADJ. aimless; haphazard; digressing at random. In prison Malcolm X set himself the task of reading straight through the dictionary; to him, reading was purposeful, not *desultory*.

deterrent N. something that discourages; hindrance. Does the threat of capital punishment serve as a *deterrent* to potential killers? also ADJ.

diatribe N. bitter scolding; invective. During the lengthy *diatribe* delivered by his opponent he remained calm and self-controlled.

dichotomy N. split; branching into two parts (especially contradictory ones). Willie didn't know how to resolve the *dichotomy* between his ambition to go to college and his childhood longing to run away and join the circus. Then he heard about Ringling Brothers Circus College, and he knew he'd found his school.

diffidence N. shyness. You must overcome your *diffidence* if you intend to become a salesperson.

diffuse ADJ. wordy; rambling; spread out (like a gas). If you pay authors by the word, you tempt them to produce *diffuse* manuscripts rather than brief ones. also V. diffusion, N.

digression N. wandering away from the subject. Nobody minded when Professor Renoir's lectures wandered away from their official theme; his *digressions* were always more fascinating than the topic of the day. digress, V.

dirge N. lament with music. The funeral *dirge* stirred us to tears.

disabuse V. correct a false impression; undeceive. I will attempt to *disabuse* you of your impression of my client's guilt; I know he is innocent.

discerning ADJ. mentally quick and observant; having insight. Though no genius, the star was sufficiently *discerning* to tell her true friends from the countless phonies who flattered her.

discordant ADJ. not harmonious; conflicting. Nothing is quite so *discordant* as the sound of a junior high school orchestra tuning up.

discredit V. defame; destroy confidence in; disbelieve. The campaign was highly negative in tone; each candidate tried to *discredit* the other.

discrepancy N. lack of consistency; difference. The police noticed some *discrepancies* in his description of the crime and did not believe him.

discrete ADJ. separate; unconnected. The universe is composed of *discrete* bodies.

disingenuous ADJ. lacking genuine candor; insincere. Now that we know the mayor and his wife are engaged in a bitter divorce fight, we find their earlier remarks regretting their lack of time together remarkably *disingenuous*.

disinterested ADJ. unprejudiced. Given the judge's political ambitions and the lawyers' financial interest in the case, the only *disinterested* person in the courtroom may have been the court reporter.

disjointed ADJ. disconnected. His remarks were so *disjointed* that we could not follow his reasoning.

dismiss V. eliminate from consideration; reject. Believing in John's love for her, she *dismissed* the notion that he might be unfaithful. (secondary meaning)

disparage V. belittle. A doting mother, Emma was more likely to praise her son's crude attempts at art than to *disparage* them.

disparate ADJ. basically different; unrelated. Unfortunately, Tony and Tina have *disparate* notions of marriage: Tony sees it as a carefree extended love affair, while Tina sees it as a solemn commitment to build a family and a home.

dissemble V. disguise; pretend. Even though John tried to *dissemble* his motive for taking modern dance, we all knew he was there not to dance but to meet girls.

disseminate V. distribute; spread; scatter (like seeds). By their use of the Internet, propagandists have been able to *disseminate* their pet doctrines to new audiences around the globe.

dissolution N. breaking of a union; decay; termination. Which caused King Lear more suffering: the *dissolution* of his kingdom into warring factions, or the *dissolution* of his aged, failing body? dissolve, V.

dissonance N. discord; opposite of harmony. Composer Charles Ives often used *dissonance*—clashing or unresolved chords—for special effects in his musical works. dissonant, ADJ.

distend V. expand; swell out. I can tell when he is under stress by the way the veins *distend* on his forehead.

distill V. purify; refine; concentrate. A moonshiner *distills* mash into whiskey; an epigrammatist *distills* thoughts into quips.

diverge V. vary; go in different directions from the same point. The spokes of the wheel *diverge* from the hub.

divest V. strip; deprive. He was *divested* of his power to act and could no longer govern. divestiture, N.

document V. provide written evidence. She kept all the receipts from her business trip in order to *document* her expenses for the firm. also N.

dogmatic ADJ. opinionated; arbitrary; doctrinal. We tried to discourage Doug from being so *dogmatic,* but never could convince him that his opinions might be wrong.

dormant ADJ. sleeping; lethargic; latent. At fifty her long-*dormant* ambition to write flared up once more; within a year she had completed the first of her great historical novels. dormancy, N.

dupe N. someone easily fooled. While the gullible Watson often was made a *dupe* by unscrupulous parties, Sherlock Holmes was far more difficult to fool.

ebullient ADJ. showing excitement; overflowing with enthusiasm. Amy's *ebullient* nature could not be repressed; she was always bubbling over with excitement. ebullience, N.

eclectic ADJ. selective; composed of elements drawn from disparate sources. His style of interior decoration was *eclectic:* bits and pieces of furnishings from widely divergent periods, strikingly juxtaposed to create a unique decor. eclecticism, N.

efficacy N. power to produce desired effect. The *efficacy* of this drug depends on the regularity of the dosage. efficacious, ADJ.

effrontery N. insolent boldness; temerity. The classic example of unmitigated *effrontery* or "chutzpah" is the man who killed his parents and then asked the judge for mercy because he was an orphan.

elegy N. poem or song expressing lamentation. On the death of Edward King, Milton composed the *elegy* "Lycidas." elegiacal, ADJ.

elicit V. draw out by discussion. The detectives tried to *elicit* where he had hidden his loot.

embellish V. adorn; ornament; enhance, as a story. The costume designer *embellished* the leading lady's ball gown with yards and yards of ribbon and lace.

empirical ADJ. based on experience. He distrusted hunches and intuitive flashes; he placed his reliance entirely on *empirical* data.

emulate V. imitate; rival. In a brief essay, describe a person you admire, someone whose virtues you would like to *emulate.*

endemic ADJ. prevailing among a specific group of people or in a specific area or country. This disease is *endemic* in this part of the world; more than 80 percent of the population are at one time or another affected by it.

enervate V. weaken. She was slow to recover from her illness; even a short walk to the window *enervated* her. enervation, N.

engender V. cause; produce. To receive praise for real accomplishments *engenders* self-confidence in a child.

enhance V. increase; improve. You can *enhance* your chances of being admitted to the college of your choice by learning to write well; an excellent essay can *enhance* any application.

ephemeral ADJ. short-lived; fleeting. The mayfly is an *ephemeral* creature: its adult life lasts little more than a day.

equanimity N. calmness of temperament; composure. Even the inevitable strains of caring for an ailing mother did not disturb Bea's *equanimity.*

equivocate V. intentionally mislead; attempt to conceal the truth. Rejecting the candidate's attempts to *equivocate* about his views on abortion, the reporters pressed him to state clearly where he stood on the issue. equivocal, ADJ.

erudite ADJ. learned; scholarly. Though his fellow students thought him *erudite,* Paul knew he would have to spend many years in serious study before he could consider himself a scholar. erudition, N.

esoteric ADJ. hard to understand; known only to the chosen few. *New Yorker* short stories often include *esoteric* allusions to obscure people and events; the implication is, if you are in the in-crowd, you'll get the reference; if you come from Cleveland, you won't. esoterica, N.

eulogy N. expression of praise, often on the occasion of someone's death. Instead of delivering a spoken *eulogy* at Genny's memorial service, Jeff sang a song he had written in her honor. eulogize, V.

euphemism N. mild expression in place of an unpleasant one. The expression "he passed away" is a *euphemism* for "he died."

exacerbate v. worsen; embitter. The latest bombing *exacerbated* England's already existing bitterness against the IRA, causing the Prime Minister to break off the peace talks abruptly. exacerbation, N.

exculpate v. clear from blame. She was *exculpated* of the crime when the real criminal confessed.

exigency N. urgent state; demand or requirement. Given the *exigency* of the current near-riot conditions, the mayor felt it necessary to call for federal help. Packing enough food and fuel to last the week, the hiker felt well prepared to face the *exigencies* of wilderness life. exigent. ADJ.

extrapolation N. projection; conjecture. Based on their *extrapolation* from the results of the primaries on Super Tuesday, the networks predicted that George Bush would be the Republican candidate for the presidency. extrapolate, v.

facetious ADJ. joking (often inappropriately); humorous. I'm serious about this project; I don't need any *facetious,* smart-alecky cracks about do-good little rich girls.

facilitate v. help bring about; make less difficult. Rest and proper nourishment should *facilitate* the patient's recovery.

fallacious ADJ. false; misleading. Paradoxically, *fallacious* reasoning does not always yield erroneous results; even though your logic may be faulty, the answer you get may be correct. fallacy, N.

fatuous ADJ. foolish; inane. She is far too intelligent to utter such *fatuous* remarks.

fawning ADJ. courting favor by cringing and flattering. She was constantly surrounded by a group of *fawning* admirers who hoped to win her favor. fawn, v.

felicitous ADJ. apt; suitably expressed; well chosen. Famous for his *felicitous* remarks, he was called upon to serve as master-of-ceremonies at many a banquet.

fervor N. glowing ardor; intensity of feeling. At the protest rally, the students cheered the strikers and booed the dean with equal *fervor.*

flag v. droop; grow feeble. When the opposing hockey team scored its third goal only minutes into the first period, the home team's spirits *flagged.* flagging, ADJ.

fledgling ADJ. inexperienced. While it is necessary to provide these *fledgling* poets with an opportunity to present their work, it is not essential that we admire everything they write. also N.

flout v. reject; mock. The headstrong youth *flouted* all authority; he refused to be curbed.

foment v. stir up; instigate. Cher's archenemy Heather spread some nasty rumors that *fomented* trouble in the club. Do you think Cher's foe meant to *foment* such discord?

forestall v. prevent by taking action in advance. By setting up a prenuptial agreement, the prospective bride and groom hoped to *forestall* any potential arguments about money in the event of a divorce.

frugality N. thrift; economy. In these economically difficult days businesses must practice *frugality* or risk bankruptcy. frugal, ADJ.

futile ADJ. useless; hopeless; ineffectual. It is *futile* for me to try to get any work done around here while the telephone is ringing every 30 seconds. futility, N.

gainsay v. deny. She was too honest to *gainsay* the truth of the report.

garrulous ADJ. loquacious; wordy; talkative. My Uncle Henry can out-talk any other three people I know. He is the most *garrulous* person in Cayuga County. garrulity, N.

goad v. urge on. She was *goaded* by her friends until she yielded to their wishes. also N.

gouge v. overcharge. During the World Series, ticket scalpers tried to *gouge* the public, asking astronomical prices even for bleacher seats.

grandiloquent ADJ. pompous; bombastic; using high-sounding language. The politician could never speak simply; she was always *grandiloquent.*

gregarious ADJ. sociable. Typically, party-throwers are *gregarious;* hermits are not.

guileless ADJ. without deceit. He is naive, simple, and *guileless;* he cannot be guilty of fraud.

gullible ADJ. easily deceived. *Gullible* people have only themselves to blame if they fall for con artists repeatedly. As the saying goes, "Fool me once, shame on you. Fool me twice, shame on me."

harangue N. long, passionate, and vehement speech. In her lengthy *harangue,* the principal berated the offenders. also v.

homogeneous ADJ. of the same kind. Because the student body at Elite Prep was so *homogeneous,* Sara and James decided to send their daughter to a school that offered greater cultural diversity. homogeneity, N.

hyperbole N. exaggeration; overstatement. As far as I'm concerned, Apple's claims about the new computer are pure *hyperbole*; no machine is that good! hyperbolic, ADJ.

iconoclastic ADJ. attacking cherished traditions. Deeply *iconoclastic,* Jean Genet deliberately set out to shock conventional theatergoers with his radical plays. iconoclasm, N.

idolatry N. worship of idols; excessive admiration. Little Johnny's adoration of his babysitter verged on idolatry; in his eyes, Lydia could do no wrong.

immutable ADJ. unchangeable. All things change over time; nothing is *immutable.*

impair V. injure; hurt. Drinking alcohol can *impair* your ability to drive safely; if you're going to drink, don't drive.

impassive ADJ. without feeling; imperturbable; stoical. Refusing to let the enemy see how deeply shaken he was by his capture, the prisoner kept his face *impassive.*

impede V. hinder; block. The special prosecutor determined that the Attorney General, though inept, had not intentionally set out to *impede* the progress of the investigation.

impermeable ADJ. impervious; not permitting passage through its substance. This new material is *impermeable* to liquids; it will be an excellent fabric for raincoats.

imperturbable ADJ. calm; placid. Wellington remained *imperturbable* and in full command of the situation in spite of the hysteria and panic all around him. imperturbability, N.

impervious ADJ. impenetrable; incapable of being damaged or distressed. The carpet salesman told Simone that his most expensive brand of floor covering was warranted to be *impervious* to ordinary wear and tear. Having read so many negative reviews of his acting, the movie star had learned to ignore them, and was now *impervious* to criticism.

implacable ADJ. incapable of being pacified. Madame Defarge was the *implacable* enemy of the Evremonde family.

implicit ADJ. understood but not stated. Jack never told Jill he adored her; he believed his love was *implicit* in his deeds.

implode V. burst inward. If you break a vacuum tube, the glass tube *implodes.* implosion, N.

inadvertently ADV. unintentionally; by oversight; carelessly. Judy's great fear was that she might *inadvertently* omit a question on the exam and mismark her whole answer sheet.

inchoate ADJ. recently begun; rudimentary; elementary. Before the Creation, the world was an *inchoate* mass.

incongruity N. lack of harmony; absurdity. The *incongruity* of his wearing sneakers with formal attire amused the observers. incongruous, ADJ.

inconsequential ADJ. insignificant; unimportant. Brushing off Ali's apologies for having broken the wine glass, Tamara said, "Don't worry about it; it's *inconsequential.*"

incorporate V. introduce something into a larger whole; combine; unite. Breaking with precedent, President Truman ordered the military to *incorporate* blacks into every branch of the armed services. also ADJ.

indeterminate ADJ. uncertain; not clearly fixed; indefinite. That interest rates shall rise appears certain; when they will do so, however, remains *indeterminate.*

indigence N. poverty. Neither the economists nor the political scientists have found a way to wipe out the inequities of wealth and eliminate *indigence* from our society.

indolent ADJ. lazy. Couch potatoes lead an *indolent* life lying back in their Lazyboy recliners watching TV. indolence, N.

inert ADJ. inactive; lacking power to move. "Get up, you lazybones," Tina cried to Tony, who lay in bed *inert.* inertia, N.

ingenuous ADJ. naive and trusting; young; unsophisticated. The woodsman did not realize how *ingenuous* Little Red Riding Hood was until he heard that she had gone off for a walk in the woods with the Big Bad Wolf. ingenue, N.

inherent ADJ. firmly established by nature or habit. Katya's *inherent* love of justice caused her to champion anyone she considered to be treated unfairly by society.

innocuous ADJ. harmless. An occasional glass of wine with dinner is relatively *innocuous* and should have no ill effect on most people.

insensible ADJ. unconscious; unresponsive. Sherry and I are very different; at times when I would be covered with embarrassment, she seems *insensible* to shame.

insinuate V. hint; imply; creep in. When you said I looked robust, did you mean to *insinuate* that I'm getting fat?

insipid ADJ. lacking in flavor; dull. Flat prose and flat ginger ale are equally *insipid;* both lack sparkle.

insularity N. narrow-mindedness; isolation. The *insularity* of the islanders manifested itself in their suspicion of anything foreign. insular, ADJ.

intractable ADJ. unruly; stubborn; unyielding. Charlie Brown's friend Pigpen was *intractable;* he absolutely refused to take a bath.

intransigence N. refusal of any compromise; stubbornness. The negotiating team had not expected such *intransigence* from the striking workers, who rejected any hint of a compromise. intransigent, ADJ.

inundate V. overwhelm; flood; submerge. This semester I am *inundated* with work; you should see the piles of paperwork flooding my desk. Until the great dam was built, the waters of the Nile used to *inundate* the river valley every year.

inured ADJ. accustomed; hardened. Although she became *inured* to the Alaskan cold, she could not grow accustomed to the lack of sunlight.

invective N. abuse. He had expected criticism but not the *invective* that greeted his proposal.

irascible ADJ. irritable; easily angered. Miss Minchin's *irascible* temper intimidated the younger schoolgirls, who feared she'd burst into a rage at any moment.

irresolute ADJ. uncertain how to act; weak. Once you have made your decision, don't waver; a leader should never appear *irresolute.*

itinerary N. plan of a trip. Disliking sudden changes in plans when she traveled abroad, Ethel refused to make any alterations in her *itinerary.*

laconic ADJ. brief and to the point. Many of the characters portrayed by Clint Eastwood are *laconic* types: strong men of few words.

lassitude N. languor; weariness. After a massage and a long soak in the hot tub, I surrendered to my growing *lassitude* and lay down for a nap.

latent ADJ. potential but undeveloped; dormant; hidden. Polaroid pictures are popular at parties because you can see the *latent* photographic image gradually appear before your eyes. latency, N.

laud V. praise. The NFL *lauded* Boomer Esiason's efforts to raise money to combat cystic fibrosis. also N. laudable, laudatory, ADJ.

lethargic ADJ. drowsy; dull. The stuffy room made her *lethargic:* she felt as if she was about to nod off. lethargy, N.

levee N. earthen or stone embankment to prevent flooding. As the river rose and threatened to overflow the *levee,* emergency workers rushed to reinforce the walls with sandbags.

levity N. lack of seriousness or steadiness; frivolity. Stop giggling and wriggling around in the pew; such *levity* is improper in church.

log N. record of a voyage or flight; record of day-to-day activities. "Flogged two seamen today for insubordination," wrote Captain Bligh in the *Bounty's log.* To see how much work I've accomplished recently, just take a look at the number of new files listed on my computer *log.* also V.

loquacious ADJ. talkative. Though our daughter barely says a word to us these days, put a phone in her hand and see how *loquacious* she can be; our phone bills are out of sight! loquacity, N.

lucid ADJ. easily understood; clear; intelligible. Lexy makes an excellent teacher; her explanations of technical points are *lucid* enough for a child to grasp. lucidity, N.

luminous ADJ. shining; issuing light. The sun is a *luminous* body.

magnanimity N. generosity. Noted for his *magnanimity,* philanthropist Eugene Lang donated millions to charity. magnanimous, ADJ.

malingerer N. one who feigns illness to escape duty. The captain ordered the sergeant to punish all *malingerers* and force them to work. malinger, V.

malleable ADJ. capable of being shaped by pounding; impressionable. Gold is a *malleable* metal, easily shaped into bracelets and rings. Fagin hoped Oliver was a *malleable* lad, easily shaped into a thief.

maverick N. rebel; nonconformist. To the masculine literary establishment, George Sand with her insistence on wearing trousers and smoking cigars was clearly a *maverick* who fought her proper womanly role.

mendacious ADJ. lying; habitually dishonest. Distrusting Huck from the start, Miss Watson assumed he was *mendacious* and refused to believe a word he said. mendacity, N.

metamorphosis N. change of form. The *metamorphosis* of caterpillar to butterfly is typical of many such changes in animal life. metamorphose, V.

meticulous ADJ. excessively careful; painstaking; scrupulous. Martha Stewart was a *meticulous* housekeeper, fussing about each and every detail that went into making up her perfect home.

misanthrope N. one who hates mankind. In *Gulliver's Travels*, Swift portrays human beings as vile, degraded beasts; for this reason, various critics consider him a *misanthrope*. misanthropic, ADJ.

mitigate V. appease; moderate. Nothing Jason did could *mitigate* Medea's anger; she refused to forgive him for betraying her.

mollify V. soothe. The airline customer service representative tried to *mollify* the angry passenger by offering her a seat in first class.

morose ADJ. ill-humored; sullen; melancholy. Forced to take early retirement, Bill acted *morose* for months; then, all of a sudden, he shook off his gloom and was his usual cheerful self.

mundane ADJ. worldly as opposed to spiritual; everyday. Uninterested in philosophical or spiritual discussions, Tom talked only of *mundane* matters such as the daily weather forecast or the latest basketball results.

negate V. cancel out; nullify; deny. A sudden surge of adrenalin can *negate* the effects of fatigue; there's nothing like a good shock to wake you up. negation, N.

neophyte N. recent convert; beginner. This mountain slope contains slides that will challenge experts as well as *neophytes.*

obdurate ADJ. stubborn. He was *obdurate* in his refusal to listen to our complaints.

obsequious ADJ. slavishly attentive; servile; sycophantic. Helen valued people who behaved as if they respected themselves; nothing irritated her more than an excessively *obsequious* waiter or a fawning salesclerk.

obviate V. make unnecessary; prevent problems. If you can house-sit for me for the next two weeks, that will *obviate* my need to find someone to feed the cats while I am gone.

occlude V. shut; close. A blood clot partially *occluded* a coronary artery, obstructing the flow of arterial blood. occlusion, N.

officious ADJ. meddlesome; excessively pushy in offering one's services. After her long flight, Jill just wanted to nap, but the *officious* bellboy was intent on showing her all the special features of the deluxe suite.

onerous ADJ. burdensome. She asked for an assistant because her work load was too *onerous.*

opprobrium N. infamy; vilification. He refused to defend himself against the slander and *opprobrium* hurled against him by the newspapers; he preferred to rely on his record.

oscillate V. vibrate pendulumlike; waver. It is interesting to note how public opinion *oscillates* between the extremes of optimism and pessimism.

ostentatious ADJ. showy; pretentious; trying to attract attention. Trump's latest casino in Atlantic City is the most *ostentatious* gambling palace in the East; it easily out-glitters its competitors. ostentation, N.

paragon N. model of perfection. Her fellow students disliked Lavinia because Miss Minchin always pointed her out as a *paragon* of virtue.

partisan ADJ. one-sided; prejudiced; committed to a party. Rather than joining forces to solve our nation's problems, the Democrats and Republicans spend their time on *partisan* struggles. also N.

pathological ADJ. related to the study of disease; diseased or markedly abnormal. Jerome's *pathological* fear of germs led him to wash his hands a hundred times a day. pathology, N.

paucity N. scarcity. They closed the restaurant because the *paucity* of customers made it uneconomical to operate.

pedantic ADJ. showing off learning; bookish. Leavening her decisions with humorous, down-to-earth anecdotes, Judge Judy was not at all the *pedantic* legal scholar. pedantry, N.

penchant N. strong inclination; liking. Dave has a *penchant* for taking risks; one semester he went steady with three girls, two of whom were stars on the school karate team.

penury N. severe poverty; stinginess. When his pension fund failed, George feared he would end his days in *penury.* He became such a penny-pincher that he turned into a closefisted, *penurious* miser.

perennial N. something long-lasting. These plants are hardy *perennials* and will bloom for many years. also ADJ.

perfidious ADJ. treacherous; disloyal. When Caesar realized that Brutus had betrayed him, he reproached his *perfidious* friend. perfidy, N.

perfunctory ADJ. superficial; not thorough; lacking interest, care, or enthusiasm. The auditor's *perfunctory* inspection of the books overlooked many errors.

permeable ADJ. penetrable; porous; allowing liquids or gas to pass through. If your jogging clothes weren't made out of *permeable* fabric, you'd drown in your own sweat (figuratively speaking). permeate, V.

pervasive ADJ. spread throughout. Despite airing them for several hours, she could not rid her clothes of the *pervasive* odor of mothballs that clung to them. pervade, V.

phlegmatic ADJ. calm; not easily disturbed. The nurse was a cheerful but *phlegmatic* person, unexcited in the face of sudden emergencies.

piety N. devoutness; reverence for God. Living her life in prayer and good works, Mother Teresa exemplified the true spirit of *piety*. pious, ADJ.

placate V. pacify; conciliate. The store manager tried to *placate* the angry customer, offering to replace the damaged merchandise or to give back her money.

plasticity N. ability to be molded. When clay dries out, it loses its *plasticity* and becomes less malleable.

platitude N. trite remark; commonplace statement. In giving advice to his son, old Polonius expressed himself only in *platitudes;* every word out of his mouth was a truism.

plethora N. excess; overabundance. She offered a *plethora* of excuses for her shortcomings.

plummet V. fall sharply. Stock prices *plummeted* as Wall Street reacted to the rise in interest rates.

porous ADJ. full of pores; like a sieve. Dancers like to wear *porous* clothing because it allows the ready passage of water and air.

pragmatic ADJ. practical (as opposed to idealistic); concerned with the practical worth or impact of something. This coming trip to France should provide me with a *pragmatic* test of the value of my conversational French class.

preamble N. introductory statement. In the *Preamble* to the Constitution, the purpose of the document is set forth.

precarious ADJ. uncertain; risky. Saying the stock was currently overpriced and would be a *precarious* investment, the broker advised her client against purchasing it.

precipitate ADJ. rash; premature; hasty; sudden. Though I was angry enough to resign on the spot, I had enough sense to keep myself from quitting a job in such a *precipitate* fashion.

precursor N. forerunner. Though Gray and Burns share many traits with the Romantic poets who followed them, most critics consider them *precursors* of the Romantic Movement, not true Romantics.

presumptuous ADJ. overconfident; impertinently bold; taking liberties. Matilda thought it *presumptuous* of the young man to address her without first being introduced. Perhaps manners were freer here in the New World. presumption, N.

prevaricate V. lie. Some people believe that to *prevaricate* in a good cause is justifiable and regard such misleading prevarications as "white lies."

pristine ADJ. characteristic of earlier times; primitive, unspoiled. This area has been preserved in all its *pristine* wildness.

probity N. uprightness; incorruptibility. Everyone took his *probity* for granted; his defalcations, therefore, shocked us all.

problematic ADJ. doubtful; unsettled; questionable; perplexing. Given the way building costs have exceeded estimates for the job, whether the arena will ever be completed is *problematic*.

prodigal ADJ. wasteful; reckless with money. Don't be so *prodigal* spending my money; when you've earned some money, you can waste as much of it as you want! also N.

profound ADJ. deep; not superficial; complete. Freud's remarkable insights into human behavior caused his fellow scientists to honor him as a *profound* thinker. profundity, N.

prohibitive ADJ. tending to prevent the purchase or use of something; inclined to prevent or forbid. Susie wanted to buy a new Volvo but had to settle for a used Dodge because the new car's price was *prohibitive*. prohibition, N.

proliferate V. grow rapidly; spread; multiply. Times of economic hardship inevitably encourage countless get-rich-quick schemes to *proliferate*. proliferation, N.

propensity N. natural inclination. Convinced of his own talent, Sol has an unfortunate *propensity* to belittle the talents of others.

propitiate V. appease. The natives offered sacrifices to *propitiate* the angry gods.

propriety N. fitness; correct conduct. Miss Manners counsels her readers so that they may behave with *propriety* in any social situation and not embarrass themselves.

proscribe V. ostracize; banish; outlaw. Antony, Octavius, and Lepidus *proscribed* all those who had conspired against Julius Caesar.

pungent ADJ. stinging; sharp in taste or smell; caustic. The *pungent* odor of ripe Limburger cheese appealed to Simone but made Stanley gag. pungency, N.

qualified ADJ. limited; restricted. Unable to give the candidate full support, the mayor gave him only a *qualified* endorsement. (secondary meaning)

quibble N. minor objection or complaint. Aside from a few hundred teensy-weensy *quibbles* about the set, the script, the actors, the director, the costumes, the lighting, and the props, the hypercritical critic loved the play. also V.

quiescent ADJ. at rest; dormant; temporarily inactive. After the devastating eruption, fear of Mount Etna was great; people did not return to cultivate its rich hillside lands until the volcano had been *quiescent* for a full two years. quiescence, N.

rarefied ADJ. made less dense [of a gas]. The mountain climbers had difficulty breathing in the *rarefied* atmosphere. rarefy, V. rarefaction, N.

recalcitrant ADJ. obstinately stubborn; determined to resist authority; unruly. Which animal do you think is more *recalcitrant*, a pig or a mule?

recant V. disclaim or disavow; retract a previous statement; openly confess error. Hoping to make Joan of Arc *recant* her sworn testimony, her English captors tried to convince her that her visions had been sent to her by the Devil.

recluse N. hermit; loner. Disappointed in love, Miss Emily became a *recluse;* she shut herself away in her empty mansion and refused to see another living soul. reclusive, ADJ.

recondite ADJ. difficult to understand; profound; secret. While Holmes happily explored arcane subjects such as paleography and ancient Near Eastern languages, Watson claimed they were far too *recondite* for a simple chap like him.

refractory ADJ. stubborn; unmanageable. The *refractory* horse was eliminated from the race when he refused to obey the jockey.

refute V. disprove. The defense called several respectable witnesses who were able to *refute* the false testimony of the prosecution's only witness. refutation, N.

relegate V. banish to an inferior position; delegate; assign. After Ralph dropped his second tray of drinks that week, the manager swiftly *relegated* him to a minor post cleaning up behind the bar.

reproach V. express disapproval or disappointment. He never could do anything wrong without imagining how the look on his mother's face would *reproach* him afterwards. also N. reproachful, ADJ.

reprobate N. scoundrel; person lacking moral principles. In Twain's *Adventures of Huckleberry Finn*, the Duke and the Dauphin are a pair of drunken *reprobates*, con men ready to swindle a poor widow out of her last dollar.

repudiate V. disown; disavow. On separating from Tony, Tina announced that she would *repudiate* all debts incurred by her soon-to-be ex-husband.

rescind V. cancel. Because of the public outcry against the new taxes, the senator proposed a bill to *rescind* the unpopular financial measure.

resolution N. determination. Nothing could shake his *resolution* to succeed despite all difficulties. resolute, ADJ.

resolve N. determination; firmness of purpose. How dare you question my *resolve* to take up sky-diving! Of course I haven't changed my mind! also V.

reticent ADJ. reserved; uncommunicative; inclined to silence. Fearing his competitors might get advance word about his plans from talkative staff members, Hughes preferred *reticent* employees to loquacious ones. reticence, N.

reverent ADJ. respectful; worshipful. Though I bow my head in church and recite the prayers, sometimes I don't feel properly *reverent*. revere, V. reverence, N.

sage N. person celebrated for wisdom. Hearing tales of a mysterious Master of All Knowledge who lived in the hills of Tibet, Sandy was possessed with a burning desire to consult the legendary *sage*. also ADJ.

salubrious ADJ. healthful. Many people with hay fever move to more *salubrious* sections of the country during the months of August and September.

sanguine — cheerfully optimistic, hopeful, confident

sanction v. approve; ratify. Nothing will convince me to *sanction* the engagement of my daughter to such a worthless young man.

satiate v. satisfy fully. Having stuffed themselves until they were *satiated*, the guests were so full they were ready for a nap.

saturate v. soak thoroughly. Thorough watering is the key to lawn care; you must *saturate* your new lawn well to encourage its growth.

savor v. enjoy; have a distinctive flavor, smell, or quality. Relishing his triumph, Costner especially *savored* the chagrin of the critics who had predicted his failure.

secrete v. hide away or cache; produce and release a substance into an organism. The pack rat *secretes* odds and ends in its nest; the pancreas *secretes* insulin in the islets of Langerhans.

shard N. fragment, generally of pottery. The archaeologist assigned several students the task of reassembling earthenware vessels from the *shards* he had brought back from the expedition.

skeptic N. doubter; person who suspends judgment until having examined the evidence supporting a point of view. I am a *skeptic* about the new health plan; I want some proof that it can work. skeptical, ADJ. skepticism, N.

solicitous ADJ. worried, concerned. The employer was very *solicitous* about the health of her employees as replacements were difficult to get. solicitude, N.

soporific ADJ. sleep-causing; marked by sleepiness. Professor Pringle's lectures were so *soporific* that even he fell asleep in class. also N.

specious ADJ. seemingly reasonable but incorrect; misleading (often intentionally). To claim that, because houses and birds both have wings, both can fly is extremely *specious* reasoning.

spectrum N. colored band produced when a beam of light passes through a prism. The visible portion of the *spectrum* includes red at one end and violet at the other.

sporadic ADJ. occurring irregularly. Although you can still hear *sporadic* outbursts of laughter and singing outside, the big Halloween parade has passed; the party's over till next year.

stigma N. token of disgrace; brand. I do not attach any *stigma* to the fact that you were accused of this crime; the fact that you were acquitted clears you completely. stigmatize, N.

stint v. be thrifty; set limits. "Spare no expense," the bride's father said, refusing to *stint* on the wedding arrangements.

stipulate v. make express conditions, specify. Before agreeing to reduce American military forces in Europe, the president *stipulated* that NATO teams be allowed to inspect Soviet bases.

stolid ADJ. dull; impassive. The earthquake shattered Stuart's usual *stolid* demeanor; trembling, he crouched on the no longer stable ground. stolidity, N.

striated ADJ. marked with parallel bands; grooved. The glacier left many *striated* rocks. striate, V.

strut N. pompous walk. His *strut* as he marched about the parade ground revealed him for what he was: a pompous buffoon. also V.

strut N. supporting bar. The engineer calculated that the *strut* supporting the rafter needed to be reinforced. (secondary meaning)

subpoena N. writ of summoning a witness to appear. The prosecutor's office was ready to serve a *subpoena* on the reluctant witness. also V.

subside v. settle down; descend; grow quiet. The doctor assured us that the fever would eventually *subside.*

substantiate v. establish by evidence; verify; support. These endorsements from satisfied customers *substantiate* our claim that Barron's *How to Prepare for the GRE* is the best GRE-prep book on the market.

supersede v. cause to be set aside; replace; make obsolete. Bulk mailing postal regulation 326D *supersedes* bulk mailing postal regulation 326C. If, in bundling your bulk mailing, you follow regulation 326C, your bulk mailing will be returned. supersession, N.

supposition N. hypothesis; surmise. I based my decision to confide in him on the *supposition* that he would be discreet. suppose, V.

tacit ADJ. understood; not put into words. We have a *tacit* agreement based on only a handshake.

tangential ADJ. peripheral; only slightly connected; digressing. Despite Clark's attempts to distract her with *tangential* remarks, Lois kept on coming back to her main question: why couldn't he come out to dinner with Superman and her?

tenuous ADJ. thin; rare; slim. The allegiance of our allies is held by rather *tenuous* ties; let us hope they will remain loyal.

tirade N. extended scolding; denunciation; harangue. Every time the boss holds a meeting, he goes into a lengthy *tirade,* scolding us for everything from tardiness to padding our expenses.

torpor N. lethargy; sluggishness; dormancy. Throughout the winter, nothing aroused the bear from his *torpor*; he would not emerge from hibernation until spring. torpid, ADJ.

tortuous ADJ. winding; full of curves. Because this road is so *tortuous,* it is unwise to go faster than twenty miles an hour on it.

tractable ADJ. docile; easily managed. Although Susan seemed a *tractable* young woman, she had a stubborn streak of independence that occasionally led her to defy the powers-that-be when she felt they were in the wrong. tractability, N.

transgression N. violation of a law; sin. Forgive us our *transgressions;* we know not what we do. transgress, V.

truculence N. aggressiveness; ferocity. Tynan's reviews were noted for their caustic attacks and general tone of *truculence.* truculent, ADJ.

vacillate V. waver; fluctuate. Uncertain which suitor she ought to marry, the princess *vacillated,* saying now one, now the other. vacillation, N.

venerate V. revere. In Tibet today, the common people still *venerate* their traditional spiritual leader, the Dalai Lama.

veracious ADJ. truthful. Did you believe that Kato Kaelin was *veracious* when he testified about what he heard the night Nicole Brown Simpson was slain? Some people question his *veracity*.

verbose ADJ. wordy. We had to make some major cuts in Senator Foghorn's speech because it was far too *verbose.* verbosity, N.

viable ADJ. practical or workable; capable of maintaining life. That idea won't work. Let me see whether I can come up with a *viable* alternative. viability. N.

viscous ADJ. sticky, gluey. Melted tar is a *viscous* substance. viscosity, N.

vituperative ADJ. abusive; scolding. He became more *vituperative* as he realized that we were not going to grant him his wish.

volatile ADJ. changeable; explosive; evaporating rapidly. The political climate today is extremely *volatile*; no one can predict what the electorate will do next. Maria Callas's temper was extremely *volatile*; the only thing you could predict was that she would blow up. Acetone is an extremely *volatile* liquid; it evaporates instantly. volatility, N.

warranted ADJ. justified; authorized. Before the judge issues the injunction, you must convince her this action is *warranted*.

wary ADJ. very cautious. The spies grew *wary* as they approached the sentry.

welter N. turmoil; bewildering jumble. The existing *welter* of overlapping federal and state programs cries out for immediate reform.

whimsical N. capricious; fanciful. In *Mrs. Doubtfire,* the hero is a playful, *whimsical* man who takes a notion to dress up as a woman so that he can look after his children, who are in the custody of his ex-wife. whimsy, N.

zealot N. fanatic; person who shows excessive zeal. Though Glenn was devout, he was no *zealot;* he never tried to force his religious beliefs on his friends.

5

ANALYTICAL ABILITY: TACTICS AND PRACTICE

The analytical ability section of the GRE is the longest of the three sections, both in terms of time allotted (60 minutes) and the number of questions (35). This section has two types of questions: 26 analytical reasoning questions and nine logical reasoning questions. The analytical reasoning questions are presented in groups of four or five questions, each group based on a single set of conditions. The logical reasoning questions are interspersed throughout the section. The groups of analytical reasoning questions could be separated by one, two, or three logical reasoning questions. Occasionally, there are two logical reasoning questions based on the same passage, but most often there is just one. A typical analytical ability section might be broken up as follows:

Question 1	a logical reasoning question
Questions 2–5	four analytical reasoning questions
Questions 6–8	three logical reasoning questions
Questions 9–13	five analytical reasoning questions
Question 14	a logical reasoning question
Questions 15–18	four analytical reasoning questions
Question 19	a logical reasoning question
Questions 20–23	four analytical reasoning questions
Questions 24–28	five analytical reasoning questions
Questions 29–30	two logical reasoning questions
Questions 31–34	four analytical reasoning questions
Question 35	a logical reasoning question

Each analytical reasoning question is a logical puzzle based on a given set of conditions. Most students have never seen questions like this and have no idea how to even begin solving such puzzles; consequently, they find this section to be the most difficult part of the GRE. Fortunately, there are several easy-to-learn strategies that can help you solve these puzzles. In going through this, you will learn all of them. The most valuable thing you can do to master analytical reasoning questions is to practice. Therefore, be sure to do the sample questions, all of which have complete solutions.

Each logical reasoning question requires you to analyze an argument presented in a short passage. Often you are asked either to find a conclusion which is a logical consequence of the passage, or to choose a statement which, if true, would strengthen or weaken the argument presented in the passage. The various tactics for handling this type of question are presented in the second part of this along with several practice questions. For each sample question, not only will you be given an explanation for the correct choice, you will be told why each of the other choices is incorrect. As you go through the sample questions in this chapter, be sure to read the full explanations; don't just check the answers.

If you study the tactics and do all of the problems in this chapter, you will be well prepared for the analytical ability section of the GRE, and should have the confidence you need to earn a high score.

ANALYTICAL REASONING

Before beginning their preparation for the GRE, the vast majority of college students have never even seen an analytical reasoning question. As we stated in Chapter 1, on first reading, these questions seem mind-boggling and hopelessly complicated. It is likely that when you took the diagnostic test you felt overwhelmed and intimidated by them. Don't panic! On the next several pages we will explain all of the techniques needed for correctly answering analytical reasoning questions, and by the time you finish reading this chapter you should feel completely at ease with them.

When you take the test, the only directions for answering analytical reasoning questions are the following three sentences, which will appear on the screen at the beginning of the section:

<u>Directions</u>: Each group of questions is based on a passage, graph, table, or set of conditions. In answering some of the questions, it might be useful to draw a rough diagram. For each question, select the best answer choice given.

As always, you should immediately click on "Dismiss the Instructions," not only to save the time it takes to read them, but because they are useless. They give you absolutely no insight into how to answer these questions. The first sentence is misleading, because, in fact, almost all questions are based on a short introductory passage, followed by a list of several conditions — very few questions, if any, are based on graphs or tables. The second sentence is correct; drawing a diagram, chart, table, or other pictorial representation of the situation is often helpful. In this chapter you will learn when and how you should do this. Finally, these questions don't have two or three reasonable answers, of which one is *best;* like math questions, they have *exactly one correct answer,* which is what you are to select.

Tactic 1

Be Familiar with the Most Common Types of Analytical Reasoning Questions

As you will see, there is a great variety of types of analytical reasoning questions that can be asked on the GRE. However, there are four types that occur much more frequently than the others, and when you see them, you should immediately know what you need to do to answer them.

- **Which of the following *could* be true?**
  If only one of the answer choices *could* be true, then each of the other four choices *must be false;* that is, each one must violate at least one of the given conditions.
- **Which of the following *must* be true?**
  Since only one of the answer choices *must* be true, then for each of the other choices, either it is false or it is possibly (but not definitely) true.
- **Which of the following *cannot* be true?**
  Since only one of the answer choices *cannot* be true, then each of the other choices could be or must be true. The correct answer is

the only choice which violates at least one of the given conditions or is otherwise inconsistent with what we know must be true.

- **How many possibilities are there?**
  This question asks, "How many different ways are there to satisfy all of the given conditions?" Here, you must systematically count or list all of the possibilities that do not violate the conditions.

Tactic 2

Simplify the Information by Using Abbreviations and Symbols

The analytical reasoning questions are not intended to be ambiguous or deceptive. In fact, the testmakers take great pains to use language precisely and to word the set of conditions describing a particular relationship so carefully that only one interpretation is possible. In doing so, however, they use so many words that it is easy to get lost. To see the situation clearly, you need to replace those words with symbols. There are two reasons for this. First, it is very difficult to keep looking at the list of conditions on the screen, especially when you have to scroll down to see them all. So you can't solve most analytical reasoning questions until you write the conditions on your scrap paper, and writing full sentences would be far too time-consuming. Second, it is much easier to work with a few symbols than with lengthy sentences.

The first step is to strip away all of the excess verbiage and then to abbreviate the remaining key words with single letters. GRE questions sometimes help in this process by using letters rather than words; for example, "six floats—C, D, E, F, G, and H are lined up for a parade," or "five singers—P, Q, R, S, and T are auditioning for a part in an opera." Other times, words are used. When this occurs, you must immediately replace each word with an uppercase letter. For example, if a question states that "five musicians—a bassist, a drummer, a guitarist, a pianist, and a trumpeter—are performing in a talent show," you should immediately abbreviate them B, D, G, P, and T; and if a question refers to "three girls—Amanda, Brianne, and Cindy, and four boys—Dave, Ed, Frank, and George," immediately write: "girls: A B C   boys: D E F G" on your scrap paper.

Here are some symbols that many students find useful. You do not have to use all of them and are certainly free to use others if you prefer. However, you must symbolize and abbreviate the conditions to avoid getting lost.

MEANING	SYMBOL
is equal to; is the same (weight, height, age, etc.) as	$V or$ $=$
is not equal to; is not the same (weight, height, age, etc.) as	~false; not $\neq$
is less than; is (lighter, shorter, younger, etc.) than; is to the left of; is in front of; precedes; etc.	⊂ if, then $<$
is immediately (to the left of, in front of, etc.); immediately precedes	$<<$
is greater than; is (heavier, taller, older, etc.) than; is to the right of; is behind; follows; etc.	$>$
is immediately (to the right of, behind, etc.); immediately follows; etc.	$>>$
is going to; is connected to (by a one-way street); etc.	$\rightarrow$
is connected to (by a two-way street); etc.	$\leftrightarrow$

Observe how we reduce the following set of conditions to a few manageable symbolic statements.

A college is sponsoring a variety show. Auditions were held for eight students: Alan, Beth, Carol, Diane, Ellen, Frank, George, and Hank. The director will choose six of them to perform in the show. So far, the following decisions have been made:

Alan will perform immediately after Diane does.

The show must open with Ellen's comedy routine.

Since Frank and Hank both play the piano, at most one of them will be permitted to perform.

> Carol will not perform unless Beth performs earlier in the program.
>
> If Beth is chosen to do her ballet, she will perform after Diane does her dance number, with only one intervening act.

First, replace the name of each student by its initial letter.

Alan	=	A
Beth	=	B
Carol	=	C
Diane	=	D

Ellen	=	E
Frank	=	F
George	=	G
Hank	=	H

Second, using logical symbols, on your scrap paper write down what you know about the students who have auditioned for the show.

Let X < Y signify that X will perform before Y, and X << Y signify that X will perform immediately before Y.

D << A	Diane performs immediately before Alan.
E = 1	Ellen performs first.
F → ~H	If Frank performs, then Hank doesn't.
H → ~F	If Hank performs, then Frank doesn't.
C → (B < C)	If Carol performs, then Beth performs before Carol does.
B → (D << x << B)	If Beth performs, then someone (x) performs immediately after Diane and before Beth.

Consider the last condition in conjunction with the first. Since Diane immediately precedes Alan, x = A, and the last condition can be written B → (D << A << B).

So, if Beth is selected, you know the exact order of three of the performers.

Having translated each of the given conditions into symbols, you should *never* look at the conditions on the computer screen again. You should answer every question based on this set of conditions by referring to the symbolic statements on your scrap paper.

Tactic 3

Pay Careful Attention to the Key Words that Serve to Limit the Situation

Look at the set of conditions presented in the discussion of Tactic 2. Note the words that limit the situations presented. The show *must* open with Ellen's comedy routine;...*at most one* of Frank and Hank will be permitted to perform; Alan will perform *immediately* after Diane;...there will be *only one* intervening act between Diane and Beth.

Certain words are critical to your understanding of the situation. Take particular note of them, and be sure to incorporate them in your symbols.

FREQUENTLY USED KEY WORDS

after	if and only if
all	immediately
always	impossible
at least n (n, $n + 1$,	last
$n + 2$, ...)	less, least
at most n (0, 1, 2, ... , n)	more, most
before	must be
but	no
can be	no fewer than n (= at
cannot be	least n)
consecutive	no more than n (= at
different	most n)
directly	only
each	possible
entire	same
every	some
exactly	the least (smallest, shortest,
except	youngest, etc.)
fewer	the most (greatest, tallest,
first	oldest, etc.)
if	unless

Note that certain of these key words have only one function—to rule out a potential ambiguity. These words so precisely define the situation that only one interpretation is possible. Take, for example, *immediately*. What does the statement "Alan will perform after Diane does" tell you? It tells you that Diane will perform sometime earlier in the program than Alan. What does the statement "Alan will perform immediately after Diane does" tell you? It tells you the exact relationship between Alan and Diane, letting you know that Diane is the person who performs right before Alan with nobody else coming between them.

Tactic 4

First, Eliminate Answer Choices Ruled Out by Individual Conditions; Then, Work Through the Remaining Choices

Pay special attention to any conditions phrased in unambiguous terms—*always, never, all, none.* Because they allow only one interpretation of the situation, you may be able to use them to instantly rule out several answer choices.

See how each of the given conditions concerning the variety show can be used to eliminate one or more of the choices in Question 1. Remember to refer only to the symbolic statements we wrote down; do not refer back to the original list of conditions.

---

1. Which of the following program listings satisfies each of the director's requirements?

(A) Diane, Alan, Beth, Carol, Hank, George
(B) Ellen, Diane, Alan, Hank, Beth, Carol
(C) Beth, Diane, Frank, George, Alan, Ellen
(D) Ellen, Diane, Alan, Beth, Frank, Hank
(E) Ellen, Frank, Diane, Alan, Beth, George

SOLUTION.

- The first condition is: D << A. So eliminate Choice C, in which Diane does not *immediately* precede Alan.
- The next condition is: E = 1. Therefore, we can eliminate Choice A, in which Ellen is not the first performer. (Note that Ellen is not first in Choice C either, but C has already been eliminated, and so we never have to consider it again).

- The third condition states that F → ~H; so eliminate Choice D, in which both Frank and Hank appear.
- The next condition, C → (B < C), doesn't apply. This condition says what must be true *if Carol is selected;* but Carol is not listed in either of the two remaining choices—B and E.
- Finally, recall from our discussion in Tactic 2 that we determined that if Beth is selected to perform, we must have the sequence D << A << B somewhere in the program. Hence we can eliminate Choice B.

By the process of elimination, we now know that the answer is Choice E. In fact, the program

$$E, F, D, A, B, G$$

does *not* violate any of the given conditions, and so *is* acceptable.

Tactic 5

Study Conditions Not Merely for What They State But Also for What They Imply

Certain analytical reasoning questions resemble the inference questions you find in the reading comprehension section of the GRE. To answer them correctly, you must understand not only what the conditions state explicitly, but what they imply.

Consider the following question based on the same set of conditions given in the discussion of Tactic 2.

> **2.** Which of the following students could not be the last person to perform in the program?
> (A) Alan   (B) Beth   (C) Carol   (D) Diane   (E) Ellen

SOLUTION. Note that none of the conditions discusses who will be the last to perform. However, the correct *implication* can easily be made by referring to the first condition: D << A. This tells us that Alan must perform immediately after Diane does, and so Diane cannot be the last performer on the program. The answer is D.

Tactic 6

Organize Information in a List or Table

Often the key to answering analytical reasoning questions is to organize the given information in a list or table. Notice that we did not do this in the questions about the students auditioning for the variety show. As you go through lots of different types of analytical reasoning questions, you will begin to sense intuitively when making a list or a table will be helpful.

Consider the following set of conditions. Before attempting to answer any of the questions based on it, we will enter as much information as possible into a table.

At a high school science fair, the four top winners were a freshman, a sophomore, a junior, and a senior. Each of the winners did a project in a different field: astronomy, biology, chemistry, and geology. The names of the four winners were: Ken, Larry, Mary, and Nancy.

Through discussions with various students, the following facts were ascertained.

The geology project won neither first nor second prize.

Mary won second prize.

The junior won first prize.

The chemistry project, which was done by the senior, won fourth prize.

Ken did the astronomy project.

First use Tactic 2 to abbreviate all of the words. Clearly, we will let K, L, M, and N represent the four names, and A, B, C, and G represent the four subject areas. Since both *sophomore* and *senior* begin with S, we could use So. for *sophomore* and Sr. for *senior*, or we could just use 9, 10, 11, and 12 to represent the four grades.

The most convenient way to display the given information is in a table. You should set up a blank table, and use each of the given conditions to enter information.

Start with a blank grid, and read each condition in order.

Prize	Grade	Subject	Name
1st			
2nd			
3rd			
4th			

Since the geology project won neither first nor second prize, the G must go in the third or fourth row.

Prize	Grade	Subject	Name
1st			
2nd			
3rd		G	
4th		G	

Since Mary won second prize, put an M in the second row.

Prize	Grade	Subject	Name
1st			
2nd			M
3rd		G	
4th		G	

Since the junior won first prize, put an 11 in the first row.

Prize	Grade	Subject	Name
1st	11		
2nd			M
3rd		G	
4th		G	

The chemistry project, which was done by the senior, won fourth prize. Therefore, in the fourth row we can replace the G with a C and enter a 12.

Prize	Grade	Subject	Name
1st	11		
2nd			M
3rd		G	
4th	12	C	

Since Ken did the astronomy project, Ken didn't win third or fourth prize (they went to the geology and chemistry projects), and Mary won second prize; so Ken's astronomy project won first prize.

Prize	Grade	Subject	Name
1st	11	A	K
2nd			M
3rd		G	
4th	12	C	

We do not have complete information, but this is all we can deduce from the given conditions, and so we will have to use it in answering the questions.

---

3. Which of the following statements *must* be true?
(A) The freshman won second prize.
(B) Larry is a sophomore.
(C) Mary did the biology report.
(D) Nancy is a senior.
(E) Ken won fourth prize.

SOLUTION. Looking at our final table, we see that Choice E is definitely wrong (Ken won first prize, not fourth). Choices A, B, and D are all possible; they do not violate the entries in the table, and so *could* be true, but none of them *must* be true. Choice C, on the other hand, *must* be true. The only science not listed is biology, so it *must* go in the second row, next to Mary.

Prize	Grade	Subject	Name
1st	11	A	K
2nd		B	M
3rd		G	
4th	12	C	

Tactic 7

Do Not Use Information Specific to One Question in a Subsequent Question

We will now answer two more questions based on the set of conditions discussed in Tactic 6.

specific only to only this question

---

4. If Nancy is a sophomore, which of the following is the correct order of the winners, from first place to fourth place?

(A) Ken, Mary, Larry, Nancy
(B) Mary, Ken, Nancy, Larry
(C) Larry, Ken, Nancy, Mary
(D) Ken, Mary, Nancy, Larry
(E) Ken, Larry, Nancy, Mary

does Nancy not

SOLUTION. Question 4 adds another condition which we must now take into account, namely that Nancy is a sophomore. Start with the last table we used in Tactic 6, and put in this additional information.

Rows 1 and 2 are already taken by Ken and Mary, and row 4 is reserved for a senior. Therefore, Nancy must go in row 3.

Prize	Grade	Subject	Name
1st	11	A	K
2nd		B	M
3rd	10	G	N
4th	12	C	

We can now complete the table.

The freshman must go in row 2, and Larry must go in row 4.

Prize	Grade	Subject	Name
1st	11	A	K
2nd	9	B	M
3rd	10	G	N
4th	12	C	L

It is now an easy task to answer question 4. Choice D is the correct order:

Ken, Mary, Nancy, Larry.

We have now answered two questions on this set of conditions. Suppose the third question is question 5, below.

---

5. Which of the following statements must be true?
   I. Mary is a freshman.
   II. Larry won fourth prize.
   III. Both the freshman and the sophomore placed higher than the senior.
   (A) None (B) I only (C) III only (D) I and III only
   (E) I, II, and III

Be careful! Looking at the complete table that we created in answering question 4, it appears that all of the statements are true, and that the answer is E. However, our final table was based on a condition stated in question 4 that was not one of the original conditions—namely, that Nancy is a sophomore. That condition applied to question 4 *only*. We may not rely on it in answering question 5. We must go back to the table we had after question 3—the table that was created based only on the original set of conditions:

Solution.

Prize	Grade	Subject	Name
1st	11	A	K
2nd		B	M
3rd		G	
4th	12	C	

From this table it is clear that although statements I and II *could* be true, they are not necessarily true. Statement III, on the other hand, *must* be true. (Both the freshman and sophomore placed higher than the senior, who, we know, won fourth prize.) The correct answer is Choice C: III only.

Tactic 8

Draw a Simple Picture or Diagram That Correctly Illustrates the Given Set of Conditions

On some analytical reasoning questions, an excellent way to deal with the information is to draw a simple diagram, picture, or map. This is particularly helpful when you are dealing with the physical or temporal order of things. It is much easier to tell whether person A can be seated opposite person B if you have sketched a diagram of the table; it is easier to know whether person C is older or younger than person D if you have entered all of the given information on a time line; and it is easier to determine whether town E is east of town W if you have drawn a simple map.

Questions 6–9 are based on the following set of conditions.

> The chairperson and vice-chairperson of a congressional committee are seated opposite one another at the ends of a rectangular conference table. The other six members of the committee are seated around the table, three on each side.
>
> The chairperson is a senator; the vice-chairperson a representative.
> Each senator must be seated next to at least one representative, and vice versa.

Rep. Adams is seated at the vice-chairperson's right, next to Sen. Byrd.

Rep. Cohen, who is not the vice-chairperson, is sitting opposite Sen. Davis.

Sen. Evans is sitting between two representatives.

Only one person is sitting between Rep. Frank and Rep. Gold.

Remember that on the GRE, the preceding set of conditions would appear on the left-hand side of a split screen, and the first question would be on the right-hand side. However, you should not even read that question until you have drawn a rectangle to represent the table. Then reread each of the given conditions, in order, filling in the new information on your drawing as you proceed. Use a dash (—) to represent a seat at the table, and let *r* = representative, and *s* = senator.

The chairperson and vice-chairperson are seated opposite one another at the ends of the table.

The chairperson is a senator; the vice-chairperson a representative.

Each senator must be seated next to at least one representative, and vice versa.

This condition does not help us here, but we will use it as we proceed.

Rep. Adams is seated at the vice-chairperson's right, next to Sen. Byrd.

We now know a senator is to the vice-chairperson's left.

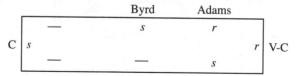

Rep. Cohen, who is not the vice-chairperson, is sitting opposite Sen. Davis.

Cohen is not the vice-chairperson, and cannot be the chairperson, since the chairperson is a senator. Since he is sitting opposite Davis, he cannot sit opposite Byrd or Adams. So he must be on either side of the chairperson. If he were to the right of the chairperson, Sen. Davis would be between two senators, which is not allowed. So Cohen is to the left of the chairperson. Also, a representative is to the right of Davis.

Cohen	Byrd	Adams	
r	*s*	*r*	
C *s*			*r* V-C
s	*r*	*s*	
Davis			

Sen. Evans is sitting between two representatives.

The only place for Evans to sit is opposite Adams. He is then between the vice-chairperson, a representative, and another representative, who is still unknown.

Cohen	Byrd	Adams	
r	*s*	*r*	
C *s*			*r* V-C
s	*r*	*s*	
Davis		Evans	

Only one person is sitting between Rep. Frank and Rep. Gold.

Representatives Frank and Gold are the only representatives missing in the previous diagram. It is clear that they are to sit on either side of Sen. Evans; but there is no way to determine which one is the vice-chairman and which one is seated opposite Sen. Byrd. Therefore, there are two possible seating arrangements.

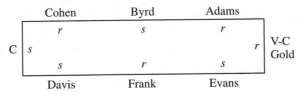

Cohen	Byrd	Adams	
r	*s*	*r*	
C *s*			*r* V-C / Gold
s	*r*	*s*	
Davis	Frank	Evans	

or

Note that the chair is a senator whose name is not mentioned in the set of conditions.

Having created an accurate picture of the situation, you can now easily answer *any* question based on this set of conditions. Without this diagram, you would have to constantly refer back to the original statements, and the solutions would be much less obvious. Now refer to the final diagrams to answer each of questions 6–9.

---

6. How many senators are not sitting next to another senator?

(A) 0   (B) 1   (C) 2   (D) 3   (E) 4

SOLUTION. Only two senators—Byrd and Evans—are not sitting next to a senator. They are each between two representatives. The answer is Choice C.

---

7. Which of the following statements concerning Sen. Harris, the eighth member of the committee, must be true?

I. He is the chairperson.

II. He is sitting opposite Rep. Frank.

III. A senator is sitting on his right.

(A) I only   (B) II only   (C) I and II only
(D) I and III only   (E) I, II, and III

SOLUTION. The only place for Sen. Harris is in the chairperson's seat. I is true. Rep. Frank *could* be the vice-chairperson, in which case he would be opposite Sen. Harris; but the vice-chairperson could also be Rep. Gold, so it is not true that Sen. Harris *must* be sitting opposite Rep. Frank. II is false. From the diagram, we see that Sen. Davis is sitting to the right of the chairperson. III is true. The answer is Choice D: I and III only.

> **8.** Which committee member is the vice-chairperson?
> (A) Adams   (B) Cohen   (C) Frank   (D) Gold
> (E) It cannot be determined from the information given.

SOLUTION. We have seen that the vice-chairperson could be either Frank or Gold, so the answer is Choice E: It cannot be determined from the information given.

> **9.** If Sen. Jones is added to the committee, where could she be seated without violating any of the given conditions?
> (A) Immediately to the right of Sen. Evans
> (B) Immediately to the left of Sen. Evans
> (C) Immediately to the right of Sen. Davis
> (D) Immediately to the left of Sen. Davis
> (E) Immediately to the right of Sen. Byrd

SOLUTION. If Sen. Jones is seated on either side of Sen. Evans, there would be two people between Representatives Frank and Gold. So neither Choice A nor B is correct. If Sen. Jones is seated to the right of Sen. Davis, then Sen. Davis would be between two senators, whereas if she is seated to the left of Sen. Davis, she would be between two senators. Eliminate choices C and D. The answer is Choice E: sitting to the right of Sen. Byrd would not violate any condition.

LOGICAL REASONING

Tactic 9

Look at the Questions Before You Look at the Argument

We have seen that in analytical reasoning questions we always analyze the set of conditions completely, before even looking at the first question. With logical reasoning questions, however, the situation is different. Rather than jumping in blindly and analyzing each and every aspect of the argument—assumptions, central point, evidence, conclusions, logical flaws—do no more work than necessary. Look at the question stem. Then examine the argument. Know what aspect of the argument you are to concentrate on, and focus on it. You will save time and effort.

The logical reasoning question that follows consists of a short passage, followed by the question, "Which of the following best serves as an assumption that would make the argument above logically correct?" If you read the question before you read the passage, you will know that, as presented, the argument is faulty. As a result, you will be looking for the flaw as you read the passage, and may already realize what's wrong before reading through the five choices. If you read the passage first, you may not catch the subtle flaw, and you may find the conclusion perfectly reasonable. Then when you read the question, and learn that the argument was not logically correct, you will be forced to go back and reread the passage, wasting valuable time.

CAUTION: Read only the question itself—*do not read the choices* before reading the passage. Doing so will confuse you and waste time.

In order to save $500,000 in this year's budget, the city council voted to freeze the salaries of its school building inspectors. This short-sighted decision is yet another example of the council being penny wise and pound foolish. The cursory inspections that will result from this action will cause many structural defects to go undetected, resulting in millions more dollars being spent on repairs in the future.

In order for his argument to be logically correct, the author of the above argument used which of the following statements as an unstated underlying assumption?

(A) City inspectors are already overpaid and so the wage freeze is warranted.

(B) The city council cares less about the safety of the school children than it does about saving money.

(C) If they do not receive an increase in their wages, school inspectors will become lax in performing their jobs.

(D) The council does not feel that cursory inspections will necessarily result in defects going undetected.

(E) The council will not authorize repairs in the future, so it will never have to incur the extra costs.

The passage attempts to justify the conclusion that the city will eventually have to pay much more than it is now saving. Alerted to the fact that the logic is faulty (by having first read the question), you probably picked up the subtle shift from "freeze the salaries" in the first sentence to perform "cursory inspections" in the third sentence. If you did, you might have said to yourself, "the fact that the wages of the inspectors are not being raised does not necessarily mean that they will retaliate by rendering poorer service." This then is the gap in the logic. To justify the conclusion presented, we need to assume that freezing salaries will result in cursory or slipshod inspections; and this is precisely what Choice C says.

In this example, none of the other choices is an assumption upon which the argument depends. You can read and analyze each of the other choices before eliminating it, but that takes time. It is always better if you can anticipate the correct choice.

You have just seen how reading a question before reading the argument to which it refers can save you valuable time. Here are a few more typical questions followed by explanations of how you should critically read the argument in order to make the most efficient use of your time.

- Which of the following statements identifies a flaw in the reasoning in the argument above?

    If you have read the question first, you will be looking for flaws as you read the passage, whereas you might otherwise be taken in by the faulty logic presented.

- Which of the following statements, if true, best supports the conclusion of the argument?

    Now, as you read the passage, you know that the facts as stated are not sufficient to justify the conclusion, and you can actually be thinking about what else you would need to know to have more confidence in the truth of what is being claimed.

- Which of the following statements is best supported by the facts presented in the passage above?

    Having read the question first, you know that the passage does *not* reach a conclusion. Rather, you are being asked to form a conclusion based on the given statements (facts), which you are to accept as true.

Tactic 10

Learn to Spot the Major Logical Reasoning Question Types

Just as it will help you to know the major types of reading questions on the GRE, it will also help you to familiarize yourself with the major types of logical reasoning questions on the test.

If you can recognize just what a given question is asking for, you'll be better able to tell which particular approach to take to the argument at hand.

Here are six categories of logical reasoning questions you are sure to face.

1. **Assumption** Questions that test your ability to recognize the premises on which an argument is based often take the following forms:
    - The conclusion above depends on which of the following assumptions?
    - The author of the passage above makes which of the following assumptions?
    - The author of the passage above presupposes that...
    - In the passage above, the author assumes which of the following statements to be true?

2. **Inference** Questions that test your ability to go beyond the author's explicit statements and see what these statements imply may be worded like these.
    - It can be inferred from the passage above that the author believes that...
    - Which of the following is implied by the passage above?
    - From the information above, which of the following is the most reasonable inference?

3. **Conclusion** Questions that test your ability to determine what claim can logically be made on the basis of the evidence in the passage often take these forms.
    - If the statements above are true, which of the following is a conclusion that can be properly drawn?
    - Which of the following would provide the most logical conclusion for the preceding paragraph?

- The statements in the passage, if true, best support which of the following conclusions?

4. **Central Point**   Questions that test your ability to understand the thrust of an argument are often worded like these.
   - The statement cited above conveys which of the following propositions?
   - The passage above emphasizes which of the following points?
   - The author in the passage above argues that...
   - Which of the following expresses the point the author of the passage above makes?

5. **Support**   Questions that test your ability to recognize whether an assertion supports or undermines an argument are often worded like these.
   - Which of the following, if true, best supports the author's conclusion?
   - Which of the following, if true, most weakens the author's conclusion?
   - Which of the following, if true, would constitute the strongest evidence in support of the claim made above?
   - Which of the following, if true, would most weaken the persuasiveness of the claim made above?

NOTE: Implicit in the question, "Which of the following best supports (or most weakens) the conclusion?" is the fact that at least a few of the choices support (or weaken) the conclusion. Your job is to find the one that *best* supports (or *most* weakens) it.

6. **Argument Evaluation**   Questions that test your ability to judge an argument often take these forms.
   - Which of the following would be most important to know in evaluating the accuracy of the argument above?
   - Which of the following hypotheses, if true, would help resolve the apparent paradox introduced above?
   - If all of the statements above are correct, an explanation of their apparent contradiction is provided by...
   - Which of the following identifies a flaw in the speaker's reasoning?

• Knowledge of which of the following would be least useful in evaluating the claims made in the passage above?

Tactic 11

Read Each Argument Very Carefully

Some students, who find that they can answer many reading comprehension questions correctly by skimming the passage, without reading every word, attack logical reasoning questions in the same way. *This is a very poor strategy.*

First of all, the temptation to skim logical arguments should not be as strong since these passages are much shorter, and less time will be saved. More important, it is not enough to have a general idea about the argument; you must be able to analyze it very carefully.

A cursory reading is not sufficient to pick up a subtle flaw in the logic or to ascertain what unstated premise the author is assuming to be true. The importance of reading the passage carefully is underscored later in this chapter in the analysis of the sample logical reasoning question used to illustrate Tactic 13.

Tactic 12

Find the Conclusion of the Argument

It is imperative that you are absolutely clear about what conclusion the author of the argument claims to have reached. The three most common situations are as follows:

• The conclusion is the last sentence of the passage, often introduced by a word such as *therefore, so, thus, hence,* or *consequently*. Here is a simple example of this type of argument:

> Joan Smith has those qualities that we seek in our congressional leaders. She is honest, hard-working, intelligent, and dedicated. Having served for ten years in the House of Representatives, she has the requisite experience to be an effective United States Senator. Therefore, you should enthusiastically vote for Ms. Smith in this year's election.

• The conclusion is the first sentence of the passage, followed by the supporting evidence. In this case, there is no word such as *therefore* signaling the conclusion, but it is still very easy to spot. For example, the preceding argument could have been presented as follows:

> Joan Smith deserves your vote for United States Senator. She has those qualities that we seek in our congressional leaders. She is honest, hard-working, intelligent, and dedicated. In addition, having served for ten years in the House of Representatives, she has the requisite congressional experience to be an effective United States Senator.

- The conclusion is not in the passage. In this case, the question usually asks you to identify the conclusion that is implicit in the argument. For example, if in the two preceding arguments the last or first sentences, respectively, had been omitted, you would have no difficulty determining that the author of the passage wanted you to vote for Joan Smith. The question might have asked, "Which of the following five statements can most reasonably be inferred from the statements in the given passage?"

Tactic 13

Pay Particular Attention to Signal Words in the Question (and in the Argument as Well)

In answering logical reasoning questions, you must read closely both the argument and the question or questions based on it. When you do so, be on the lookout for certain signal words that can clarify the situation. In particular, be alert for:

Cause and Effect Signal Words
The following words often signal the conclusion of an argument.

accordingly
consequently
for this reason
hence
so
therefore
thus

Contrast Signal Words

The following words often signal a reversal of thought within an argument or a question stem.

    although
    but
    despite
    even though
    except
    however
    in contrast
    instead
    nevertheless
    not
    on the contrary
    on the other hand
    rather than
    unlike

Notice that in the following logical reasoning problem several of these words are present: the argument contains the words *despite*, *not*, and *consequently*, and the question stem has the word *except*. Each of these words plays a role in your reasoning.

> Despite the fact that River City increased the average class size by more than 15% in all grades two years ago, this year's average SAT scores for the junior class were the highest ever. This shows that class size is not a good determinant of student performance. Consequently, other school districts should follow River City's lead and save money by increasing the size of their classes.
>
> Each of the following statements, if true, is a valid objection to this argument EXCEPT
>
> (A) The advantages of smaller classes are more pronounced in elementary school than in high school.
>
> (B) The number of classroom discipline problems reported by teachers is directly proportional to the number of students in the classroom.

   (C) Japanese schools have a lower teacher to student ratio than American schools, and have generally better results on international standardized tests.

   (D) Three years ago, the eighth graders in River City Middle School had very high scores on their standardized tests.

   (E) The effects on students of learning in larger classes takes at least three or four years to manifest itself completely.

It is implicit in the question stem that the argument is not very persuasive, and that there are several possible objections that could be raised. In fact, you are told that four of the five statements given raise valid objections to the argument presented. Your job is to determine the only one which does not.

The conclusion that larger class sizes are not detrimental to student learning is based on a single piece of data concerning high school juniors.

Choice A raises the objection that looking at the results of high school students on the SAT does not tell the whole story and that elementary school students will suffer from the larger classes.

Choice E raises an even stronger objection. It suggests that all students may suffer the consequences of increased class sizes; it will just take more time until the results are clearly discernible.

Choice B raises a completely different objection. Even if student academic performance is not adversely affected, there are behavioral disadvantages to having large classes.

Choice D raises still another objection to the argument, the support for which is based on the performance of this year's junior class. Since three years ago, as eighth graders, they had very high scores, it is possible that this group of students is brighter than the average. It is likely that they would excel regardless of class size, whereas other students might suffer more.

Choice C is slightly harder to analyze. If the word *lower* makes you think *smaller,* Choice C seems to say that smaller classes, at least in Japan, result in higher test scores, and are thus beneficial; this then would be yet another valid objection to the given argument. If, however, you are confident in your analysis to this point, Tactic 14 that follows tells you that by the process of elimination, Choice C must be the correct answer. So look at Choice C again. In fact, it refers to a *lower teacher to student ratio*, which means more students per teacher, which translates as *larger* class sizes. Choice C then is not an objection; it supports the argument by showing that good results can occur in larger classes.

As this example shows, logical reasoning questions must be read very carefully. Do not attempt to analyze them too quickly.

Tactic 14

Always Use the Process of Elimination to Reject Incorrect Choices

From Tactic 9, you know that in logical reasoning questions you should always read the question first. This, of course, does not guarantee that you will know the correct answer before reading the choices; in fact, more often than not, you won't. What do you do then? Use the process of elimination. In the best case scenario, this will allow you to zoom in on the correct answer; at worst, it eliminates some obvious wrong choices and allows you to make an educated guess and move on.

Let's see how the process of elimination works on the next logical reasoning question.

In the United States between 1993 and 1998, the number of people on death row continued to increase, but at a rate lower than that of the general prison population.

Which of the following statements directly contradicts this claim?

(A) The number of death row inmates increased slightly from 1993 to 1998.

(B) Among people convicted of murder, the proportion who were sentenced to death decreased from 1993 to 1998.

(C) Each year from 1993 to 1998, more death row inmates were executed than in the previous year.

(D) Each year from 1993 to 1998, fewer people were sentenced to death than in the previous year.

(E) The proportion of death row inmates among the general prison population rose from 0.6% in 1993 to 0.8% in 1998.

Even though the passage is only one sentence long, you should have read the question "Which of the following statements directly contradicts this claim?" first. Unfortunately, there are many ways to contradict the claim made in that sentence. So there is no point in trying to think of one, and then looking to see if it is one of the five choices. You simply must read each choice, and then, by process of elimination, find the correct one.

CAUTION: Do not spend even one second deciding whether or not you think the claim in the passage or any of the choices is true. That is completely irrelevant. We are examining only the logic of the argument. We are looking for a statement that, if true, would mean that the claim is false. [See Tactic 15]

- The passage states that the death row population increased; Choice A confirms this (and says nothing about the general prison population). Choice A is incorrect.
- Choice B compares the proportion of new death row inmates to the number of people convicted of murder, not to the general prison population. Choice B is incorrect.
- If the number of people executed each year went up, the death row population *might* have decreased (thereby contradicting the first part of the claim), but not necessarily (not if they were replaced by many more people being sentenced to death). Choice C is incorrect.
- Choice D doesn't guarantee that the claim is true, but it comes closer to confirming it than contradicting it. Even if fewer people were sentenced to death each year, some still were, so the number of people on death row might have increased. Again, no reference is made to the general prison population. Choice D is incorrect.

Choice E is a little harder to analyze, but because it refers to an increase, many students would not choose it, thinking it confirms rather than refutes the claim. But you must. Having definitively rejected choices A, B, C, and D, you know, by the process of elimination, that Choice E *must* be the correct answer. Let's examine why, in fact, it is.

- The passage claims that the death row population increased at a slower rate than the prison population. This means that the *proportion* of death row inmates in the prison population actually *decreased*. Choice E, which states that the proportion increased, is a direct contradiction of that claim.

NOTE:

(1) Although any of choices A, B, C, and D could be true without the claim being true, none of them is inconsistent with the truth of the claim.

(2) Choices B, C, and D each introduce an extraneous issue. Neither the number of murder convictions nor the number of executions nor the number of people sentenced to death is directly relevant to the claim.

Tactic 15

In Questions About Weakening or Strengthening an Argument, Examine the Argument for Any Unstated Assumptions It Makes

An argument is based upon certain assumptions made by its author. If an argument's basic premises are sound, the argument is strengthened. If the argument's basic premises are flawed, the argument is weakened.

Pinpoint what the argument assumes. Then compare that assumption with the answer choices. If the question asks you to choose an answer that most strengthens the argument, look for the answer choice that is most in keeping with the argument's basic assumption. If the question asks you to choose an answer that most weakens the argument, look for the answer choice that casts the most doubt on that assumption.

Apply this tactic to the following question.

> In a recent speech, the president of a major college said, "It is extremely valuable for college-educated adults entering the workplace to be able to speak at least one foreign language fluently. I am, therefore, proposing that all of our students be encouraged to spend their junior year abroad."
>
> Which of the following, if true, most weakens the president's argument?
>
> (A) Most students who study abroad for a full year return home with a good working knowledge of the language spoken in the country.

(B) Only students who already know a language well will choose to study in a country where that language is spoken.

(C) Some colleges do a much better job than others in teaching foreign languages.

(D) Some students learn to speak foreign languages fluently by taking intensive immersion courses in the United States.

(E) Many students who spend their junior year abroad learn to speak the language fluently, but cannot read and write with ease.

The argument claims that, in order for students to learn to speak foreign languages well, they should study abroad. It clearly assumes a high correlation between studying in a foreign country and learning to speak the language well. It assumes, at the least, that students who have studied abroad can speak a foreign language well, and, possibly, that students who have not studied abroad cannot.

Choice A is in keeping with the assumption inherent in the president's argument. If true, it would strengthen the argument, not weaken it. Choice E, by stating that many students who study abroad do not learn to read and write the language well, seems to cast doubt on the value of the junior year abroad program. However, since the president talked only about the value of being able to speak a foreign language well, Choice E also strengthens his argument.

Choices B and C are also incorrect. They neither strengthen nor weaken the president's argument. At worst, Choice B suggests that it may be difficult to convince some students to study abroad, but it doesn't state that they shouldn't be encouraged to do so. In order to weaken the president's argument, Choice C would have to go much further than it does; it would have to state that some colleges do such a good job, that their students actually learn to speak foreign languages fluently.

The correct answer is Choice D. It states that it is possible for American students to learn to speak foreign languages fluently without studying abroad. Choice D weakens the president's argument by suggesting an alternative method by which college students could achieve the president's goal of speaking a foreign language.

PRACTICE QUESTIONS

Analytical Reasoning Questions

Questions 1–5

Six actors—Bob, Carol, Dave, Ed, Frank, and Grace—are auditioning for a part in an off-Broadway play. The auditions will take place over four consecutive days, starting on a Thursday. Each actor will have one audition. The days on which the different actors will audition must conform to the following conditions:

At least one audition will take place each day.

No more than two auditions will take place on any day.

No more than three auditions will take place on any two consecutive days.

Bob's audition must take place on Saturday.

Carol's audition must take place on the same day as another audition.

Frank's audition must take place on a day before Grace's audition.

Dave's audition must take place on a day after Ed's audition.

1. If only one audition takes place on Thursday, which actor could have that audition?

(A) Bob   (B) Carol   (C) Dave   (D) Frank   (E) Grace

2. If Bob's and Frank's auditions are on the same day, which of the following must be true?

(A) Dave's audition will take place on Thursday.

(B) Dave's audition will take place on Friday.

(C) Grace's audition will take place on Thursday.

(D) Carol's audition will take place on Sunday.

(E) Ed's audition will take place on Sunday.

3. If the director decides to hold two auditions on Thursday and two on Sunday, how many actors would be eligible to audition on Friday?

(A) 1   (B) 2   (C) 3   (D) 4   (E) 5

4. If Ed and Grace have their auditions on the same day, which of
   the following must be true?

   (A) Ed's audition will take place on Thursday.
   (B) Frank's audition will take place on Friday.
   (C) Carol's audition will take place on Saturday.
   (D) Grace's audition will take place on Saturday.
   (E) Carol's audition will take place on Sunday.

5. If Ed's audition is on Saturday, which of the following actors
   cannot audition on the same day as any other actor?

   (A) Bob   (B) Carol   (C) Ed   (D) Frank   (E) Grace

Questions 6–9

As part of their sports physicals, seven collegiate athletes—F, G, H,
I, J, K, and L—are being weighed. In announcing the results of the
physical exams, the coach has given the following information:

    None of the athletes is exactly the same weight as another athlete.
    K is heavier than L, but lighter than H.
    I is heavier than J.
    Both F and G are heavier than H.

6. Each of the following could be true EXCEPT

   (A) F is the heaviest.
   (B) G is the heaviest.
   (C) I is the heaviest.
   (D) More than three athletes are heavier than K.
   (E) More than three athletes are lighter than K.

7. Which of the following, if true, would be sufficient to determine
   which athlete is the lightest?

   (A) I is the heaviest.
   (B) I is lighter than K.
   (C) K is heavier than J.
   (D) J is heavier than K.
   (E) Exactly five students are lighter than F.

8. If J is heavier than F, how many different rankings, by weight, of the athletes are possible?

   (A) 1   (B) 2   (C) 4   (D) 6   (E) 8

9. If H is heavier than I, which of the following CANNOT be true?
   (A) I's weight is equal to the average of F's weight and G's weight.
   (B) I's weight is equal to the average of K's weight and L's weight.
   (C) J's weight is equal to the average of K's weight and L's weight.
   (D) J is the second lightest.
   (E) J is the lightest.

Questions 10–13

Jacqueline placed nine books—two biographies, two computer books, two dictionaries, two novels, and a thesaurus—in a row on a shelf over her desk. The positions of the books are numbered from 1 to 9, with the leftmost book being book 1 and the rightmost book being book 9. The following facts are known about the order in which the books were placed:

   The two biographies are next to each other.
   The fourth book is a novel.
   The two computer books are not next to each other.
   Both the first and last book are dictionaries.
   The thesaurus is not next to either novel.

10. If one of the biographies is book number 3, in what position is the other biography?

    (A) 2   (B) 4   (C) 5   (D) 6   (E) 7

11. If a novel is in position 5, each of the following could be true EXCEPT
    (A) The thesaurus is next to one of the dictionaries.
    (B) The thesaurus is in position 6.
    (C) The two computer books and the thesaurus are in three consecutive positions.
    (D) A biography is in position 2.
    (E) A biography is in position 8.

12. If a novel is in position 6, which of the following could be true?

(A) A computer book is in position 2.

(B) The thesaurus is in position 3.

(C) A biography is in position 5.

(D) The thesaurus is in position 5.

(E) A computer book is in position 7.

13. Which of the following, if true, would enable you to determine the position of every type of book?

(A) A computer book is in position 2.

(B) A computer book is in position 3.

(C) A biography is in position 5.

(D) A computer book is in position 7.

(E) A novel is in position 7.

Logical Reasoning Questions

Questions 14–15

The microwave oven has become a standard appliance in many kitchens, mainly because it offers a fast way of cooking food. Yet, some homeowners believe that the ovens are still not completely safe. Microwaves, therefore, should not be standard appliances until they are more carefully researched and tested.

14. Which one of the following, if true, would most weaken the conclusion of the passage above?

(A) Homeowners often purchase items despite knowing they may be unsafe.

(B) Those homeowners in doubt about microwave safety ought not to purchase microwaves.

(C) Research and testing of home appliances seldom reveal safety hazards.

(D) Microwaves are not as dangerous as steam irons, which are used in almost every home.

(E) Homeowners often purchase items that they do not need.

15. Which one of the following, if true, would most strengthen the conclusion of the passage above?
    (A) Homeowners often doubt the advertised safety of all new appliances.
    (B) Speed of food preparation is not the only concern of today's homeowner.
    (C) Modern homeowners have more free time than ever before.
    (D) Food preparation has become almost a science, with more complicated and involved recipes.
    (E) Many microwave ovens have been found to leak radioactive elements.

16. Ms. Weissman teaches five French classes—three beginning classes and two advanced classes. From the first marking period to the second, although the number of students earning A's in all of her classes increased by 8%, the number of students earning A's in her three beginning classes actually decreased.

    Which of the following statements can definitely be inferred from the information above?
    (A) Ms. Weissman has more students in her advanced classes than in her beginning classes.
    (B) Ms. Weissman has fewer students in her advanced classes than in her beginning classes.
    (C) The number of students earning A's in each of Ms. Weissman's advanced classes increased by more than 8%.
    (D) In at least one of Ms. Weissman's advanced classes, the number of students earning A's increased by more than 8%.
    (E) More advanced students than beginning students earned A's during the second marking period.

17. Al's GPA is higher than Bob's. Carol's GPA is lower than Bob's, but it is higher than Dan's.

    If the preceding statements are true, which of the following statements would have to be true in order to conclude that Ellen has a higher GPA than Carol?
    (A) Ellen's GPA is higher than Dan's.
    (B) Bob's GPA is lower than Ellen's.
    (C) Ellen's GPA is equal to the average of Al's GPA and Dan's GPA.

(D) Al's GPA is higher than Ellen's.

(E) Bob or Dan has a lower GPA than Ellen.

18. Years ago, a nationwide poll concluded that there are more televisions than there are bathtubs in American homes. No doubt that fact remains today, especially in light of the growing popularity of home computers. Now, in addition to owning televisions for entertainment, more and more families are purchasing TV monitors for use with a personal computer. We can safely guess that there are still many more people staring at a picture tube than singing in the shower.

Which one of the following statements can be deduced from this passage?

(A) Personal computers probably cost less than installing a shower or a bathtub.

(B) People can wash themselves without a tub or shower, but they cannot watch television unless they own a television set.

(C) TV monitors will work with personal computers in place of regular computer monitors.

(D) As many computers are sold today as television sets a few years ago.

(E) More television monitors are now used with personal computers than are used to watch commercial television broadcasts.

19. Jeremy: Since Prof. Sanchez is a brilliant teacher whose students excel, she should be granted tenure.

Alberto: Since Prof. Sanchez has not published any research, she is not widely respected in the academic community. Therefore, she should not be granted tenure.

Which of the following is an underlying assumption that Alberto has used in reaching his conclusion?

(A) Prof. Sanchez has applied for tenure.

(B) Brilliant teachers usually publish their research.

(C) Good teaching should not be considered in making tenure decisions.

(D) All professors who are respected in the academic community should be granted tenure.

(E) Being widely respected in the academic community should be a prerequisite for being granted tenure.

20. Some scientists have proposed that, over two hundred million years ago, one giant land mass—rather than various continents and islands—covered one-third of the earth. Long before there was any human life, and over vast periods of time, islands and continents drifted apart. Australia was the first to separate, while South America and Africa were late in splitting apart. Some islands, of course, were formed by volcanoes and were never part of the great land mass.

All the following would support the author's claim EXCEPT

(A) Many of the plants of the South American rain forests are markedly similar to those of the African rain forest.

(B) Australia has more animals that are not found on any other continent than have several of the much larger continents.

(C) Volcanic islands like Hawaii have ecosystems very different from those of continental lands with the same average temperature.

(D) The plants of similar conditions in South America have less in common with those of Australia than with those of Asia, Africa, or Europe.

(E) The primitive languages of Australia are unlike those of Africa, which resemble those of South America.

21. A recent study of children between 2 and 4 years old has shown that in this period of their lives, they show no preference for cereals that have been sweetened either naturally or artificially. But almost all of the same group four years later preferred sweetened cereals. This change shows that the preference for sweetened foods is acquired rather than natural, and that without the example of others using sweeteners, whether in television advertisements or in the home, children would avoid the chief causes of obesity and cavities.

Which one of the following, if true, would provide the best support for this argument?

(A) A second study showed that children who had eaten sweetened food between the ages of 2 and 4 showed no greater preference for sweetened foods at the ages of 6 to 8 than children who had not eaten sweetened foods at the younger age.

(B) A second study showed that children between 4 and 6 who had been sequestered from advertising for sweeteners preferred sugar-free cereals when they were 6 to 8 years old.

(C) Studies of children 6 to 8 who ate sweetened foods show those who live in areas where the water is fluoridated had fewer cavities than children who ate unsweetened foods and lived in areas where the water was not fluoridated.

(D) Studies have shown that the influence of parents upon their children's behavior at early ages is measurably greater than the influence of peer groups or school teachers.

(E) Contrary to what advertisers claim, both adults and children have no difficulty in distinguishing between naturally and artificially sweetened foods or beverages.

22. In America, a baseball game should be described as a series of solo performances: at any given moment, attention is focused on one player and one play. On the other hand, soccer involves all of the team most of the time: each player interacts with others constantly, so that no single individual seems responsible for success or failure. It is because spectators prefer concentrating on individual personalities that baseball remains a much more popular spectator sport than soccer.

Which one of the following, if true, can best be used to undermine the conclusion of this argument?

(A) Soccer. is more popular with spectators in France than baseball.

(B) Among the ten most televised sports in America, by far the most watched is football, and the least watched are tennis and bowling.

(C) Many people watch only the baseball teams of the city in which they live and for whom they root.

(D) Compared to football and basketball, baseball games are much cheaper to attend.

(E) In some sections of the United States, soccer leagues for children under fifteen are more popular than Little League baseball.

23. Antifreeze lowers the melting point of any liquid to which it is added so that the liquid will not freeze in cold weather. It is commonly used to maintain the cooling system in automobile radiators. Of course, the weather may become so cold that even antifreeze is not effective, but such a severe climatic condition rarely occurs in well-traveled places.

Which one of the following can be deduced from the passage?

(A) Well-traveled places have means of transportation other than automobiles.

(B) Antifreeze does not lower the melting point of certain liquids in extreme conditions.

(C) Severe climatic conditions rarely occur.

(D) It is not often that many travelers who use antifreeze have their cooling systems freeze.

(E) Antifreeze raises the melting point of some liquids.

Answers

1. **D**	7. **D**	13. **E**	19. **E**
2. **B**	8. **C**	14. **C**	20. **E**
3. **D**	9. **A**	15. **E**	21. **B**
4. **E**	10. **A**	16. **D**	22. **B**
5. **E**	11. **B**	17. **B**	23. **D**
6. **E**	12. **E**	18. **C**	

6

QUANTITATIVE ABILITY: TACTICS AND PRACTICE

FACTS AND FORMULAS

1. **Sum:** the result of an addition: 8 is the sum of 6 and 2

2. **Difference:** the result of a subtraction: 4 is the difference of 6 and 2

3. **Product:** the result of a multiplication: 12 is the product of 6 and 2

4. **Quotient:** the result of a division: 3 is the quotient of 6 and 2

5. **Remainder:** when 15 is divided by 6, the quotient is 2 and the remainder is 3: $15 = 6 \times 2 + 3$

6. **Integers:** $\{\dots, -3, -2, -1, 0, 1, 2, 3, \dots\}$

7. **Factor** or **Divisor:** any integer that leaves no remainder (i.e., a remainder of 0) when it is divided into another integer: 1, 2, 5, 10 are the factors (or divisors) of 10

8. **Multiple:** the product of one integer by a second integer: 7, 14, 21, 28, ... are multiples of 7 ($7 = 1 \times 7$, $14 = 2 \times 7$, and so on)

9. **Even integers:** the multiples of 2: $\{\dots, -4, -2, 0, 2, 4, \dots\}$

10. **Odd integers:** the non-multiples of 2: $\{\dots, -3, -1, 1, 3, 5, \dots\}$

11. **Consecutive integers:** two or more integers, written in sequence, each of which is 1 more than the preceding one. For example:

$$7, 8, 9 \qquad -2, -1, 0, 1, 2 \qquad n, n+1, n+2$$

12. **Prime number:** a positive integer that has exactly two divisors. The first few primes are 2, 3, 5, 7, 11, 13, 17. (*not* 1)

13. **Exponent:** a number written as a superscript: the 3 in 7^3. On the GRE, the only exponents you need to know about are positive integers: $2^n = 2 \times 2 \times 2 \times \dots \times 2$, where 2 appears as a factor n times.

14. Laws of Exponents:

For any numbers b and c and positive integers m and n:

(i) $b^m b^n = b^{m+n}$ (ii) $\dfrac{b^m}{b^n} = b^{m-n}$ (iii) $(b^m)^n = b^{mn}$

(iv) $b^m c^m = (bc)^m$

15. Square root of a positive number: if a is positive, $\sqrt{a}$ is the only positive number whose square is a: $\left(\sqrt{a}\right)^2 = \sqrt{a} \times \sqrt{a} = a$.

16. The product and the quotient of two positive numbers or two negative numbers are positive; the product and the quotient of a positive number and a negative number are negative.

17. • The product of an *even* number of negative factors is positive.
  • The product of an *odd* number of negative factors is negative.

18. For any positive numbers a and b:

$$\sqrt{ab} = \sqrt{a} \times \sqrt{b} \qquad \text{and} \qquad \sqrt{\dfrac{a}{b}} = \dfrac{\sqrt{a}}{\sqrt{b}}$$

19. For any real numbers a, b, and c:

  • $a(b + c) = ab + ac$ • $a(b - c) = ab - ac$

and, if $a \neq 0$,

  • $\dfrac{b + c}{a} = \dfrac{b}{a} + \dfrac{c}{a}$ • $\dfrac{b - c}{a} = \dfrac{b}{a} - \dfrac{c}{a}$

20. To compare two fractions, use your calculator to convert them to decimals.

21. To multiply two fractions, multiply their numerators and multiply their denominators:

$$\frac{3}{5} \times \frac{4}{7} = \frac{3 \times 4}{5 \times 7} = \frac{12}{35}$$

22. To divide any number by a fraction, multiply that number by the reciprocal of the fraction.

$$\frac{3}{5} \div \frac{2}{3} = \frac{3}{5} \times \frac{3}{2} = \frac{9}{10}$$

23. To add or subtract fractions with the same denominator, add or subtract the numerators and keep the denominator:

$$\frac{4}{9} + \frac{1}{9} = \frac{5}{9} \qquad \text{and} \qquad \frac{4}{9} - \frac{1}{9} = \frac{3}{9} = \frac{1}{3}$$

24. To add or subtract fractions with different denominators, first rewrite the fractions as equivalent fractions with the same denominator:

$$\frac{1}{6} + \frac{3}{4} = \frac{2}{12} + \frac{9}{12} = \frac{11}{12}$$

25. Percent: a fraction whose denominator is 100:

$$15\% = \frac{15}{100} = .15$$

26. The *percent increase* of a quantity is

$$\frac{\text{actual increase}}{\text{original amount}} \times 100\%.$$

The *percent decrease* of a quantity is

$$\frac{\text{actual decrease}}{\text{original amount}} \times 100\%.$$

27. Ratio: a fraction that compares two quantities that are measured in the same units. The ratio *2 to 3* can be written $\frac{2}{3}$ or 2:3.

28. In any ratio problem, write the letter *x* after each number and use some given information to solve for *x*.

29. Proportion: an equation that states that two ratios (fractions) are equal. Solve proportions by cross-multiplying: if $\frac{a}{b} = \frac{c}{d}$, then $ad = bc$.

30. Average of a set of *n* numbers: the sum of those numbers divided by *n*:

$$\text{average} = \frac{\text{sum of the numbers}}{n} \quad \text{or simply}$$

$$A = \frac{\text{sum}}{n}$$

31. If you know the average, *A*, of a set of *n* numbers, multiply *A* by *n* to get their sum: sum = *nA*.

32. To multiply two binomials, use the FOIL method: multiply each term in the first parentheses by each term in the second parentheses and simplify by combining terms, if possible.

$$(2x - 7)(3x + 2) = \underbrace{(2x)(3x)}_{\text{First terms}} + \underbrace{(2x)(2)}_{\text{Outer terms}} + \underbrace{(-7)(3x)}_{\text{Inner terms}} + \underbrace{(-7)(2)}_{\text{Last terms}} =$$

$$6x^2 + 4x - 21x - 14 = 6x^2 - 17x - 14$$

33. The three most important binomial products on the GRE are these:

- $(x - y)(x + y) = x^2 - y^2$
- $(x - y)^2 = (x - y)(x - y) = x^2 - 2xy + y^2$
- $(x + y)^2 = (x + y)(x + y) = x^2 + 2xy + y^2$

34. All distance problems involve one of three variations of the same formula:

$$\text{distance} = \text{rate} \times \text{time} \qquad \text{rate} = \frac{\text{distance}}{\text{time}}$$

$$\text{time} = \frac{\text{distance}}{\text{rate}}$$

35.

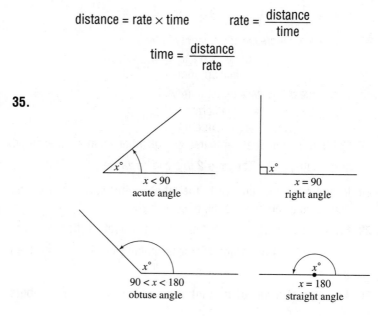

36. If two or more angles form a straight angle, the sum of their measures is 180°.

37. The sum of all the measures of all the angles around a point is 360°.

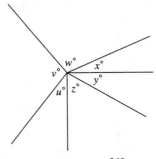

$$u + v + w + x + y + z = 360$$

38.

vertical angles

39. Vertical angles have equal measures.

$$a = c \text{ and } b = d.$$

40. If a pair of parallel lines is cut by a transversal that is *not* perpendicular to the parallel lines:
- Four of the angles are acute, and four are obtuse.
- All four acute angles are equal: $a = c = e = g$.
- All four obtuse angles are equal: $b = d = f = h$.
- The sum of any acute angle and any obtuse angle is 180°: for example, $d + e = 180$, $c + f = 180$, $b + g = 180$,….

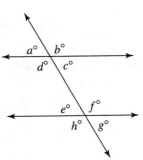

41. In any triangle, the sum of the measures of the three angles is 180°: $x + y + z = 180$.

42. The measure of an exterior angle of a triangle is equal to the sum of the measures of the two opposite interior angles.

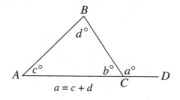

43. In any triangle:
- the longest side is opposite the largest angle;
- the shortest side is opposite the smallest angle;
- sides with the same length are opposite angles with the same measure.

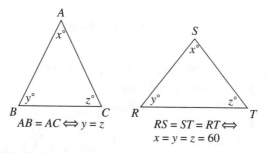

44. In any right triangle, the sum of the measures of the two acute angles is 90°.

45.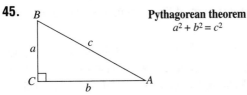

Pythagorean theorem
$$a^2 + b^2 = c^2$$

46. In a 45-45-90 right triangle, the sides are x, x, and $x\sqrt{2}$.

47. In a 30-60-90 right triangle the sides are x, $x\sqrt{3}$, and $2x$.

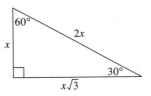

48. The sum of the lengths of any two sides of a triangle is greater than the length of the third side.

The difference between the lengths of any two sides of a triangle is less than the length of the third side.

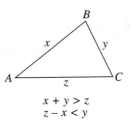

$$x + y > z$$
$$z - x < y$$

49. The area of a triangle is given by $A = \dfrac{1}{2}bh$, where b = base and h = height.

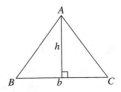

50. If A represents the area of an equilateral triangle with side s, then $A = \dfrac{s^2\sqrt{3}}{4}$.

51. In any quadrilateral, the sum of the measures of the four angles is 360°.

52. A *parallelogram* is a quadrilateral in which both pairs of opposite sides are parallel. A *rectangle* is a parallelogram in which all four angles are right angles. A *square* is a rectangle in which all four sides have the same length.

53. In any parallelogram:

- Opposite sides are equal: *AB* = *CD* and *AD* = *BC*.
- Opposite angles are equal: *a* = *c* and *b* = *d*.
- Consecutive angles add up to 180°: *a* + *b* = 180, *b* + *c* = 180, and so on.
- The two diagonals bisect each other: *AE* = *EC* and *BE* = *ED*.

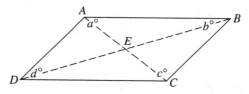

54. In any rectangle:

- The measure of each angle in a rectangle is 90°.
- The diagonals of a rectangle have the same length: *AC* = *BD*.

55. In any square:

- All four sides have the same length.
- Each diagonal divides the square into two 45-45-90 right triangles.
- The diagonals are perpendicular to each other: *AC* ⊥ *BD*.

56. Formulas for perimeter and area:

- For a parallelogram: $A = bh$ and $P = 2(a + b)$.
- For a rectangle: $A = \ell w$ and $P = 2(\ell + w)$.
- For a square: $A = s^2$ or $A = \frac{1}{2} d^2$ and $P = 4s$.

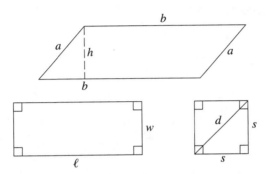

57. Let r be the radius, d the diameter, C the circumference, and A the area of a circle, then

$$d = 2r \quad C = \pi d = 2\pi r \quad A = \pi r^2$$

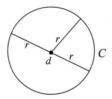

58. The formula for the volume of a rectangular solid is $V = \ell wh$.

In a cube, all the edges are equal. Therefore, if e is the edge, the formula for the volume is $V = e^3$.

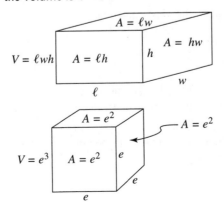

59. The formula for the surface area of a rectangular solid is $A = 2(\ell w + \ell h + wh)$. The formula for the surface area of a cube is $A = 6e^2$.

60. The formula for the volume, V, of a cylinder is $V = \pi r^2 h$. The surface area, A, of the side of the cylinder is $A = 2\pi rh$. The area of the top and bottom are each πr^2.

61. The distance, d, between two points, $A(x_1, y_1)$ and $B(x_2, y_2)$, can be calculated using the distance formula:

$$d = \sqrt{(x_2 - x_1)^2 + (y_2 - y_1)^2}.$$

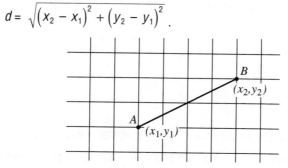

62. The slope of the line is given by:

$$\text{slope} = \frac{y_2 - y_1}{x_2 - x_1}$$

63. • The slope of any horizontal line is 0.
   • The slope of any line that goes up as you move from left to right is positive.
   • The slope of any line that goes down as you move from left to right is negative.

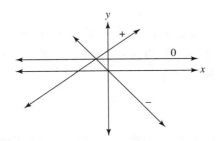

64. **The Counting Principle:** If two jobs need to be completed and there are *m* ways to do the first job and *n* ways to do the second job, then there are *m* × *n* ways to do one job followed by the other. This principle can be extended to any number of jobs.

65. If *E* is any event, the **probability** that *E* will occur is given by

$$P(E) = \frac{\text{number of favorable outcomes}}{\text{total number of possible outcomes}},$$

assuming that all of the possible outcomes are equally likely.

66.–69. Let *E* be an event, and let *P(E)* be the probability that it will occur.

66. If *E* is *impossible,* then **P(E) = 0**.

67. If it is *certain* that *E* will occur, then **P(E) = 1**.

68. In all other cases, **0 < P(E) < 1**.

69. The probability that event *E* will *not* occur is **1 – P(E)**.

70. If an experiment is done 2 (or more) times, the probability that first one event will occur, and then a second event will occur, is the product of the probabilities.

GENERAL MATH TACTICS

Tactic 1

Draw a Diagram

On any geometry question for which a figure is not provided, draw one (as accurately as possible) on your scrap paper. If a diagram is provided, copy it onto your scrap paper, unless you *instantly* see the solution.

Let's consider some examples.

Example 1

What is the area of a rectangle whose length is twice its width and whose perimeter is equal to that of a square whose area is 1?

(A) 1   (B) 6   (C) $\frac{2}{3}$ (D) $\frac{4}{3}$ (E) $\frac{8}{9}$

Solution

Don't even think of answering this question until you have drawn a square and a rectangle and labeled each of them: each side of the square is 1; and if the width of the rectangle is w, its length is $2w$.

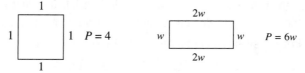

Now, write the required equation and solve it:

$$6w = 4 \Rightarrow w = \frac{4}{6} = \frac{2}{3} \Rightarrow 2w = \frac{4}{3}$$

The area of the rectangle = $lw = \left(\frac{4}{3}\right)\left(\frac{2}{3}\right) = \frac{8}{9}$ (E).

Drawings should not be limited, however, to geometry questions; there are many other questions on which drawings will help.

Example 2

A jar contains 10 red marbles and 30 green ones. How many red marbles must be added to the jar so that 60% of the marbles will be red?

(A) 25   (B) 30   (C) 35   (D) 40   (E) 60

Solution

Draw a diagram and label it. From the diagram it is clear that there are now $40 + x$ marbles in the jar, of which $10 + x$ are red. Since we want the fraction of red marbles to be

$60\% \left(= \frac{3}{5}\right)$, we have $\frac{10 + x}{40 + x} = \frac{3}{5}$.

Cross-multiplying, we get:

$$50 + 5x = 120 + 3x \Rightarrow 2x = 70 \Rightarrow x = 35 \text{ (C)}.$$

Of course, you could have set up the equation and solved it without the diagram, but the drawing makes the solution easier and you are less likely to make a careless mistake.

Tactic 2

Trust a Diagram that Appears To Be Drawn to Scale

Example 3

In the figure at the right, what is the sum of the measures of all of the marked angles?

(A) 360°   (B) 540°
(C) 720°   (D) 900°
(E) 1080°

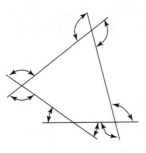

Solution

Make your best estimate of each angle, and add up the values. The five choices are so far apart that, even if you're off by 15° or more on some of the angles, you'll get the right answer. The sum of the estimates shown is 690°, so the correct answer *must* be 720° (C).

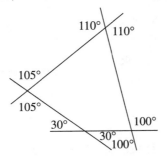

<u>Column A</u>   <u>Column B</u>

Example 4

| x | 170 |

Solution

Since the diagram appears to be drawn to scale (the angle labeled 35° looks to be about 35°), trust it. Look at x: it appears to be *about* 90 + 50 = 140; it is *definitely* less than 170.

Also, y, drawn above is clearly more than 10, so x is less than 170. Choose (B).

Tactic 3

When Necessary, Change a Diagram, and then Trust Your Figure

Example 5

In △ACB, what is the value of x?

(A) 75   (B) 60   (C) 45
(D) 30   (E) 15

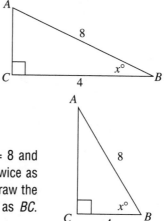

Solution

The figure provided is useless. $AB = 8$ and $BC = 4$, but in the figure AB is *not* twice as long as BC. On your scrap paper redraw the triangle so that AB *is* twice as long as BC. Now, just look: x is about 60 (B).

In fact, x is exactly 60. If the hypotenuse of a right triangle is twice the length of one of the legs, you have a 30-60-90 triangle, and the angle formed by the hypotenuse and that leg is 60°.

Example 6

AB

10

Solution

Again, the diagram cannot be trusted. Actually, there are two things wrong: $\angle C$ is labeled 40°, but looks much more like 60° or 70°, and AC and BC are each labeled 10, but BC is drawn much longer. On your scrap paper redraw the triangle with a 40° angle and two sides of the same length. Now, it's clear that $AB < 10$. Choose (B).

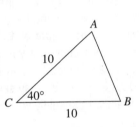

Tactic 4

Add a Line to a Diagram

Occasionally, after staring at a diagram, you still have no idea how to solve the problem to which it applies. It looks as though there isn't enough given information. When this happens, it often helps to draw another line in the diagram.

Example 7

In the figure at the right, Q is a point on the circle whose center is O and whose radius is r, and $OPQR$ is a rectangle. What is the length of diagonal PR?

(A) r (B) r^2 (C) $\dfrac{r^2}{\pi}$ (D) $\dfrac{r\sqrt{2}}{\pi}$

(E) It cannot be determined from the information given.

Solution

If, after staring at the diagram and thinking about rectangles, circles, and the Pythagorean theorem, you're still lost, don't give up. Ask yourself, "Can I add another line to this diagram?" As soon as you think to draw in *OQ*, the other diagonal, the problem becomes easy: the two diagonals are equal, and, since *OQ* is a radius, it is equal to *r* (A).

Tactic 5

Subtract to Find Shaded Regions

Whenever part of a figure is white and part is shaded, the straight-forward way to find the area of the shaded portion is to find the area of the entire figure and then subtract from it the area of the white region. Of course, if you are asked for the area of the white region, you can, instead, subtract the shaded area from the total area. Occasionally, you may see an easy way to calculate the shaded area directly, but usually you should subtract.

Example 8

In the figure below, *ABCD* is a rectangle, and *BE* and *CF* are arcs of circles centered at *A* and *D*. What is the area of the shaded region?

(A) $10 - \pi$ (B) $2(5 - \pi)$ (C) $2(5 - 2\pi)$ (D) $6 + 2\pi$ (E) $5(2 - \pi)$

Solution

The entire region is a 2×5 rectangle whose area is 10. Since each white region is a quarter-circle of radius 2, the combined area of these regions is that of a semicircle of radius 2:

$$\frac{1}{2}\pi(2)^2 = 2\pi.$$

Therefore, the area of the shaded region is $10 - 2\pi = 2(5 - \pi)$ (B).

Tactic 6

Don't Do More Than You Have To
Look for shortcuts. Since a problem can often be solved in more than one way, you should always look for the easiest method. Consider the following examples.

Example 9

If $5(3x - 7) = 20$, what is $3x - 8$?

(A) $\frac{11}{3}$ (B) 0   (C) 3   (D) 14   (E) 19

It's not difficult to solve for x:
$$5(3x - 7) = 20 \Rightarrow 15x - 35 = 20 \Rightarrow 15x = 55 \Rightarrow x = \frac{55}{15} = \frac{11}{3}$$

But it's too much work. Besides, once you find that $x = \frac{11}{3}$, you still have to multiply to get $3x$: $3\frac{11}{3} = 11$, and then subtract to get $3x - 8$: $11 - 8 = 3$.

Solution

The key is to recognize that you don't need x. Finding $3x - 7$ is easy (just divide the original equation by 5), and $3x - 8$ is just 1 less:
$$5(3x - 7) = 20 \Rightarrow 3x - 7 = 4 \Rightarrow 3x - 8 = 3.$$

<u>Column A</u>	<u>Column B</u>

Example 10

Zach worked from 9:47 A.M. until 12:11 P.M.
Sam worked from 9:11 A.M. until 12:47 P.M.

The number of minutes Zach worked	The number of minutes Sam worked

Solution

Don't spend any time calculating how many minutes either boy worked. You need to know only which column is greater; and since Sam started earlier and finished later, he clearly worked longer. The answer is B.

Tactic 7

Pay Attention to Units

Often the answer to a question must be in units different from those used in the given data. As you read the question, write down and underline or circle exactly what you are being asked. Do the examiners want hours or minutes or seconds, dollars or cents, feet or inches, meters or centimeters? On multiple-choice questions an answer with the wrong units is almost always one of the choices.

Example 11

At a speed of 48 miles per hour, how many minutes will be required to drive 32 miles?

(A) $\frac{2}{3}$ (B) $\frac{3}{2}$ (C) 40   (D) 45   (E) 2400

Solution

This is a relatively easy question. Just be attentive. Since $\frac{32}{48} = \frac{2}{3}$, it will take $\frac{2}{3}$ of an *hour* to drive 32 miles. Choice A is $\frac{2}{3}$; but that is *not* the correct answer because you are asked how many *minutes* will be required. The correct answer is $\frac{2}{3}(60) = 40$ (C).

Tactic 8

Systematically Make Lists

When a question asks "how many," often the best strategy is to make a list of all the possibilities. It is important that you make the list in a *systematic* fashion so that you don't inadvertently leave something out. Often, shortly after starting the list, you can see a pattern developing and can figure out how many more entries there will be without writing them all down.

Example 12

The product of three positive integers is 300. If one of them is 5, what is the least possible value of the sum of the other two?

Solution

Since one of the integers is 5, the product of the other two is 60 (5 × 60 = 300). Systematically, list all possible pairs, (a, b), of positive integers whose product is 60, and check their sums. First, let $a = 1$, then 2, and so on.

a	b	$a + b$
1	60	61
2	30	32
3	20	23
4	15	19
5	12	17
6	10	16

The answer is 16.

Example 13

A palindrome is a number, such as 93539, that reads the same forward and backward. How many palindromes are there between 100 and 1000?

Solution. First, write down the numbers in the 100's that end in 1:

101, 111, 121, 131, 141, 151, 161, 171, 181, 191

Now write the numbers beginning and ending in 2:

202, 212, 222, 232, 242, 252, 262, 272, 282, 292

By now you should see the pattern: there are 10 numbers beginning with 1, and 10 beginning with 2, and there will be 10 beginning with 3, 4, ..., 9 for a total of 9 × 10 = 90 palindromes.

PRACTICE QUESTIONS

Multiple-Choice Questions

1. In the figure below, if the radius of circle O is 10, what is the length of diagonal AC of rectangle $OABC$?

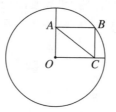

(A) $\sqrt{2}$ (B) $\sqrt{10}$ (C) $5\sqrt{2}$ (D) 10   (E) $10\sqrt{2}$

2. In the figure below, $ABCD$ is a square and AED is an equilateral triangle. If $AB = 2$, what is the area of the shaded region?

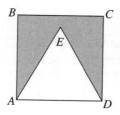

(A) $\sqrt{3}$ (B) 2   (C) 3   (D) $4 - 2\sqrt{3}$ (E) $4 - \sqrt{3}$

3. If $5x + 13 = 31$, what is the value of $\sqrt{5x + 31}$?

(A) $\sqrt{13}$ (B) $\sqrt{\dfrac{173}{5}}$ (C) 7   (D) 13   (E) 169

4. At Nat's Nuts a $2\frac{1}{4}$-pound bag of pistachio nuts costs \$6.00. At this rate, what is the cost, in cents, of a bag weighing 9 ounces?

(A) 1.5   (B) 24   (C) 150   (D) 1350   (E) 2400

5. In the figure below, three circles of radius 1 are tangent to one another. What is the area of the shaded region between the circles?

(A) $\frac{\pi}{2} - \sqrt{3}$ (B) 1.5   (C) $\pi - \sqrt{3}$ (D) $\sqrt{3} - \frac{\pi}{2}$

(E) $2 - \frac{\pi}{2}$

Quantitative Comparison Questions

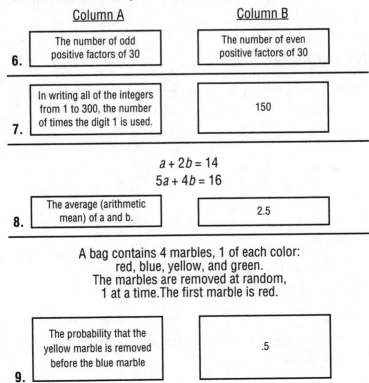

Column A	Column B
6. The number of odd positive factors of 30	The number of even positive factors of 30
7. In writing all of the integers from 1 to 300, the number of times the digit 1 is used.	150

$a + 2b = 14$
$5a + 4b = 16$

8. The average (arithmetic mean) of a and b.	2.5

A bag contains 4 marbles, 1 of each color:
red, blue, yellow, and green.
The marbles are removed at random,
1 at a time. The first marble is red.

9. The probability that the yellow marble is removed before the blue marble	.5

<u>Column A</u>   <u>Column B</u>

The area of circle *O* is 12.

10. | The area of the shaded sector | | $\frac{\pi}{2}$ |
|---|---|---|

Answer Key

1. **D**	3. **C**	5. **D**	7. **A**	9. **C**
2. **E**	4. **C**	6. **C**	8. **C**	10. **B**

Answer Explanations

1. **D.** There is nothing wrong with the diagram, so trust it. *AC* is clearly longer than *OC*, and very close to radius *OE*.

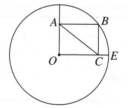

Therefore, *AC* must be about 10. Check the choices. They are approximately as follows:

(A) $\sqrt{2} = 1.4$; (B) $\sqrt{10} = 3.1$; (C) $5\sqrt{2} = 7$;

(D) 10; (E) $10\sqrt{2} = 14$. The answer must be 10.

**The answer *is* 10. The two diagonals are equal, and diagonal *OB* is a radius.

2. **E.** Use Tactic 5: subtract to find the shaded area. The area of square *ABCD* is 4. By Fact 50, the area of $\triangle AED$ is $\dfrac{2^2 \sqrt{3}}{4} = \dfrac{4\sqrt{3}}{4} = \sqrt{3}$. Then the area of the shaded region is $4 - \sqrt{3}$..

3. **C.** Use Tactic 6: don't do more than you have to. In particular, don't solve for *x*. Here

   $5x + 13 = 31 \Rightarrow 5x = 18 \Rightarrow 5x + 31 =$
   $18 + 31 = 49 \Rightarrow \sqrt{5x + 31} = \sqrt{49} = 7$.

4. **C.** This is a relatively simple ratio, but use Tactic 7 and make sure you get the units right. You need to know that there are 100 cents in a dollar and 16 ounces in a pound.

   $\dfrac{\text{price}}{\text{weight}} : \dfrac{6 \text{ dollars}}{2.25 \text{ pounds}} = \dfrac{600 \text{ cents}}{36 \text{ ounces}} = \dfrac{x \text{ cents}}{9 \text{ ounces}}$

   Now cross-multiply and solve: $36x = 5400 \Rightarrow x = 150$.

5. **D.** Use Tactic 4 and add some lines: connect the centers of the three circles to form an equilateral triangle whose sides are 2. Now use Tactic 5 and find the shaded area by subtracting the area of the three sectors from the area of the triangle, which is $\dfrac{2^2 \sqrt{3}}{4} = \sqrt{3}$ (Fact 50). Each sector is $\dfrac{1}{6}$ of a circle of radius 1. Together the three sectors form $\dfrac{1}{2}$ of such a circle, so their total area is $\dfrac{1}{2}\pi(1)^2 = \dfrac{\pi}{2}$. Finally, subtract: the area of the shaded region is $\sqrt{3} - \dfrac{\pi}{2}$.

6. **C.** Use Tactic 8. Systematically list all the factors of 30, either individually or in pairs: 1, 30, 2, 15, 3, 10, 5, 6. Of the 8 factors, 4 are even and 4 are odd. The columns are equal (C).

7. **A.** Use Tactic 8. Systematically list the numbers that contain the digit 1, writing as many as you need to see the pattern. Between 1 and 99 the digit 1 is used 10 times as the units

digit (1, 11, 21, ..., 91) and 10 times as the tens digit (10, 11, 12, ..., 19) for a total of 20 times. From 200 to 299, there are 20 more times (the same 20 but preceded by 2). Finally, from 100 to 199 there are 20 more plus 100 numbers where the digit 1 is used in the hundreds place. The total is 20 + 20 + 20 + 100 = 160. Column A is greater.

8. **C.** Use Tactic 6: don't do more than is necessary. You don't need to solve this system of equations; you don't need to know the values of a and b, only their average. Adding the two equations gives

$$6a + 6b = 30 \Rightarrow a + b = 5 \Rightarrow \frac{a+b}{2} = \frac{5}{2}.$$

The columns are equal (C).

9. **C.** Use Tactic 8. Systematically list all of the orders in which the marbles could be drawn. With 4 colors, there would ordinarily have been 24 orders, but since the first marble drawn was red, there are only 6 arrangements for the other 3 colors: BYG, BGY, YGB, YBG, GYB, GBY. In 3 of these 6 the yellow comes before the blue, and in the other 3 the blue comes before the yellow. Therefore, the probability that the yellow marble will be removed before the blue marble is $\frac{3}{6} = \frac{1}{2} = .5$.

The columns are equal (C).

10. **B.** The shaded sector is $\frac{45}{360} = \frac{1}{8}$ of the circle, so its area is $\frac{1}{8}$ of 12: $\frac{12}{8} = \frac{3}{2} = 1.5$. Since $\pi > 3$, $\frac{\pi}{2} > 1.5$. Column B is greater.

DISCRETE QUANTITATIVE QUESTIONS

Ten of the mathematics questions on the GRE are multiple-choice questions.

In this section you will learn important strategies you need to help you answer multiple-choice questions on the GRE. However, as invaluable as these tactics are, use them only when you need them. *If you know how to solve a problem and are confident that you can do so accurately and reasonably quickly, JUST DO IT!*

Tactic 9

Test the Choices, Starting with C

Tactic 9, often called *backsolving*, is useful when you are asked to solve for an unknown and you understand what needs to be done to answer the question, but you want to avoid doing the algebra. The idea is simple: test the various choices to see which one is correct.

NOTE: On the GRE the answers to virtually all numerical multiple-choice questions are listed in either increasing or decreasing order. Consequently, in applying Tactic 9, *you should always start with the middle value,* (what we call C). For example, assume that choices A, B, C, D, and E are given in increasing order. Try (C). If it works, you've found the answer. If (C) doesn't work, you should now know whether you need to test a larger number or a smaller one, and that information permits you to eliminate two more choices. If (C) is too small, you need a larger number, so (A) and (B) are out; if (C) is too large, you can eliminate (D) and (E), which are even larger.

Examples 14 and 15 illustrate the proper use of Tactic 9.

Example 14

If the average (arithmetic mean) of 2, 7, and x is 12, what is the value of x?

(A) 9   (B) 12   (C) 21   (D) 27   (E) 36

Solution

Use Tactic 9. Test Choice C: $x = 21$.

- Is the average of 2, 7, and 21 equal to 12?

- No: $\dfrac{2 + 7 + 21}{3} = \dfrac{30}{3} = 10$, which is *too small*.

- Eliminate (C); also, since, for the average to be 12, *x* must be *greater* than 21, eliminate (A) and (B).

- Try Choice D: *x* = 27. Is the average of 2, 7, and 27 equal to 12?

- Yes: $\dfrac{2 + 7 + 27}{3} = \dfrac{36}{3} = 12$. The answer is D.

Every problem that can be solved using Tactic 9 can be solved directly, usually in less time. Therefore, we stress: *if you are confident that you can solve a problem quickly and accurately, just do so.*

Example 15

If the sum of five consecutive odd integers is 735, what is the largest of these integers?

(A) 155   (B) 151   (C) 145   (D) 143   (E) 141

Solution

Use Tactic 9. Test Choice C: 145.

- If 145 is the largest of the five integers, the integers are 145, 143, 141, 139, and 137. Quickly add them on your calculator. The sum is 705.
- Since 705 is too small, eliminate (C), (D), and (E).
- If you noticed that the amount by which 705 is too small is 30, you should realize that each of the five numbers needs to be increased by 6; therefore, the largest is 151 (B).
- If you didn't notice, just try 151, and see that it works.

This solution is easy, and it avoids having to set up and to solve the required equation:

$$n + (n + 2) + (n + 4) + (n + 6) + (n + 8) = 735.$$

Tactic 10

Replace Variables with Numbers

Mastery of Tactic 10 is critical for anyone developing good test-taking skills. This tactic can be used whenever the five choices involve the variables in the question. There are three steps:

1. Replace each letter with an easy-to-use number.

2. Solve the problem using those numbers.

3. Evaluate each of the five choices with the numbers you picked to see which choice is equal to the answer you obtained.

Examples 16–17 illustrate the proper use of Tactic 10.

Example 16

If *a* is equal to *b* multiplied by *c*, which of the following is equal to *b* divided by *c*?

(A) $\dfrac{a}{bc}$ (B) $\dfrac{ab}{c}$ (C) $\dfrac{a}{c}$ (D) $\dfrac{a}{c^2}$ (E) $\dfrac{a}{bc^2}$

Solution

• Pick three easy-to-use numbers that satisfy $a = bc$: for example, $a = 6$, $b = 2$, $c = 3$.

• Solve the problem with these numbers: $b \div c = \dfrac{b}{c} = \dfrac{2}{3}$.

• Check each of the five choices to see which one is equal to $\dfrac{2}{3}$:

• (A) $\dfrac{a}{bc} = \dfrac{6}{(2)(3)} = 1$: NO.   (B) $\dfrac{ab}{c} = \dfrac{(6)(2)^1}{3_1} = 6$: NO.

(C) $\dfrac{a}{c} = \dfrac{6}{3} = 2$: NO.   (D) $\dfrac{a}{c^2} = \dfrac{6}{3^2} = \dfrac{6}{9} = \dfrac{2}{3}$: YES!

Still check (E): $\dfrac{a}{bc^2} = \dfrac{6}{2(3^2)} = \dfrac{6}{2(3^2)} = \dfrac{6}{18} = \dfrac{1}{3}$: NO.

• The answer is (D).

Example 17

If the sum of four consecutive odd integers is *s*, then, in terms of *s*, what is the greatest of these integers?

(A) $\dfrac{s-12}{4}$ (B) $\dfrac{s-6}{4}$ (C) $\dfrac{s+6}{4}$ (D) $\dfrac{s+12}{4}$ (E) $\dfrac{s+16}{4}$

Solution

• Pick four easy-to-use consecutive odd integers: say, 1, 3, 5, 7. Then *s*, their sum, is 16.

- Solve the problem with these numbers: the greatest of these integers is 7.

- When $s = 10$, the five choices are $\dfrac{s-12}{4} = \dfrac{4}{4}$, $\dfrac{s-6}{4} = \dfrac{10}{4}$, $\dfrac{s+6}{4} = \dfrac{22}{4}$, $\dfrac{s+12}{4} = \dfrac{28}{4}$, $\dfrac{s+16}{4} = \dfrac{32}{4}$.

- Only $\dfrac{28}{4}$, Choice D, is equal to 7.

Of course, Examples 16 and 17 can be solved without using Tactic 10 *if your algebra skills are good.*

The important point is that, if you are uncomfortable with the correct algebraic solution, you can use Tactic 10 and *always* get the right answer.

Example 18 is somewhat different. You are asked to reason through a word problem involving only variables. Most students find problems like these mind-boggling. Here, the use of Tactic 10 is essential.

Helpful Hint

Replace the letters with numbers that are easy to use, not necessarily ones that make sense. It is perfectly OK to ignore reality. A school can have five students, apples can cost $10 each, trains can go 5 miles per hour or 1000 miles per hour—it doesn't matter.

Example 18

If a school cafeteria needs c cans of soup each week for each student, and if there are s students in the school, for how many weeks will x cans of soup last?

(A) $\dfrac{cx}{s}$ (B) $\dfrac{xs}{c}$ (C) $\dfrac{s}{cx}$ (D) $\dfrac{x}{cs}$ (E) csx

Solution

- Replace c, s, and x with three easy-to-use numbers. If a school cafeteria needs 2 cans of soup each week for each student, and if there are 5 students in the school, how many weeks will 20 cans of soup last?

- Since the cafeteria needs $2 \times 5 = 10$ cans of soup per week, 20 cans will last for 2 weeks.
- Which of the choices equals 2 when $c = 2$, $s = 5$, and $x = 20$?
- The five choices become: $\frac{cx}{x} = 8$, $\frac{xs}{c} = 50$, $\frac{x}{cs} = \frac{1}{8}$, $\frac{x}{cs} = 2$, $csx = 200$. The answer is (D).

Tactic 11

Choose an Appropriate Number

Tactic 11 is similar to Tactic 10 in that we pick convenient numbers. However, here no variable is given in the problem. Tactic 11 is especially useful in problems involving fractions, ratios, and percents.

Helpful Hint

In problems involving fractions, the best number to use is the least common denominator of all the fractions. In problems involving percents, the easiest number to use is 100.

Example 19

At Central High School each student studies exactly one foreign language. Three-fifths of the students take Spanish, and one-fourth of the remaining students take Italian. If all of the others take French, what <u>percent</u> of the students take French?

(A) 10   (B) 15   (C) 20   (D) 25   (E) 30

Solution

The least common denominator of $\frac{3}{5}$ and $\frac{1}{4}$ is 20, so assume that there are 20 students at Central High. (Remember that the numbers you choose don't have to be realistic.) Then the number of students taking Spanish is 12 $\left(\frac{3}{5} \text{ of } 20\right)$. Of the remaining 8 students, 2 $\left(\frac{1}{4} \text{ of } 8\right)$ take Italian. The other 6 take French. Finally, 6 is 30% of 20. The answer is (E).

Example 20

From 1994 to 1995 the sales of a book decreased by 80%. If the sales in 1996 were the same as in 1994, by what percent did they increase from 1995 to 1996?

(A) 80%   (B) 100%   (C) 120%   (D) 400%   (E) 500%

Solution

Use Tactic 12, and assume that 100 copies were sold in 1994 (and 1996). Sales dropped by 80 (80% of 100) to 20 in 1995 and then increased by 80, from 20 back to 100, in 1996. The percent increase was

$$\frac{\text{actual increase}}{\text{original amount}} \times 100\% = \frac{80}{20} \times 100\% = 400\% \text{ (D)}.$$

Tactic 12

Add Equations

When a question involves two equations, either add them or subtract them. If there are three or more equations, add them.

Helpful Hint

Very often, answering a question does not require you to solve the equations. Remember Tactic 6: Do not do any more than is necessary.

Example 21

If $3x + 5y = 14$ and $x - y = 6$, what is the average of x and y?

(A) 0   (B) 2.5   (C) 3   (D) 3.5   (E) 5

Solution

Add the equations:

$$\begin{array}{r} 3x + 5y = 14 \\ + \quad x - y = 6 \\ \hline 4x + 4y = 20 \end{array}$$

Divide each side by 4: $x + y = 5$

The average of x and y is their sum divided by 2:

$$\frac{x + y}{2} = 2.5$$

The answer is (B).

Example 22

If $a - b = 1$, $b - c = 2$, and $c - a = d$, what is the value of d?

(A) −3   (B) −1   (C) 1   (D) 3

(E) It cannot be determined from the information given.

Solution

Add the three equations:

$$\begin{aligned} a - b &= 1 \\ b - c &= 2 \\ + \; c - a &= d \\ \hline 0 = 3 + d &\Rightarrow d = -3 \end{aligned}$$

The answer is (A).

Tactic 13

Eliminate Absurd Choices, and Guess

When you have no idea how to solve a problem, eliminate all the absurd choices and *guess* from among the remaining ones.

Example 23

The average of 5, 10, 15, and x is 20. What is x?

(A) 0   (B) 20   (C) 25   (D) 45   (E) 50

Solution

If the average of four numbers is 20, and three of them are less than 20, the other one must be greater than 20. Eliminate A and B and guess. If you further realize that, since 5 and 10 are *a lot* less than 20, x will probably be *a lot* more than 20, you can eliminate (C), as well. Then guess either (D) or (E).

Example 24

If 25% of 220 equals 5.5% of w, what is w?

(A) 10   (B) 55   (C) 100   (D) 110   (E) 1000

Solution

Since 5.5% of w equals 25% of 220, which is surely greater than 5.5% of 220, w must be *greater* than 220. Eliminate choices A, B, C, and D. The answer *must* be (E)!

PRACTICE QUESTIONS

1. Judy is now twice as old as Adam but 6 years ago she was 5 times as old as he was. How old is Judy now?

(A) 10   (B) 16   (C) 20   (D) 24   (E) 32

2. If $a < b$ and c is the sum of a and b, which of the following is the positive difference between a and b?

(A) $2a - c$ (B) $2b - c$ (C) $c - 2b$ (D) $c - a + b$ (E) $c - a - b$

3. If w widgets cost c cents, how many widgets can you get for d dollars?

(A) $\dfrac{100dw}{c}$ (B) $\dfrac{dw}{100c}$ (C) $100cdw$ (D) $\dfrac{dw}{c}$ (E) cdw

4. If 120% of a is equal to 80% of b, which of the following is equal to $a + b$?

(A) $1.5a$ (B) $2a$ (C) $2.5a$ (D) $3a$ (E) $5a$

5. In the figure at the right, $WXYZ$ is a square whose sides are 12. AB, CD, EF, and GH are each 8, and are the diameters of the four semicircles. What is the area of the shaded region?

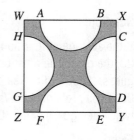

(A) $144 - 128\pi$ (B) $144 - 64\pi$
(C) $144 - 32\pi$ (D) $144 - 16\pi$
(E) 16π

6. What is a divided by a% of a?

(A) $\dfrac{a}{100}$ (B) $\dfrac{100}{a}$ (C) $\dfrac{a^2}{100}$ (D) $\dfrac{100}{a^2}$ (E) $100a$

7. On a certain Russian-American committee, $\frac{2}{3}$ of the members are men, and $\frac{3}{8}$ of the men are Americans. If $\frac{3}{5}$ of the committee members are Russian, what fraction of the members are American women?

(A) $\frac{3}{20}$ (B) $\frac{11}{60}$ (C) $\frac{1}{4}$ (D) $\frac{2}{5}$ (E) $\frac{5}{12}$

8. Nadia will be x years old y years from now. How old was she z years ago?

(A) $x + y + z$ (B) $x + y - z$ (C) $x - y - z$
(D) $y - x - z$ (E) $z - y - x$

9. If $12a + 3b = 1$ and $7b - 2a = 9$, what is the average (arithmetic mean) of a and b?

(A) 0.1   (B) 0.5   (C) 1   (D) 2.5   (E) 5

10. If $x\%$ of y is 10, what is y?

(A) $\frac{10}{x}$ (B) $\frac{100}{x}$ (C) $\frac{1000}{x}$ (D) $\frac{x}{100}$ (E) $\frac{x}{10}$

Answer Key

1. **B**	3. **A**	5. **C**	7. **A**	9. **B**
2. **B**	4. **C**	6. **B**	8. **C**	10. **C**

Answer Explanations

1. **B.** Use Tactic 9: backsolve, starting with (C). If Judy is now 20, Adam is 10; 6 years ago, they would have been 14 and 4, which is less than 5 times as much. Eliminate C, D, and E, and try a smaller value. If Judy is now 16, Adam is 8; 6 years ago, they would have been 10 and 2. That's it; 10 is 5 times 2.

2. **B.** Use Tactic 10. Pick simple values for a, b, and c. Let $a = 1$, $b = 2$, and $c = 3$. Then $b - a = 1$. Only $2b - c$ is equal to 1.

3. **A.** Use Tactic 10: replaces variables with numbers. If 2 widgets cost 10 cents, then widgets cost 5 cents each; and for 3 dollars, you can get 60 widgets. Which of the choices equals 60 when $w = 2$, $c = 10$, and $d = 3$?

    Only $\dfrac{100dw}{c}$.

4. **C.** Use Tactic 11: choose appropriate numbers. Since 120% of 80 = 80% of 120, let $a = 80$ and $b = 120$. Then $a + b = 200$, and $200 \div 80 = 2.5$.

5. **C.** If you don't know how to solve this, you must use Tactic 13: eliminate the absurd choices and guess. Which choices are absurd? Certainly, (A) and (B), both of which are negative. Also, since Choice D is about 94, which is much more than half the area of the square, it is much too large. Guess between (C) (about 43) and (E) (about 50). If you remember that the way to find shaded areas is to subtract, guess (C): $144 - 32\pi$.

6. **B.** Use Tactics 10 and 11: replace a by a number, and use 100 since the problem involves percents.

    $$100 \div (100\% \text{ of } 100) = 100 \div 100 = 1.$$

    Test each choice; which one equals 1 when $a = 100$? A and B: $\dfrac{100}{100} = 1$. Eliminate (C), (D), and (E); and test (A) and (B) with another value, 50, for a:

    $$50 \div (50\% \text{ of } 50) = 50 \div (25) = 2.$$

    Now, only $\dfrac{100}{a}$, works: $\dfrac{100}{50} = 2$.

7. **A.** Use TACTIC 11: choose appropriate numbers. The LCM of all the denominators is 120, so assume that the committee has 120 members. Then there are $\dfrac{2}{3} \times 120 = 80$ men and 40 women. Of the 80 men, 30 $\left(\dfrac{3}{8} \times 80\right)$ are American. Since there are 72 $\left(\dfrac{3}{5} \times 120\right)$ Russians, there are $120 - 72 = 48$ Americans, of whom 30 are men, so the other 18 are women. Finally, the fraction of American women is $\dfrac{18}{120} = \dfrac{3}{20}$.

8. **C.** Use Tactic 10: replace x, y, and z with easy-to-use numbers. Assume Nadia will be 10 in 2 years. How old was she 3 years ago? If she will be 10 in 2 years, she is 8 now and 3 years ago was 5. Which of the choices equals 5 when $x = 10$, $y = 2$, and $z = 3$? Only $x - y - z$.

9. **B.** Use Tactic 12, and add the two equations:

$$10a + 10b = 10 \Rightarrow a + b = 1 \Rightarrow \frac{a + b}{2} = \frac{1}{2} \text{ or } 0.5.$$

10. **C.** Use Tactics 10 and 11. Since 100% of 10 is 10, let $x = 100$ and $y = 10$. When $x = 100$, choices C and E are each 10. Eliminate choices A, B, and D, and try some other numbers: 50% of 20 is 10. Of (C) and (E), only $\frac{1000}{x} = 20$ when $x = 50$.

QUANTITATIVE COMPARISON QUESTIONS

One half of the 28 questions on the quantitative section of the GRE are quantitative comparisons. It is very likely that the only time you ever encountered questions of this type before was when you were preparing for the PSAT or SAT I, in your junior or senior year of high school. Therefore, it may be at least four years since you last answered a quantitative comparison question. Even if you knew all the various strategies for answering them at the time, and it is likely that you didn't, you are probably no longer familiar with them. In this section you will learn all of the necessary tactics. If you master them, you will quickly realize that quantitative comparisons are the easiest mathematics questions on the GRE and will wish that there were more than 14 of them.

Before the first quantitative comparison question appears on the screen, you will see these instructions.

<u>Directions</u>: This question consists of two quantities, one in Column A and one in Column B. You are to compare the two quantities and decide whether

the quantity in Column A is greater;

the quantity in Column B is greater;

the two quantities are equal;

the relationship cannot be determined from the information given.

<u>Common information</u>: Information concerning one or both of the quantities to be compared is centered above the two columns. A symbol that appears in both colums represents the same thing in Column A as it does in Column B.

Before learning the different strategies for solving this type of question, let's clarify these instructions. In quantitative comparison questions there are two quantities, one in Column A and one in Column B, and it is your job to compare them.

You should click on the oval in front of	if
The quantity in Column A is greater.	The quantity in Column A is greater *all the time, no matter what.*
The quantity in Column B is greater.	The quantity in Column B is greater *all the time, no matter what.*
The two quantities are equal.	The two quantities are equal *all the time, no matter what.*
The relationship cannot be determined from the information given.	*The answer is not one of the first three choices.*

This means, for example, that *if you can find a single instance* when the quantity in Column A is greater than the quantity in Column B, then you can immediately eliminate two choices: the answer cannot be "The quantity in Column B is greater," and the answer cannot be "The two quantities are equal." In order for the answer to be "The quantity in Column B is greater," the quantity in Column B would have to be greater *all the time;* but you know of one instance when it isn't. Similarly, since the quantities are not equal *all the time,* the answer can't be "The two quantities are equal." The correct answer, therefore, is either "The quantity in Column A is greater" or "The relationship cannot be determined from the information given." If it turns out that the quantity in Column A *is* greater all the time, them that is the answer; if, however, you can find a single instance where the quantity in Column A is not greater, the answer is "The relationship cannot be determined from the information given."

By applying the tactics that you will learn in this section, you will probably be able to determine which of the choices is correct; if, however, after eliminating two of the choices, you still cannot determine which answer is correct, quickly guess between the two remaining choices and move on.

Helpful Hint

Right now, memorize the instructions for answering quantitative comparison questions. When you take the GRE, dismiss the instructions for these questions immediately—do not spend even one second reading the directions (or looking at the sample problems.)

Before learning the most important tactics for handling quantitative comparison questions, let's look at two examples to illustrate the preceding instructions.

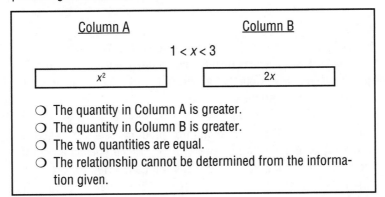

Column A	Column B

$$1 < x < 3$$

| x^2 | $2x$ |

○ The quantity in Column A is greater.
○ The quantity in Column B is greater.
○ The two quantities are equal.
○ The relationship cannot be determined from the information given.

Solution

In each column, x represents the same thing—a number between 1 and 3. If x is 2, then x^2 and $2x$ are each 4, and *in this* case the two quantities are equal. We can, therefore, eliminate the first two choices: neither Column A nor Column B is greater *all the time*. However, in order for the correct answer to be "The two quantities are equal," the columns would have to be equal *all the time*. Are they? Note that although 2 is the only *integer* between 1 and 3, it is not the only *number* between 2 and 3: x could be 1.1 or 2.5 or any of infinitely many other numbers. And in those cases the quantities are not equal (for example, $2.5^2 = 6.25$, whereas $2(2.5) = 5$). The columns are *not* always equal, and so the correct answer is the fourth choice: "The relationship cannot be determined from the information given."

Column A	Column B

p and q are primes

$p + q = 12$

p	8

○ The quantity in Column A is greater.
○ The quantity in Column B is greater.
○ The two quantities are equal.
○ The relationship cannot be determined from the information given.

Solution

Since 5 and 7 are the only primes whose sum is 12, p could be 5 or 7. In either case, p is less than 8, and so the quantity in Column B is greater, *all the time*. Note that although $1 + 11 = 12$, p cannot be 11, because 1 is not a prime.

Note: To simplify the discussion, throughout the rest of this section, in the explanations of the answers to all sample questions and the Model Tests, the four answer choices will be referred to as (A), (B), (C), and (D), respectively. For example, we will write

The correct answer is (B).

rather than

The correct answer is "The quantity
in Column B is greater."

Tactic 14

Replace Variables with Numbers

Many problems that are hard to analyze because they contain variables become easy to solve when the variables are replaced by simple numbers.

Tactic 14 is the most important tactic for quantitative comparison questions. *Be sure to master it!*

Most quantitative comparison questions contain variables. When those variables are replaced by simple numbers such as 0 and 1, the quantities in the two columns become much easier to compare.

Column A	Column B

Example 25

$$a < b < c < d$$

ab	cd

Solution

- Replace a, b, c, and d with easy-to-use numbers that satisfy the condition $a < b < c < d$: for example, $a = 1$, $b = 2$, $c = 5$, $d = 10$.
- Evaluate the two columns: $ab = (1)(2) = 2$, and $cd = (5)(10) = 50$.
- Therefore, *in this case*, the quantity in Column B is greater.
- Does that mean that (B) is the correct answer? Not necessarily. The quantity in Column B is greater this time, but will it be greater **every single time, no matter what?**
- What it does mean is that neither (A) nor (C) could possibly be the answer: Column A can't be greater **every single time, no matter what,** because it isn't greater *this* time; and the columns aren't equal **every single time, no matter what,** because they aren't equal *this* time.

The correct answer, therefore, is either (B) or (D); and in the few seconds that it took you to plug in 1, 2, 5, and 10 for a, b, c, and d, you were able to eliminate two of the four choices. If you could do nothing else, you should now guess.

But, of course, *you can and will do something else*. You will try some other numbers. But *which* numbers? Since the first numbers you chose were positive, try some negative numbers this time.

Let $a = -5$, $b = -3$, $c = -2$, and $d = -1$.

- Evaluate: $ab = (-5)(-3) = 15$ and $cd = (-2)(-1) = 2$.
- Therefore, *in this case*, the quantity in Column A is greater.
- Column B is *not* greater all the time. (B) is *not* the correct answer.
- The answer is (D).

Here are some guidelines for deciding which numbers to use when applying Tactic 14.

1. **The very best numbers to use first are 1, 0, and –1.**

2. **Often, fractions between 0 and 1 are useful.**

3. **Occasionally, "large" numbers such as 10 or 100 can be used.**

4. **If there is more than one variable, it is permissible to replace each with the same number.**

5. **If a variable appears more than once in a problem, it must be replaced by the same number each time.**

6. **Do not impose any conditions not specifically stated.** In particular, do not assume that variables must represent integers. For example, 3 is not the only number that satisfies $2 < x < 4$ (2.1, 3.95, and π all work). The expression $a < b < c < d$ does not mean that a, b, c, d are *integers*, let alone *consecutive* integers (which is why we didn't choose 1, 2, 3, and 4 in Example 14), nor does it mean that any or all of these variables are *positive*.

When you replace the variables in a quantitative comparison question with numbers, remember:

> If the value in Column A is ever greater: eliminate (B) and (C)— the answer must be (A) or (D).
> If the value in Column B is ever greater: eliminate (A) and (C)— the answer must be (B) or (D).
> If the two columns are ever equal: eliminate (A) and (B)—the answer must be (C) or (D).

Practice applying TACTIC 14 to these examples.

<u>Column A</u>   <u>Column B</u>

Example 26

$$m > 0 \text{ and } m \neq 1$$

| m^2 | | m^3 |

Example 27

| $w + 10$ | | $w - 11$ |

Solution 26

Use Tactic 14. Replace m with numbers satisfying $m > 0$ and $m \neq 1$.

	Column A	Column B	Compare	Eliminate
Let $m = 2$.	$2^2 = 4$	$2^3 = 8$	(B) is greater.	(A) and (C)
Let $m = \frac{1}{2}$.	$\left(\frac{1}{2}\right)^2 = \frac{1}{4}$	$\left(\frac{1}{2}\right)^3 = \frac{1}{8}$	(A) is greater.	(B)

The answer is (D).

Solution 27

Use Tactic 14. There are no restrictions on w, so use the best numbers: 1, 0, −1.

	Column A	Column B	Compare	Eliminate
Let $w = 1$.	$1 + 10 = 11$	$1 - 11 = -10$	(A) is greater.	(B and C)
Let $w = 0$.	$0 + 10 = 10$	$0 - 11 = -11$	(A) is greater.	
Let $w = -1$.	$-1 + 10 = 9$	$-1 - 11 = -12$	(A) is greater.	

Guess (A). We let w be a positive number, a negative number, and 0. Each time Column A was greater. That's not proof, but it justifies an educated guess.

Tactic 15

Choose an Appropriate Number

This is just like TACTIC 14. We are replacing a variable with a number, but the variable isn't mentioned in the problem.

Column A   Column B

Example 28

Every band member is either 15, 16, or 17 years old.
One-third of the band members are 16, and
twice as many band members are 16 as 15.

| The number of 17-year-old band members | The total number of 15- and 16-year-old band members |

Solution

If the first sentence of Example 28 had been "There are n students in the school band, all of whom are 15, 16, or 17 years old," the problem would have been identical to this one. Using Tactic 14, you could have replaced n with an easy-to-use number, such as 6, and solved: $\frac{1}{3}(6) = 2$ are 16 years old; then 1 is 15, and the remaining 3 are 17. The answer is (C).

Example 29

Abe, Ben, and Cal divided a cash prize.

Abe took 50% of the money and spent $\frac{3}{5}$ of what he took.

Ben took 40% of the money and spent $\frac{3}{4}$ of what he took.

| The amount that Abe spent | The amount that Ben spent |

Solution

Use Tactic 15. Assume the prize was $100. Then Abe took $50 and

spent $\frac{3}{5}(\$\overset{10}{50}) = \$30$. Ben took $40 and spent $\frac{3}{4}(\$\overset{10}{40}) = \$30$.

The answer is (C).

Tactic 16

Make the Problem Easier: Do the Same Thing to Each Column

In solving a quantitative comparison problem, you can always add the same quantity to each column or subtract the same quantity from each column. You can multiply or divide each side of an equation or inequality by the same quantity, *but in the case of inequalities you can do this only if the quantity is positive.* Since you don't know whether the columns are equal or unequal, you cannot multiply or divide by a variable *unless you know that it is positive.* If the quantities in each column are positive, you may square them or take their square roots.

Here are three examples on which to practice Tactic 16.

Column A	Column B

Example 30

$$\frac{1}{3} + \frac{1}{4} + \frac{1}{9} \qquad \qquad \frac{1}{9} + \frac{1}{3} + \frac{1}{5}$$

Example 31

a is a negative number

$$a^2 \qquad\qquad -a^2$$

Example 32

$$\frac{\sqrt{20}}{2} \qquad\qquad \frac{5}{\sqrt{5}}$$

Solution 30

Cancel (subtract)

$\frac{1}{3}$ and $\frac{1}{9}$ from

each column: $\qquad \cancel{\frac{1}{3}} + \frac{1}{4} + \cancel{\frac{1}{9}} \qquad \cancel{\frac{1}{9}} + \cancel{\frac{1}{3}} + \frac{1}{5}$

Since $\frac{1}{4} > \frac{1}{5}$, the answer is (A).

Solution 31

Add a^2 to
each column: $a^2 + a^2 = 2a^2$ $-a^2 + a^2 = 0$

Since a is negative, $2a^2$ is positive. The answer is (A).

Solution 32

Square each
column: $\left(\dfrac{\sqrt{20}}{2}\right)^2 = \dfrac{20}{4} = 5$ $\left(\dfrac{5}{\sqrt{5}}\right)^2 = \dfrac{25}{5} = 5$

The answer is (C).

Tactic 17

Ask "Could They Be Equal?" and "Must They Be Equal?"

Tactic 17 is most useful when one column contains a variable and the other contains a number. In this situation ask yourself, "Could they be equal?" If the answer is "yes," eliminate (A) and (B), and then ask, "Must they be equal?" If the second answer is "yes," then (C) is correct; if the second answer is "no," then choose (D). When the answer to "Could they be equal?" is "no," we usually know right away what the correct answer is.

Let's look at a few examples:

Column A   Column B

Example 33

The sides of a triangle are 3, 4, and x.

| x | 5 |

Example 34

Bank A has 10 tellers and bank B has 20 tellers.
Each bank has more female tellers than male tellers.

| The number of female tellers at bank A | The number of female tellers at bank B |

Column A	Column B

Example 35

| The perimeter of a rectangle whose area is 21 | 20 |

Solution 33

Could they be equal? Could *x* = 5? Of course. That's the all-important 3-4-5 right triangle. Eliminate (A) and (B). Must they be equal? Must *x* = 5? The answer is "no." Actually, *x* can be any number satisfying the inequality 1 < *x* < 7.

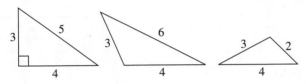

Solution 34

Could they be equal? Could the number of female tellers be the same in both banks? No. More than half (i.e., more than 10) of bank B's 20 tellers are female, but bank A has only 10 tellers in all. The answer is (B).

Solution 35

Could they be equal? Could a rectangle whose area is 21 have a perimeter of 20? Yes, if its length is 7 and its width is 3: 7 + 3 + 7 + 3 = 20. Eliminate (A) and (B). Must they be equal? If you're *not* sure, guess between (C) and (D).

There are other possibilities—lots of them; here are a 7 × 3 rectangle and a few others:

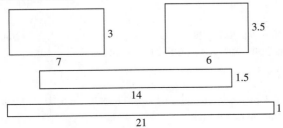

Tactic 18

Don't Calculate: Compare

Avoid unnecessary calculations. You don't have to determine the exact values of the quantities in Columns A and B; you just have to compare them.

These are problems on which poor test-takers waste time doing arithmetic and good test-takers think! Practicing Tactic 18 will help you become a good test-taker.

Now, test your understanding of Tactic 18 by solving these problems.

Column A	Column B

Example 36

The number of years from 1492 to 1929	The number of years from 1429 to 1992

Example 37

$43^2 + 27^2$	$(43 + 27)^2$

Example 38

Howie earned a 75 on each of his first three math tests and an 80 on the fourth and fifth tests.

Howie's average after four tests.	Howie's average after five tests.

Solution 36

The subtraction is easy enough, but why do it? The dates in Column B start earlier and end later. Clearly, they span more years. You don't need to know how many years. Column B is greater.

Solution 37

For *any* positive numbers a and b, $(a + b)^2 > a^2 + b^2$. You should do the calculations only if you don't know this fact. Column B is greater.

Solution 38

Remember that you want to know which average is higher, *not* what the averages are. After four tests Howie's average is clearly less than 80, so an 80 on the fifth test had to *raise* his average. Column B is greater.

PRACTICE QUESTIONS

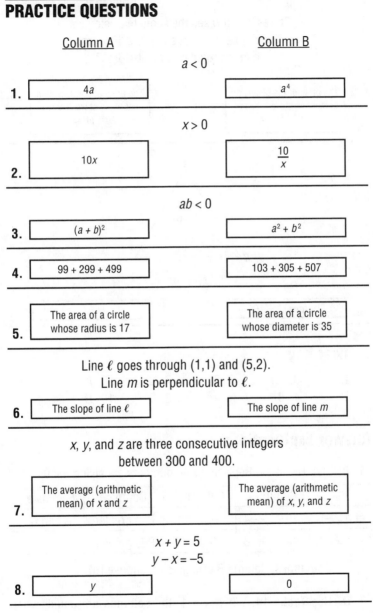

	Column A	Column B

$a < 0$

1. $4a$ | a^4

$x > 0$

2. $10x$ | $\dfrac{10}{x}$

$ab < 0$

3. $(a + b)^2$ | $a^2 + b^2$

4. $99 + 299 + 499$ | $103 + 305 + 507$

5. The area of a circle whose radius is 17 | The area of a circle whose diameter is 35

Line ℓ goes through (1,1) and (5,2).
Line m is perpendicular to ℓ.

6. The slope of line ℓ | The slope of line m

x, y, and z are three consecutive integers between 300 and 400.

7. The average (arithmetic mean) of x and z | The average (arithmetic mean) of x, y, and z

$x + y = 5$
$y - x = -5$

8. y | 0

Column A   Column B

Stores *A* and *B* sell the same television set.
The regular price at store *A* is 10% less
than the regular price at store *B*.

9.

| The price of the television set when store *A* has a 10% off sale | The price of the television set when store *B* has a 20% off sale |

AB = AC

10.

| The area of △*ABC* | 3 |

Answer Key

1. **B**	3. **B**	5. **B**	7. **C**	9. **A**
2. **D**	4. **B**	6. **A**	8. **C**	10. **D**

Answer Explanations

1. **B.** Use Tactic 14. Replace *a* with numbers satisfying $a < 0$.

	Column A	Column B	Compare	Eliminate
Let $a = -1$.	$4(-1) = -4$	$(-1)^4 = 1$	B is greater.	A and C
Let $a = -2$.	$4(-2) = -8$	$(-2)^4 = 16$	B is greater.	

Both times, Column B was greater: choose (B).

2. **D.** Use Tactic 14. When $x = 1$, the columns are equal; when $x = 2$, they aren't.

3. **B.** Use Tactic 16.

	Column A	Column B
Expand Column A:	$(a + b)^2 =$	
	$a^2 + 2ab + b^2$	$a^2 + b^2$
Subtract $a^2 + b^2$ from each column:	$2ab$	0

Since it is given that $ab < 0$, then $2ab < 0$.

4. **B.** Use Tactic 18: don't calculate; compare. Each of the three numbers in Column B is greater than the corresponding number in Column A. Column B is greater.

5. **B.** Again, use Tactic 18: don't calculate the two areas; compare them. The circle in Column A has a radius of 17, and so its diameter is 34. Since the circle in Column B has a larger diameter, its area is greater.

6. **A.** Again, use Tactic 18: don't calculate either slope. Quickly, make a rough sketch of line ℓ, going through (1,1) and (5,2), and draw line m perpendicular to it. Line ℓ has a positive slope (it slopes upward), whereas line m has a negative slope. Column A is greater.

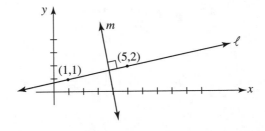

7. **C.** Use TACTIC 14: replace x, y, and z with three consecutive integers between 300 and 400—say, 318, 319, and 320, and just calculate to find the averages.

Column A: $\dfrac{318 + 320}{2} = \dfrac{638}{2} = 319.$

Column B: $\dfrac{318 + 319 + 320}{3} = \dfrac{957}{3} = 319.$

8. **C.** Use Tactic 17. Could $y = 0$? In each equation, if $y = 0$, then $x = 5$, so *y can* equal 0. Eliminate (A) and (B), and either guess between (C) and (D) or try to continue. Must $y = 0$? Yes; when you have two equations in two variables, there is only one solution, so nothing else is possible.

9. **A.** Use Tactic 15: choose an appropriate number. *The best number to use in percent problems is 100*, so assume that the regular price of the television in store *B* is 100 (the units don't matter). Since 10% of 100 is 10, the regular price in store *A* is $100 - 10 = 90$.

   Column A: 10% of 90 is 9, so the sale price in store A is $90 - 9 = 81$.

   Column B: 20% of 100 is 20, so the sale price in store B is $100 - 20 = 80$.

10. **D.** Use Tactic 17. Could the area of $\triangle ABC = 3$? Since the height is 6, the area would be 3 only if the base were 1: $\frac{1}{2}(1)(6) = 3$.

    Could $BC = 1$? Sure (see the figure). Must the base be 1? Of course not. Neither column is *always* greater, and the columns are not *always* equal (D).

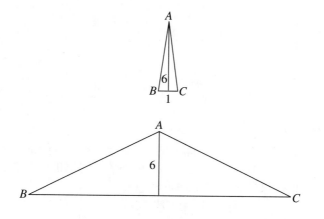

DATA INTERPRETATION QUESTIONS

Four of the 28 questions in the quantitative section are data interpretation questions. As their name suggests, these questions are always based on the information that is presented in some form of a graph or a chart. Occasionally, the data are presented in a chart or table, but much more often, they are presented graphically. The most common types of graphs are

- line graphs   • bar graphs   • circle graphs

Data interpretation questions always appear in two sets of two questions each. For example, questions 14 and 15 might refer to a particular set of graphs or charts, and then later there will be two more questions, say numbers 22 and 23, which refer to a completely different set of graphs and charts.

When the first data interpretation question appears, one or more graphs will be on the left-hand side of the screen, and the question will be on the right-hand side. It is possible that you will have to scroll down in order to see all of the data. After you confirm your answer to the first question, the second question will replace it on the right-hand side of the screen; the graphs, of course, will still be on the left-hand side for you to refer to.

The tactics discussed in this section can be applied to any type of data, no matter how they are displayed. In the practice exercises at the end of the section, there are data interpretation questions based on every type of graph that could appear on the GRE. Carefully, read through the answer explanations for each exercise, so that you learn the best way to handle each type of graph.

Infrequently, an easy data interpretation question will require only that you read the graph and find a numerical fact that is displayed. Usually, however, you will have to do some calculation on the data that you are analyzing. In harder questions, you may be given hypothetical situations and asked to make inferences based on the information provided in the given graphs.

The four questions that follow will be used to illustrate the tactics that you should use in answering data interpretation questions. Remember, however, that on the GRE there will always be exactly two questions that refer to a particular graph or set of graphs.

Sales and Earnings of XYZ Corporation 1991–1998

1998 Sales of XYZ Corporation by Category

1. What is the average (arithmetic mean) in billions of dollars of the sales of XYZ Corporation for the period 1991–1998?
   (A) 5.5   (B) 6.0   (C) 7.0   (D) 8.0   (E) 8.5

2. For which year was the percentage increase in earnings from the previous year the greatest?
   (A) 1992   (B) 1993   (C) 1994   (D) 1995   (E) 1996

3. Which of the following statements can be deduced from the data in the given charts and circle graph?
   I. Sales of major appliances in 1998 exceeded total sales in 1991.
   II. Earnings for the year in which earnings were greatest were more than sales for the year in which sales were lowest.
   III. If in 1998, the sales of major appliances had been 10% less, and the sales of computers had been 10% greater, the sales of major appliances would have been less than the sales of computers.
   (A) None   (B) I only   (C) III only   (D) I and III only
   (E) I, II, and III

4. What was the ratio of earnings to sales in 1993?

(A) $\frac{1}{40}$ (B) $\frac{1}{25}$ (C) $\frac{1}{4}$ (D) $\frac{25}{1}$ (E) $\frac{40}{1}$

Tactic 19

First Read the Titles

When the first data interpretation question appears on the screen, do not even read it! Before you attempt to answer a data interpretation question, take 15 or 30 seconds to study the graphs. Try to get a general idea about the information that is being displayed.

Observe that the bar graphs on which questions 1–4 are based present two different sets of data. The bar graph on the left-hand side provides information about the sales of XYZ Corporation, and the right-hand graph provides information about the corporation's earnings. Also, note that whereas sales are given in billions of dollars, earnings are given in millions of dollars. Finally, the circle graph gives a breakdown by category of the sales of XYZ Corporation for one particular year.

Tactic 20

Don't Confuse Percents and Numbers

Many students make mistakes on data interpretation questions because they don't distinguish between absolute numbers and percents. Although few students would look at the circle graph shown and think that XYZ Corporation sold 25 computers in 1998, many would mistakenly think that it sold 15% more major appliances than computers.

The problem is particularly serious when the questions involve percent increases or percent decreases. In question 2 you are not asked for the year in which the increase in earnings from the previous year was the greatest. You are asked for the year in which the percent increase in earnings was the greatest. A quick glance at the right-hand graph reveals that the greatest increase occurred from 1991 to 1992 when earnings jumped by $400 million. However, when we solve this problem in the discussion of Tactic 3, you will see that Choice A is not the correct answer.

NOTE: Since many data interpretation questions involve percents, you should carefully study the section devoted to them, and be sure that you know all of the tactics for solving percent problems. In particular, always try to use the number 100 or 1000, since it is so easy to mentally calculate percents of powers of 10.

Tactic 21

Whenever Possible, Estimate

Since you are not allowed to have a calculator when you take the GRE, you will not be expected to do complicated or lengthy calculations. Often, thinking and using some common sense can save you considerable time. For example, it may seem that in order to get the correct answer to question 2, you have to calculate five different percents. In fact, you only need to do one calculation, and that one you can do in your head!

Just looking at the Earnings bar graph, it is clear that the only possible answers are 1992, 1994, and 1995, the three years in which there was a significant increase in earnings from the year before. From 1993 to 1994 expenditures doubled, from $200 million to $400 million—an increase of 100%. From 1991 to 1992 expenditures increased by $400 million (from $500 million to $900 million), but that is less than a 100% increase (we don't care how much less). From 1994 to 1995 expenditures increased by $300 million (from $400 million to $700 million); but again, this is less than a 100% increase. The answer is (C).

Tactic 22

Do Each Calculation Separately

As in all Roman numeral questions, question 3 requires you to determine which of three separate statements is true. The key is to work with the statements individually.

To determine whether or not statement I is true, look at both the Sales bar graph and the circle graph. In 1998, total sales were $10 billion, and sales of major appliances accounted for 40% of the total: 40% of $10 billion = $4 billion. This exceeds the $3 billion total sales figure for 1991, so statement I is true.

In 1992, the year in which earnings were greatest, earnings were $900 million. In 1991, the year in which sales were lowest, sales were $3 billion, which is much greater than $900 million. Statement II is false.

In 1998, sales of major appliances were $4 billion. If they had been 10% less, they would have been $3.6 billion. That year, sales of computers were $2.5 billion (25% of $10 billion). If computer sales had increased by 10%, sales would have been $2.75 billion. Statement III is false.

The answer is (B): only statement I is true.

Tactic 23

Use Only the Information Given

You must base your answer to each question only on the information in the given charts and graphs. It is unlikely that you have any preconceived notion as to the sales of XYZ Corporation, but you might think that you know the population of the United States for a particular year or the percent of women currently in the workplace. If your knowledge contradicts any of the data presented in the graphs, ignore what you know. First of all, you may be mistaken; but more important, the data may refer to a different, unspecified location or year. In any event, *always* base your answers on the given data.

Tactic 24

Always Use the Proper Units

In answering question 4, observe that earnings are given in millions, while sales are in billions. If you answer too quickly, you might say that in 1993 earnings were 200 and sales were 8, and conclude that the desired ratio is $\frac{200}{8} = \frac{25}{1}$. You will avoid this mistake if you keep track of units: earnings were 200 *million dollars,* whereas sales were 8 *billion* dollars. The correct ratio is

$$\frac{200,000,000}{8,000,000,000} = \frac{2}{80} = \frac{1}{40}.$$

The answer is (A).

Tactic 25

Be Sure That Your Answer is Reasonable

Before confirming your answer, take a second to be sure that it is reasonable. For example, in question 4, choices D and E are unreasonable. From the logic of the situation, you should realize that earnings can't exceed sales. The desired ratio, therefore, must be less than 1. If you use the wrong units (see Tactic 24), your initial thought would be to choose (D). By testing your answer for reasonableness, you will realize that you made a mistake.

Remember that if you don't know how to solve a problem, you must guess in order to move on. Before guessing, however, check to see if one or more of the choices are unreasonable. If so, eliminate them. For example, if you forget how to calculate a percent increase, you would have to guess at question 2. But before guessing wildly, you should at least eliminate Choice B, since from 1992 to 1993 earnings decreased.

Tactic 26

Try to Visualize the Answer

Because graphs and tables present data in a form that enables you to readily see relationships and to make quick comparisons, you can often avoid doing any calculations. Whenever possible, use your eye instead of your computational skills.

For example, to answer question 1, rather than reading the sales figures in the bar graph on the left for each of the eight years, adding them, and then dividing by 8, visualize the situation. Where could you draw a horizontal line across the graph so that there would be the same amount of gray area above the line as white area below it? Imagine a horizontal line drawn through the 7 on the vertical axis. The portions of the bars above the line for 1993 and 1996–1998 are just about exactly the same size as the white areas below the line for 1991, 1992, and 1994. The answer is (C).

PRACTICE QUESTIONS

On the GRE there will always be exactly two questions based on any set of graphs. Accordingly, in the tests in this book, there are two pairs of data interpretation questions, each pair referring to a different set of graphs.

<u>Questions 1–2</u> refer to the following graphs.

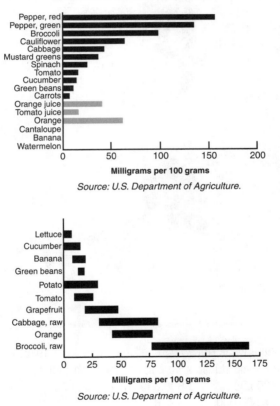

Vitamin C Content of Foods

Source: U.S. Department of Agriculture.

Source: U.S. Department of Agriculture.

1. What is the ratio of the amount of Vitamin C in 500 grams of orange to the amount of Vitamin C in 500 grams of orange juice?

    (A) 4:7   (B) 1:1   (C) 7:4   (D) 2:1   (E) 4:1

2. How many grams of tomato would you have to eat to be certain of getting more vitamin C than you would get by eating 100 grams of raw broccoli?

(A)   300   (B) 500   (C) 750   (D) 1200   (E) 1650

Questions 3–4 refer to the following graphs.

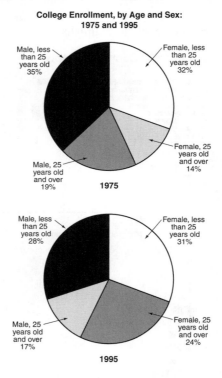

**College Enrollment, by Age and Sex:
1975 and 1995**

Male, less than 25 years old 35%
Female, less than 25 years old 32%
Female, 25 years old and over 14%
Male, 25 years old and over 19%
1975

Male, less than 25 years old 28%
Female, less than 25 years old 31%
Female, 25 years old and over 24%
Male, 25 years old and over 17%
1995

Source: U.S. Bureau of the Census, Current Population Survey.

3. If there were 10,000,000 college students in 1975, how many more male students were there than female students?
(A) 800,000   (B) 1,600,000   (C) 2,400,000
(D) 4,600,000   (E) 5,400,000

4. In 1975 what percent of female college students were at least 25 years old?
(A) 14%   (B) 31%   (C) 45%   (D) 69%   (E) 76%

Questions 5–6 refer to the following graph.

Motor Vehicle Theft in the U.S.
Percent Change from 1994 to 1998

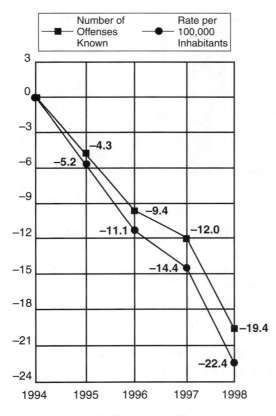

Source: U.S. Department of Justice,
Federal Bureau of Investigation.

5. If 1,000,000 vehicles were stolen in 1994, how many were stolen in 1996?
(A) 889,000   (B) 906,000   (C) 940,000
(D) 1,094,000   (E) 1,100,000

6. By what percent did the number of vehicles stolen decrease from 1997 to 1998?
(A) 7.4%   (B) 8.0%   (C) 8.4%   (D) 12.0%   (E) 19.4%

Questions 7–8 refer to the following graph.

Perceptions of Body Weight Status

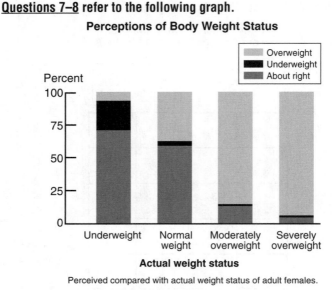

Perceived compared with actual weight status of adult females.

Source: U.S. Department of Agriculture.

7. What percent of underweight adult females perceive themselves to be underweight?
   (A) 5% (B) 22% (C) 38% (D) 50% (E) 70%

8. The members of which of the four groups had the least accurate perception of their body weight?
   (A) Underweight
   (B) Normal weight
   (C) Moderately overweight
   (D) Severely overweight
   (E) It cannot be determined from the information given in the graph.

Questions 9–10 refer to the tables on the following page.

Residents of New York City pay both New York State and New York City tax.
Residents of New York State who live and work outside of New York City pay only New York State tax.

Tax Rate Schedules for 1979

	New York State					City of New York			
Taxable Income					Taxable Income				
over	but not over		Amount of Tax		over	but not over		Amount of Tax	
$ 0	$1,000		2% of taxable income		$ 0	$1,000		0.9% of taxable income	
1,000	3,000	$20 plus	3% of excess over	$1,000	1,000	3,000	$ 9 plus	1.4% of excess over	$1,000
3,000	5,000	80 plus	4% of excess over	3,000	3,000	5,000	37 plus	1.8% of excess over	3,000
5,000	7,000	160 plus	5% of excess over	5,000	5,000	7,000	73 plus	2.0% of excess over	5,000
7,000	9,000	260 plus	6% of excess over	7,000	7,000	9,000	113 plus	2.3% of excess over	7,000
9,000	11,000	380 plus	7% of excess over	9,000	9,000	11,000	159 plus	2.5% of excess over	9,000
11,000	13,000	520 plus	8% of excess over	11,000	11,000	13,000	209 plus	2.7% of excess over	11,000
13,000	15,000	680 plus	9% of excess over	13,000	13,000	15,000	263 plus	2.9% of excess over	13,000
15,000	17,000	860 plus	10% of excess over	15,000	15,000	17,000	321 plus	3.1% of excess over	15,000
17,000	19,000	1,060 plus	11% of excess over	17,000	17,000	19,000	383 plus	3.3% of excess over	17,000
19,000	21,000	1,280 plus	12% of excess over	19,000	19,000	21,000	449 plus	3.5% of excess over	19,000
21,000	23,000	1,520 plus	13% of excess over	21,000	21,000	23,000	519 plus	3.8% of excess over	21,000
23,000		1,780 plus	14% of excess over	23,000	23,000	25,000	595 plus	4.0% of excess over	23,000
					25,000		675 plus	4.3% of excess over	25,000

9. In 1979 how much tax would a resident of New York State who lived and worked outside New York City have paid on a taxable income of $16,100?
(A) $34   (B) $110   (C) $352   (D) $970   (E) $1322

10. In 1979, how much more total tax would a resident of New York City who had a taxable income of $36,500 pay, compared to a resident of New York City who had a taxable income of $36,000?
(A) $21.50   (B) $43   (C) $70   (D) $91.50   (E) $183

Answer Key

1. **C**   6. **C**
2. **E**   7. **B**
3. **A**   8. **A**
4. **B**   9. **D**
5. **B**   10. **D**

Answer Explanations

1. **C.**   According to the graph on the left, there are approximately 70 milligrams of vitamin C in 100 grams of orange and 40 milligrams in the same amount of orange juice. This is a ratio of 70:40 = 7:4. Since the question refers to the same amount of orange and orange juice (500 grams), the ratio is unchanged.

2. **E.**   From the graph on the right, you can see that by eating 100 grams of raw broccoli, you could receive as much as 165 milligrams of vitamin C. Since 100 grams of tomato could have as little as 10 milligrams of vitamin C, you would have to eat 1650 grams of tomato to be sure of getting 165 milligrams of vitamin C.

3. **A.**   From the top graph, we see that in 1975, 54% (35% + 19%) of all college students were male, and the other 46% were female. So there were 5,400,000 males and 4,600,000 females—a difference of 800,000.

4. **B.**   In 1975, of every 100 college students, 46 were female—32 of whom were less than 25 years old, and 14 of whom were 25 years old and over. So, 14 of every 46 female students were at least 25 years old. Finally, $\frac{14}{46}$ = .30 = 30%.

5. **B.**   From 1994 to 1996 there was a 9.4% decrease in the number of vehicles stolen. Since 9.4% of 1,000,000 = 94,000, the number of vehicles stolen in 1996 was 1,000,000 – 94,000 = 906,000. If you can't solve problems such as this, you have to guess. But since the number of stolen vehicles is clearly decreasing, be sure to eliminate choices D and E first.

6. **C.**   For simplicity, assume that 1000 vehicles were stolen in 1994. By 1997, the number had decreased by 12.0% to 880 (12% of 1000 = 120, and 1000 – 120 = 880); by 1998, the number had decreased 19.4% to 806 (19.4% of 1000 = 194 and 1000 – 194 = 806). So from 1997 to 1998, the number of vehicles stolen decreased by 74 from 880 to 806. This represents a decrease of $\frac{74}{880}$ = .084 = 8.4%.

7. **B.**   The bar representing underweight adult females who perceive themselves to be underweight extends from about 70% to about 95%, a range of approximately 25%. Choice B is closest.

8. **A.** Almost all overweight females correctly considered themselves to be overweight; and more than half of all females of normal weight correctly considered themselves "about right." But nearly 70% of underweight adult females inaccurately considered themselves "about right."

9. **D.** Referring only to the New York State table, we see that the amount of tax on a taxable income between $15,000 and $17,000 was $860 plus 10% of the excess over $15,000. Therefore, the tax on $16,100 is $860 plus 10% of $1,100 = $860 + $110 = $970.

10. **D.** According to the tables, each additional dollar of taxable income over $25,000 was subject to a New York State tax of 14% and a New York City tax of 4.3%, for a total tax of 18.3%. Therefore, an additional $500 in taxable income would have incurred an additional tax of $0.183 \times 500 = $91.50.

7

TEST YOURSELF: THREE PRACTICE TESTS

This chapter contains three full-length practice tests. The format of each test is identical to the computer-based GRE that you will take, in that it has exactly the same number of verbal, quantitative, and analytical questions that an actual test has. Within each section, there is also exactly the same breakdown of question types. For example, on the verbal section there are the same number of analogies and antonyms as on a real test; in the quantitative section there are four data interpretation questions and 14 quantitative comparisons; and there are nine logical reasoning questions in the analytical ability section. Directions will appear only the first time a given type of question is introduced in each test; after that, only the type of question will appear. What is different, of course, is that this test is not computer adaptive.

After taking the test, score your answers and evaluate your results, using the self-rating guides provided. (Be sure also to read the answer explanations for questions you answered incorrectly and questions you answered correctly but found difficult.)

Simulate Test Conditions

To best simulate actual test conditions, find a quiet place to work. Have a stop watch or a clock handy so that you can keep perfect track of the time. Go through each section by answering the questions in the order in which they appear. If you don't know the answer to a question, guess (making an educated guess, if possible) and move on. Do not return to a question that you were unsure of, and do not go back to check your work if you have some time left over at the end of a section. (It isn't possible to do that on a real GRE.) Knowing how much time you have for each section and how many questions there are, try to pace yourself so that you use all your time and just finish each section in the time allowed. Do not spend too much time on any one question. Again, if you get stuck, just guess and go on to the next question.

Answer Sheet—Test 1

Section 1

1. Ⓐ Ⓑ Ⓒ Ⓓ Ⓔ
2. Ⓐ Ⓑ Ⓒ Ⓓ Ⓔ
3. Ⓐ Ⓑ Ⓒ Ⓓ Ⓔ
4. Ⓐ Ⓑ Ⓒ Ⓓ Ⓔ
5. Ⓐ Ⓑ Ⓒ Ⓓ Ⓔ
6. Ⓐ Ⓑ Ⓒ Ⓓ Ⓔ
7. Ⓐ Ⓑ Ⓒ Ⓓ Ⓔ
8. Ⓐ Ⓑ Ⓒ Ⓓ Ⓔ
9. Ⓐ Ⓑ Ⓒ Ⓓ Ⓔ
10. Ⓐ Ⓑ Ⓒ Ⓓ Ⓔ

11. Ⓐ Ⓑ Ⓒ Ⓓ Ⓔ
12. Ⓐ Ⓑ Ⓒ Ⓓ Ⓔ
13. Ⓐ Ⓑ Ⓒ Ⓓ Ⓔ
14. Ⓐ Ⓑ Ⓒ Ⓓ Ⓔ
15. Ⓐ Ⓑ Ⓒ Ⓓ Ⓔ
16. Ⓐ Ⓑ Ⓒ Ⓓ Ⓔ
17. Ⓐ Ⓑ Ⓒ Ⓓ Ⓔ
18. Ⓐ Ⓑ Ⓒ Ⓓ Ⓔ
19. Ⓐ Ⓑ Ⓒ Ⓓ Ⓔ
20. Ⓐ Ⓑ Ⓒ Ⓓ Ⓔ

21. Ⓐ Ⓑ Ⓒ Ⓓ Ⓔ
22. Ⓐ Ⓑ Ⓒ Ⓓ Ⓔ
23. Ⓐ Ⓑ Ⓒ Ⓓ Ⓔ
24. Ⓐ Ⓑ Ⓒ Ⓓ Ⓔ
25. Ⓐ Ⓑ Ⓒ Ⓓ Ⓔ
26. Ⓐ Ⓑ Ⓒ Ⓓ Ⓔ
27. Ⓐ Ⓑ Ⓒ Ⓓ Ⓔ
28. Ⓐ Ⓑ Ⓒ Ⓓ Ⓔ
29. Ⓐ Ⓑ Ⓒ Ⓓ Ⓔ
30. Ⓐ Ⓑ Ⓒ Ⓓ Ⓔ

Section 2

1. Ⓐ Ⓑ Ⓒ Ⓓ Ⓔ
2. Ⓐ Ⓑ Ⓒ Ⓓ Ⓔ
3. Ⓐ Ⓑ Ⓒ Ⓓ Ⓔ
4. Ⓐ Ⓑ Ⓒ Ⓓ Ⓔ
5. Ⓐ Ⓑ Ⓒ Ⓓ Ⓔ
6. Ⓐ Ⓑ Ⓒ Ⓓ Ⓔ
7. Ⓐ Ⓑ Ⓒ Ⓓ Ⓔ
8. Ⓐ Ⓑ Ⓒ Ⓓ Ⓔ
9. Ⓐ Ⓑ Ⓒ Ⓓ Ⓔ
10. Ⓐ Ⓑ Ⓒ Ⓓ Ⓔ

11. Ⓐ Ⓑ Ⓒ Ⓓ Ⓔ
12. Ⓐ Ⓑ Ⓒ Ⓓ Ⓔ
13. Ⓐ Ⓑ Ⓒ Ⓓ Ⓔ
14. Ⓐ Ⓑ Ⓒ Ⓓ Ⓔ
15. Ⓐ Ⓑ Ⓒ Ⓓ Ⓔ
16. Ⓐ Ⓑ Ⓒ Ⓓ Ⓔ
17. Ⓐ Ⓑ Ⓒ Ⓓ Ⓔ
18. Ⓐ Ⓑ Ⓒ Ⓓ Ⓔ
19. Ⓐ Ⓑ Ⓒ Ⓓ Ⓔ
20. Ⓐ Ⓑ Ⓒ Ⓓ Ⓔ

21. Ⓐ Ⓑ Ⓒ Ⓓ Ⓔ
22. Ⓐ Ⓑ Ⓒ Ⓓ Ⓔ
23. Ⓐ Ⓑ Ⓒ Ⓓ Ⓔ
24. Ⓐ Ⓑ Ⓒ Ⓓ Ⓔ
25. Ⓐ Ⓑ Ⓒ Ⓓ Ⓔ
26. Ⓐ Ⓑ Ⓒ Ⓓ Ⓔ
27. Ⓐ Ⓑ Ⓒ Ⓓ Ⓔ
28. Ⓐ Ⓑ Ⓒ Ⓓ Ⓔ

Section 3

1. Ⓐ Ⓑ Ⓒ Ⓓ Ⓔ
2. Ⓐ Ⓑ Ⓒ Ⓓ Ⓔ
3. Ⓐ Ⓑ Ⓒ Ⓓ Ⓔ
4. Ⓐ Ⓑ Ⓒ Ⓓ Ⓔ
5. Ⓐ Ⓑ Ⓒ Ⓓ Ⓔ
6. Ⓐ Ⓑ Ⓒ Ⓓ Ⓔ
7. Ⓐ Ⓑ Ⓒ Ⓓ Ⓔ
8. Ⓐ Ⓑ Ⓒ Ⓓ Ⓔ
9. Ⓐ Ⓑ Ⓒ Ⓓ Ⓔ
10. Ⓐ Ⓑ Ⓒ Ⓓ Ⓔ
11. Ⓐ Ⓑ Ⓒ Ⓓ Ⓔ
12. Ⓐ Ⓑ Ⓒ Ⓓ Ⓔ

13. Ⓐ Ⓑ Ⓒ Ⓓ Ⓔ
14. Ⓐ Ⓑ Ⓒ Ⓓ Ⓔ
15. Ⓐ Ⓑ Ⓒ Ⓓ Ⓔ
16. Ⓐ Ⓑ Ⓒ Ⓓ Ⓔ
17. Ⓐ Ⓑ Ⓒ Ⓓ Ⓔ
18. Ⓐ Ⓑ Ⓒ Ⓓ Ⓔ
19. Ⓐ Ⓑ Ⓒ Ⓓ Ⓔ
20. Ⓐ Ⓑ Ⓒ Ⓓ Ⓔ
21. Ⓐ Ⓑ Ⓒ Ⓓ Ⓔ
22. Ⓐ Ⓑ Ⓒ Ⓓ Ⓔ
23. Ⓐ Ⓑ Ⓒ Ⓓ Ⓔ
24. Ⓐ Ⓑ Ⓒ Ⓓ Ⓔ

25. Ⓐ Ⓑ Ⓒ Ⓓ Ⓔ
26. Ⓐ Ⓑ Ⓒ Ⓓ Ⓔ
27. Ⓐ Ⓑ Ⓒ Ⓓ Ⓔ
28. Ⓐ Ⓑ Ⓒ Ⓓ Ⓔ
29. Ⓐ Ⓑ Ⓒ Ⓓ Ⓔ
30. Ⓐ Ⓑ Ⓒ Ⓓ Ⓔ
31. Ⓐ Ⓑ Ⓒ Ⓓ Ⓔ
32. Ⓐ Ⓑ Ⓒ Ⓓ Ⓔ
33. Ⓐ Ⓑ Ⓒ Ⓓ Ⓔ
34. Ⓐ Ⓑ Ⓒ Ⓓ Ⓔ
35. Ⓐ Ⓑ Ⓒ Ⓓ Ⓔ

Model Test 1
Section 1—Verbal Ability
30 Questions—30 Minutes

<u>Antonym Directions</u>: In each of the following antonym questions, a word printed in capital letters precedes five lettered words or phrases. From these five lettered words or phrases, pick the one most nearly *opposite* in meaning to the capitalized word.

1. PRODIGAL:
- (A) nomad
- (B) sycophant
- (C) gifted child
- (D) economical person
- (E) antagonist

2. ARTIFICE:
- (A) edifice
- (B) sincerity
- (C) prejudice
- (D) creativity
- (E) affirmation

<u>Sentence Completion Directions</u>: Each of the following sentence completion questions contains one or two blanks. These blanks signify that a word or set of words has been left out. Below each sentence are five words or sets of words. For each blank, pick the word or set of words that *best* reflects the sentence's overall meaning.

3. The earth is a planet bathed in light; it is therefore ---- that many of the living organisms that have evolved on the earth have ---- the biologically advantageous capacity to trap light energy.
- (A) anomalous...engendered
- (B) unsurprising...developed
- (C) predictable...forfeited
- (D) problematic...exhibited
- (E) expectable...relinquished

4. Relatively few politicians willingly forsake center stage, although a touch of ---- on their parts now and again might well increase their popularity with the voting public.
    (A) garrulity
    (B) misanthropy
    (C) self-effacement
    (D) self-dramatization
    (E) self-doubt

Analogy Directions: Each of the following analogy questions presents a related pair of words linked by a colon. Five lettered pairs of words follow the linked pair. Choose the lettered pair of words whose relationship is *most like* the relationship expressed in the original linked pair.

5. CIRCUITOUS : ROUTE ::
    (A) problematic : solution   (D) judicious : selection
    (B) devious : argument   (E) profound : depth
    (C) elliptical : brevity

6. HELPFUL : OFFICIOUS ::
    (A) dutiful : assiduous   (D) enigmatic : dumbfounded
    (B) effusive : gushing   (E) deferential : sycophantic
    (C) gullible : incredulous

Reading Comprehension Directions: Each of the following reading comprehension questions is based on the content of the following passage. Read the passage and then determine the best answer choice for each question. Base your choice on what this passage *states directly* or *implies,* not on any information you may have gained elsewhere.

James's first novels used conventional narrative techniques: explicit characterization, action which related events in distinctly phased sequences, settings firmly outlined and specifi-
Line cally described. But this method gradually gave way to a sub-
(5) tler, more deliberate, more diffuse style of accumulation of minutely discriminated details whose total significance the

reader can grasp only by constant attention and sensitive inference. His later novels play down scenes of abrupt and prominent action, and do not so much offer a succession of
(10) sharp shocks as slow piecemeal additions of perception. The curtain is not suddenly drawn back from shrouded things, but is slowly moved away.

Such a technique is suited to James's essential subject, which is not human action itself but the states of mind which
(15) produce and are produced by human actions and interactions. James was less interested in what characters do, than in the moral and psychological antecedents, realizations, and conse- quences which attend their doings. This is why he more often speaks of "cases" than of actions. His stories, therefore, grow
(20) more and more lengthy while the actions they relate grow sim- pler and less visible; not because they are crammed with adventitious and secondary events, digressive relief, or super- numerary characters, as overstuffed novels of action are; but because he presents in such exhaustive detail every nuance of
(25) his situation. Commonly the interest of a novel is in the variety and excitement of visible actions building up to a climactic event which will settle the outward destinies of characters with storybook promise of permanence. A James novel, however, possesses its characteristic interest in carrying the reader
(30) through a rich analysis of the mental adjustments of characters to the realities of their personal situations as they are slowly revealed to them through exploration and chance discovery.

7. The passage supplies information for answering which of the following questions?
(A) Did James originate the so-called psychological novel?
(B) Is conventional narrative technique strictly chronological in recounting action?
(C) Can novels lacking overtly dramatic incident sustain the reader's interest?
(D) Were James's later novels more acceptable to the general public than his earlier ones?
(E) Is James unique in his predilection for exploring psycho- logical nuances of character?

8. According to the passage, James's later novels differ from his earlier ones in their
   (A) preoccupation with specifically described settings
   (B) ever-increasing concision and tautness of plot
   (C) levels of moral and psychological complexity
   (D) development of rising action to a climax
   (E) subordination of psychological exploration to dramatic effect

9. The author's attitude toward the novel of action appears to be one of
   (A) pointed indignation
   (B) detached neutrality
   (C) sharp derision
   (D) strong partisanship
   (E) mild disapprobation

Antonyms

10. EQUIVOCATE:
    (A) yield
    (B) distinguish
    (C) condescend
    (D) pledge
    (E) denounce

11. OPULENCE:
    (A) transience
    (B) penury
    (C) solitude
    (D) generosity
    (E) transparency

Analogies

12. EPHEMERAL : PERMANENCE ::
    (A) erratic : predictability
    (B) immaculate : cleanliness
    (C) commendable : reputation
    (D) spurious : emulation
    (E) mandatory : obedience

13. NONPLUSSED : BAFFLEMENT ::
  - (A) discomfited : embarrassment
  - (B) parsimonious : extravagance
  - (C) disgruntled : contentment
  - (D) despicable : contempt
  - (E) surly : harassment

14. OGLE : OBSERVE ::
  - (A) haggle : outbid
  - (B) clamor : dispute
  - (C) discern : perceive
  - (D) flaunt : display
  - (E) glare : glower

Sentence Completion

15. It may be useful to think of character in fiction as a function of two ---- impulses: the impulse to individualize and the impulse to ----.
  - (A) analogous...humanize
  - (B) disparate...aggrandize
  - (C) divergent...typify
  - (D) comparable...delineate
  - (E) related...moralize

16. There are any number of theories to explain these events and, since even the experts disagree, it is ---- the rest of us in our role as responsible scholars to ---- dogmatic statements.
  - (A) paradoxical for...abstain from
  - (B) arrogant of...compensate with
  - (C) incumbent on...refrain from
  - (D) opportune for...quarrel over
  - (E) appropriate for...issue forth

Reading Comprehension

According to the theory of plate tectonics, the lithosphere (earth's relatively hard and solid outer layer consisting of the crust and part of the underlying mantle) is divided into a few dozen plates
Line that vary in size and shape; in general, these plates move in rela-
(5) tion to one another. They move away from one another at a mid-ocean ridge, a long chain of sub-oceanic mountains that forms a

boundary between plates. At a mid-ocean ridge, new lithospheric material in the form of hot magma pushes up from the earth's interior. The injection of this new lithospheric material from below (10) causes the phenomenon known as sea-floor spreading.

Given that the earth is not expanding in size to any appreciable degree, how can "new" lithosphere be created at a mid-ocean ridge? For new lithosphere to come into being in one region, an equal amount of lithospheric material must be destroyed some- (15) where else. This destruction takes place at a boundary between plates called a subduction zone. At a subduction zone, one plate is pushed down under another into the red-hot mantle, where over a span of millions of years it is absorbed into the mantle.

In the early 1960's, well before scientists had formulated the (20) theory of plate tectonics, Princeton University professor Harry H. Hess proposed the concept of sea-floor spreading. Hess's original hypothesis described the creation and spread of ocean floor by means of the upwelling and cooling of magma from the earth's interior. Hess, however, did not mention rigid lithospheric (25) plates. The subsequent discovery that the oceanic crust contains evidence of periodic reversals of the earth's magnetic field helped confirm Hess's hypothesis. According to the explanation formulated by Princeton's F.J. Vine and D.H. Matthews, whenever magma wells up under a mid-ocean ridge, the ferromagnetic (30) minerals within the magma become magnetized in the direction of the geomagnetic field. As the magma cools and hardens into rock, the direction and the polarity of the geometric field are recorded in the magnetized volcanic rock. Thus, when reversals of the earth's magnetic field occur, as they do at intervals of from (35) 10,000 to around a million years, they produce a series of magnetic stripes paralleling the axis of the rift. Thus, the oceanic crust is like a magnetic tape recording, but instead of preserving sounds or visual images, it preserves the history of earth's geomagnetic field. The boundaries between stripes reflect reversals (40) of the magnetic field; these reversals can be dated independently. Given this information, geologists can deduce the rate of sea-floor spreading from the width of the stripes. (Geologists, however, have yet to solve the mystery of exactly how the earth's magnetic field comes to reverse itself periodically.)

17. According to the passage, a mid-ocean ridge differs from a subduction zone in that
   (A)   it marks the boundary line between neighboring plates
   (B)   only the former is located on the ocean floor
   (C)   it is a site for the emergence of new lithospheric material
   (D)   the former periodically disrupts the earth's geomagnetic field
   (E)   it is involved with lithospheric destruction rather than lithospheric creation

18. It can be inferred from the passage that as new lithospheric material is injected from below
   (A)   the plates become immobilized in a kind of gridlock
   (B)   it is incorporated into an underwater mountain ridge
   (C)   the earth's total mass is altered
   (D)   it reverses its magnetic polarity
   (E)   the immediately adjacent plates sink

19. According to the passage, lithospheric material at the site of a subduction zone
   (A)   rises and is polarized
   (B)   sinks and is reincorporated
   (C)   slides and is injected
   (D)   spreads and is absorbed
   (E)   diverges and is consumed

Antonyms

20. HONE:
   (A)   broaden   (D)   weld
   (B)   twist   (E)   break
   (C)   dull

21. PHLEGMATIC:
   (A)   dogmatic   (D)   self-assured
   (B)   ardent   (E)   abstracted
   (C)   haphazard

22. BANALITY:
- (A) tentative interpretation
- (B) concise summation
- (C) accurate delineation
- (D) laudatory remark
- (E) novel expression

Analogies

23. THIRST : DRIVE ::
- (A) inebriety : excess
- (B) success : ambition
- (C) indifference : passion
- (D) taste : gusto
- (E) smell : sense

24. SKULDUGGERY : SWINDLER ::
- (A) surgery : quack
- (B) quandary : craven
- (C) chicanery : trickster
- (D) forgery : speculator
- (E) cutlery : butcher

Sentence Completion

25. According to one optimistic hypothesis, the dense concentration of entrepreneurs and services in the cities would incubate new functions, ---- them, and finally export them to other areas, and so the cities, forever breeding fresh ideas, would ---- themselves repeatedly.
- (A) immunize...perpetuate
- (B) isolate...revitalize
- (C) foster...deplete
- (D) spawn...imitate
- (E) nurture...renew

26. Man is a ---- animal, and much more so in his mind than in his body: he may like to go alone for a walk, but he hates to stand alone in his ----.
- (A) gregarious...opinions
- (B) conceited...vanity
- (C) singular...uniqueness
- (D) solitary...thoughts
- (E) nomadic...footsteps

Antonyms

27. ERUDITE:
    (A) unhealthy
    (B) ignorant
    (C) impolite
    (D) indifferent
    (E) imprecise

28. EFFRONTERY:
    (A) obscurity
    (B) indolence
    (C) separation
    (D) diffidence
    (E) fluctuation

Reading Comprehension

The stability that had marked the Iroquois Confederacy's generally pro-British position was shattered with the overthrow of
James II in 1688, the colonial uprisings that followed in
Line Massachusetts, New York, and Maryland, and the commence-
(5) ment of King William's War against Louis XIV of France. The
increasing French threat to English hegemony in the interior of
North America was signalized by French-led or French-inspired
attacks on the Iroquois and on outlying colonial settlements in
New York and New England. The high point of the Iroquois
(10) response was the spectacular raid of August 5, 1689, in which
the Iroquois virtually wiped out the French village of Lachine, just
outside Montreal. A counterraid by the French on the English village of Schenectady in March, 1690, instilled an appropriate
measure of fear among the English and their Iroquois allies.
(15)   The Iroquois position at the end of the war, which was formal-
ized by treaties made during the summer of 1701 with the British
and the French, and which was maintained throughout most of
the eighteenth century, was one of "aggressive neutrality"
between the two competing European powers. Under the new
(20) system the Iroquois initiated a peace policy toward the "far
Indians," tightened their control over the nearby tribes, and
induced both English and French to support their neutrality toward
the European powers by appropriate gifts and concessions.
    By holding the balance of power in the sparsely settled border-
(25) lands between English and French settlements, and by their will-

ingness to use their power against one or the other nation if not appropriately treated, the Iroquois played the game of European power politics with effectiveness. The system broke down, however, after the French became convinced that the Iroquois were
(30) compromising the system in favor of the English and launched a full-scale attempt to establish French physical and juridical presence in the Ohio Valley, the heart of the borderlands long claimed by the Iroquois. As a consequence of the ensuing Great War for Empire, in which Iroquois neutrality was dissolved and European
(35) influence moved closer, the play-off system lost its efficacy and a system of direct bargaining supplanted it.

29. The author's primary purpose in this passage is to
- (A) denounce the imperialistic policies of the French
- (B) disprove the charges of barbarism made against the Indian nations
- (C) expose the French government's exploitation of the Iroquois balance of power
- (D) describe and assess the effect of European military power on the policy of an Indian nation
- (E) show the inability of the Iroquois to engage in European-style diplomacy

30. With which of the following statements would the author be LEAST likely to agree?
- (A) The Iroquois were able to respond effectively to French acts of aggression.
- (B) James II's removal from the throne caused dissension to break out among the colonies.
- (C) The French begrudged the British their alleged high standing among the Iroquois.
- (D) Iroquois negotiations involved playing one side against the other.
- (E) The Iroquois ceased to hold the balance of power early in the eighteenth century.

Section 2—Quantitative Ability

28 Questions—45 Minutes

<u>Quantitative Comparison Directions</u>: In the following type of question, two quantities appear, one in Column A and one in Column B. You must compare them. The correct answer to the question is

> A if the quantity in Column A is greater
> B if the quantity in Column B is greater
> C if the two quantities are equal
> D if it is impossible to determine which quantity is greater

<u>Notes</u>: Sometimes information about one or both of the quantities is centered above the two columns. If the same symbol appears in both columns, it represents the same thing each time.

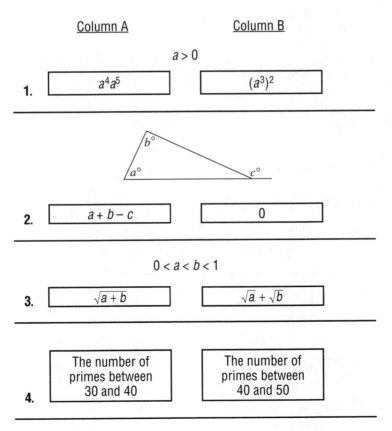

Column A | Column B

$a > 0$

1. | $a^4 a^5$ | $(a^3)^2$

2. | $a + b - c$ | 0

$0 < a < b < 1$

3. | $\sqrt{a + b}$ | $\sqrt{a} + \sqrt{b}$

4. | The number of primes between 30 and 40 | The number of primes between 40 and 50

Discrete Quantitative and Data Interpretation Directions: In the following questions, choose the best answer from the five choices listed.

5. In the figure at the right, what
is the value of $a + b + c$?

   (A) 210   (D) 270

   (B) 220   (E) 280

   (C) 240

6. Of the 200 seniors at Monroe High School, exactly 40 are in the
band, 60 are in the orchestra, and 10 are in both. How many
students are in neither the band nor the orchestra?

   (A)   80   (D) 110

   (B)   90   (E) 120

   (C) 100

7. Twenty children were sharing equally the cost of a present for
their teacher. When 4 of the children decided not to contribute,
each of the other children had to pay $1.50 more. How much
did the present cost, in dollars?

   (A)   50   (D) 120

   (B)   80   (E) 150

   (C) 100

Quantitative Comparison

Column A	Column B
10^{20}	20^{10}

8.

There are 250 people lined up outside a theater.
Jack is the 25th person from the front, and
Jill is the 125th person from the front.

The number of people between Jack and Jill	100

9.

Data Interpretation

10. What is the value of n if $3^{10} \times 27^2 = 9^2 \times 3^n$?

(A) 6
(B) 10
(C) 12

(D) 15
(E) 30

Quantitative Comparison

<u>Column A</u>   <u>Column B</u>

$90 < x$

11.

| The perimeter of △AOB | 17 |

$$\frac{a-b}{c-a} = 1$$

12.

| The average (arithmetic mean) of b and c | a |

13.

| The area of a square whose sides are 10 | The area of a square whose diagonals are 15 |

Data Interpretation

<u>**Questions 14–15**</u> refer to the following graphs.

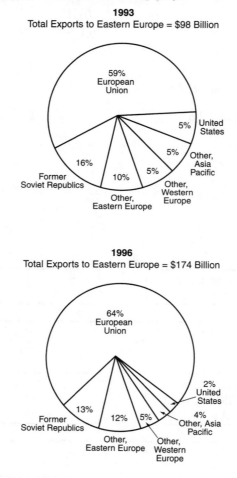

1993
Total Exports to Eastern Europe = $98 Billion

1996
Total Exports to Eastern Europe = $174 Billion

14. Which of the following statements concerning the value of exports to Eastern Europe from other Eastern European countries from 1993 to 1996 is the most accurate?

(A) They increased by 2%.

(B) They increased by 12%.

(C) They increased by 20%.

(D) They increased by 50%.

(E) They increased by 100%.

15. France is one of the countries in the European Union. If in 1996 France's exports to Eastern Europe were four times those of the United States, then what percent of the European Union's exports to Eastern Europe came from France that year?

(A) 5%

(B) 8%

(C) 12.5%

(D) 20%

(E) 25%

Quantitative Comparison

Column A	Column B

16.

The average (arithmetic mean) of the measures of the three angles of a triangle whose largest angle measures 75°	The average (arithmetic mean) of the measures of the three angles of a triangle whose largest angle measures 105°

In the figure above, all of the line segments meet to form right angles.

17.

The perimeter of the figure	52

Discrete Quantitative

18. Given that $x \neq y$ and that $(x - y)^2 = x^2 - y^2$, which of the following must be true?

       I. $x = 0$
      II. $y = 0$
      III. $x = -y$

(A) I only   (D) I and II
(B) II only   (E) I, II, and III
(C) III only

19. Let the lengths of the sides of a triangle be represented by $x + 3$, $2x - 3$, and $3x - 5$. If the perimeter of the triangle is 25, what is the length of the shortest side?

(A) 5   (D) 8
(B) 6   (E) 10
(C) 7

Data Interpretation

Questions 20–21 refer to the graph below.

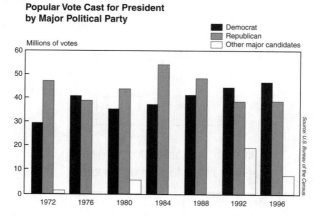

Popular Vote Cast for President by Major Political Party

20. In which presidential election between 1972 to 1996 inclusive, was the percent of votes received by the winning candidate the lowest?

(A) 1976   (D) 1992
(B) 1980   (E) 1996
(C) 1988

21. In which year between 1972 and 1996 inclusive were the greatest number of votes cast for president?

(A) 1980   (D) 1992
(B) 1984   (E) 1996
(C) 1988

Discrete Quantitative

22. In 1990, twice as many boys as girls at Adams High School earned varsity letters. From 1990 to 2000 the number of girls earning varsity letters increased by 25% while the number of boys earning varsity letters decreased by 25%. What was the ratio in 2000 of the number of girls to the number of boys who earned varsity letters?

(A) $\dfrac{5}{3}$ (D) $\dfrac{5}{6}$

(B) $\dfrac{6}{5}$ (E) $\dfrac{3}{5}$

(C) $\dfrac{1}{1}$

Quantitative Comparison

Column A   Column B

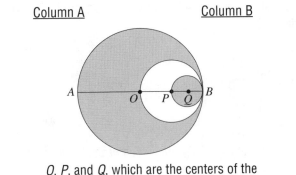

O, P, and *Q,* which are the centers of the three circles, all lie on diameter *AB.*

23.

| The area of the entire shaded region | 4 times the area of the white region |

Column A　　　　　　　Column B

In 1980, Elaine was 8 times as old as Adam,
and Judy was 3 times as old as Adam.
Elaine is 20 years older than Judy.

24. | Adam's age in 1988 |　　| 12 |

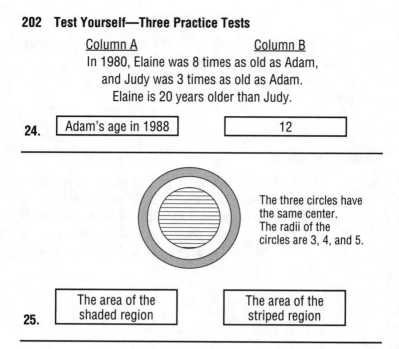

The three circles have
the same center.
The radii of the
circles are 3, 4, and 5.

25. | The area of the
shaded region |　　| The area of the
striped region |

Discrete Quantitative

26. A square and an equilateral triangle each have sides of length
5. What is the ratio of the area of the square to the area of the
triangle?

(A) $\dfrac{4}{3}$　　　　　　　(D) $\dfrac{4\sqrt{3}}{3}$

(B) $\dfrac{16}{9}$　　　　　　　(E) $\dfrac{16\sqrt{3}}{9}$

(C) $\dfrac{\sqrt{3}}{4}$

27. If $x + 2y = a$ and $x - 2y = b$, which of the following expressions
is equal to xy?

(A) ab　　　　　　　(D) $\dfrac{a^2 - b^2}{4}$

(B) $\dfrac{a + b}{2}$　　　　　　　(E) $\dfrac{a^2 - b^2}{8}$

(C) $\dfrac{a - b}{2}$

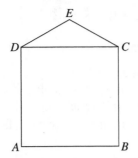

28. In the figure above, the area of square *ABCD* is 100, the area of
     triangle *DEC* is 10, and *EC* = *ED*. What is the distance from *A* to
     E?

     (A)   11   (D)   13
     (B)   12   (E) $\sqrt{244}$
     (C) $\sqrt{146}$

Section 3—Analytical Ability

35 Questions—60 Minutes

<u>Directions</u>: In this section, each set of questions is based on a short passage or a set of conditions. Sometimes, in answering these questions, you might want to make a table or diagram. For each question, choose the best answer from the five choices listed.

Logical Reasoning

1. The nursing shortage in this country is a phony one, caused by the concentration of nurses in the geographical regions with the highest paid and most generous fringe benefits for nurses. In addition, the League of American Nurses has artificially worsened the shortage by encouraging nursing schools to keep enrollments low in order to boost nurses' salaries to even higher levels.

All of the following statements, if true, would tend to weaken the argument above except:
- (A) Although nurses are paid less in Texas than in Connecticut, there are 35% more nurses in Texas than in Connecticut.
- (B) Nationwide, the salaries of nurses have risen at a slower rate than inflation over the last ten years.
- (C) The number of students who earned degrees in nursing last year was almost double the number six years ago.
- (D) Those areas of the country with the highest pay for nurses have the highest living costs.
- (E) The League of American Nurses has almost no influence on the policies of American nursing schools.

Analytical Reasoning

<u>Questions 2–5</u>
Every night Jillian has homework in four subjects: algebra, biology, English, and history. Once she starts an assignment, she always completes it, before beginning another one. She does not do her homework in the same order each night, but she does adhere to the following two rules:
> She always does her algebra before her biology.
> She always does her English before her history.

2. Each of the following is an order in which Jillian could do her assignments EXCEPT
   (A)   Algebra, biology, English, history
   (B)   Algebra, English, biology, history
   (C)   English, algebra, biology, history
   (D)   English, history, algebra, biology
   (E)   English, biology, algebra, history

3. In how many different orders can Jillian do her homework assignments?
   (A) 2   (D) 12
   (B) 3   (E) 24
   (C) 6

4. Which of the following, if adopted by Jillian as an additional rule, would mean that she has to do her homework in the exact same order each night?
   (A)   She always does her algebra before her history.
   (B)   She always does her algebra before her English.
   (C)   She always does her biology before her history.
   (D)   She always does her history before her algebra.
   (E)   She always does her history before her biology.

5. If one night in addition to her other assignments, Jillian has to write a book report, and she decides to do that immediately after completing her algebra homework and immediately before doing her history homework, which of the following CANNOT be true?
   (A)   She does her English homework first.
   (B)   She does her algebra homework second.
   (C)   She does her book report third.
   (D)   She does her biology homework last.
   (E)   She does her history homework last.

Logical Reasoning

6. Student participation in a voluntary community service program at John Adams High School increased every year, from 20% in 1995 to 40% in 2000.

    If the preceding statement is true, which of the following statements CANNOT be true about the student population at John Adams High School between 1995 and 2000?
    (A) The number of students in the school increased, and the number of students participating in the community service program increased.
    (B) The number of students in the school decreased, and the number of students participating in the community service program increased.
    (C) The number of students in the school increased, and the number of students participating in the community service program decreased.
    (D) The number of students participating in the community service program increased by 40%.
    (E) The number of students participating in the community service program remained the same.

Questions 7–8
The internal combustion engine, which powers all private motorized vehicles, should be banned. It burns up petroleum products that are needed to produce plastics, synthetics, and many medicines. Once all the oil is gone, we will no longer be able to produce these valuable commodities. Yet we do not have to burn gasoline to satisfy our transportation needs. Other kinds of engines could be developed if the oil companies would stop blocking research efforts.

7. The argument above would be most weakened by the development of which of the following?
    (A) An internal combustion engine that operated on one-tenth the gasoline used in a normal engine
    (B) A car that operated on solar energy stored in special batteries
    (C) A method of producing plastic that used no petroleum products
    (D) A synthetic oil with all the properties of natural oil
    (E) A means of locating numerous undiscovered oil fields

8. The argument above would be most strengthened if which of the following were true?
   - (A) One of the oil companies has suppressed the discovery of an engine that burns only alcohol.
   - (B) Some of the medicines that require petroleum for their production help to control and cure several of the world's most deadly diseases.
   - (C) The world's current oil reserves are about half of what they were 30 years ago.
   - (D) In high-pollution areas, automobile exhaust fumes have been shown to cause high rates of lung cancer and heart disease.
   - (E) When gasoline is burned inside an auto engine, less than one-fourth of the energy produced is used to propel the vehicle.

Analytical Reasoning

Questions 9–13

At Bayside High School, each of the seven math teachers—F, G, H, I, J, K, and L—are required to give one extra help class each day. These classes can take place either before school, during lunch period, or after school. In scheduling these classes the chairperson of the math department must follow the following rules:

At least two teachers must hold their classes before school.
At least three teachers must hold their classes after school.
H is not available after school, and J is available only after school.
I always gives extra help during her lunch period.
G will give help before school only if F is also scheduled then.

9. If L gives extra help during lunch, which of the following must be true?
   - (A) F gives help before school.
   - (B) H gives help before school.
   - (C) J gives help before school.
   - (D) K gives help during lunch.
   - (E) G gives help after school.

10. Which of the following could be a complete list of the teachers who give help before school?

(A) G   (D) F, G, K
(B) G, H   (E) F, G, H, K
(C) F, G, I

11. All of the following statements could be true EXCEPT

(A)   The same number of teachers give help before school as after school.
(B)   The same number of teachers give help before school as during lunch.
(C)   Twice as many teachers give help after school as before.
(D)   Twice as many teachers give help after school as during lunch.
(E)   Four times as many teachers give help after school as during lunch.

12. If F is the only teacher not yet scheduled, and without violating any of the given conditions he could be scheduled in any of the three time slots, then which of the following must be true?

(A)   G gives help after school.
(B)   K gives help before school.
(C)   H gives help at lunch.
(D)   K gives help after school.
(E)   L gives help after school.

13. If G and H are both scheduled to give help before school, which of the following CANNOT be true?

(A)   F gives help before school.
(B)   K gives help at lunch.
(C)   Only I gives help at lunch.
(D)   K gives help after school.
(E)   L gives help after school.

Logical Reasoning

14. *Governor:* Compared with children in other states, infants born in California weigh more, survive the first years in greater numbers, and live longer. The hysteria about the danger of pesticides in California has attracted attention simply because a few Hollywood stars have appeared on television talk shows. Pesticides are the responsibility of the California Department of Food and Agriculture, and we can be sure its members are doing their job.

The governor's argument would be weakened if all of the following were shown to be true EXCEPT

(A) in California rates of melanoma and some forms of leukemia linked to exposure to pesticides are above national norms

(B) the three highest positions at the California Department of Food and Agriculture are held by farm owners

(C) synthetic pesticide residues in food cause more cancer than do "natural pesticides" that the plants themselves produce

(D) more Californians suffer the consequences of air pollution than do the citizens in any other state

(E) children of farm workers are three times more likely to suffer childhood cancers than children of urban parents

Analytical Reasoning

Questions 15–18

Four women—Alice, Bette, Carol, and Diane—and four men—Eric, Frank, George, and Harry—are at a formal dinner party, seated around a rectangular table. The host and hostess are at opposite ends of the table, and there are three guests on each side.

Each man is sitting next to at least one woman, and each woman is sitting next to at least one man.
Harry is sitting opposite Diane, who is not the hostess.
George is sitting opposite a woman and has a woman on his right.
Alice is at the hostess's right, next to Frank.

15. Which of the following statements could be true?

      I. Eric is the host.

      II. Bette is the hostess.

      III. Each man is sitting opposite his wife.

(A) I only   (D) II and III only

(B) I and II only   (E) I, II, and III

(C) I and III only

16. If each man is sitting opposite his wife, which of the following pairs must be married to one another?

(A) Eric and Bette   (D) George and Alice

(B) Eric and Carol   (E) George and Diane

(C) Frank and Carol

17. How many people are sitting between two people of the opposite sex?

(A) 0   (D) 3

(B) 1   (E) 4

(C) 2

18. If during dinner George and Diane exchange seats, which of the following statements must be true of the new seating arrangement?

      I. No one is sitting between two people of the opposite sex.

      II. One side of the table consists entirely of people of the same sex.

      III. A single straight line can be drawn on the table so that all the women are on one side and all the men on the other side.

(A) I only   (D) I and III only

(B) II only   (E) II and III only

(C) I and II only

Logical Reasoning

19. If Rorie wakes up after 7:00 on a school day, she just grabs a granola bar for breakfast. When she wakes up after 7:00 on a day that there is no school, she makes herself an omelette.

If the preceding statements are true, and if Rorie did not have a granola bar for breakfast today, which of the following statements must be true?

(A) Today is a school day.
(B) Today is not a school day.
(C) Rorie had an omelette today.
(D) Either today is a school day or Rorie woke up after 7:00.
(E) Either today is not a school day or Rorie woke up before 7:00.

Analytical Reasoning

Questions 20–23

The Sociology department at the State University consists of three untenured professors—Q, R, and S—and seven tenured professors—T, U, V, W, X, Y, and Z. At the beginning of a new academic year, Z, the chairperson of the department, decided to reorganize the curriculum and budget committees by assigning each of the other nine professors to exactly one of the two committees. In making her assignments, the chairperson adheres to the following conditions:

> The budget committee will have five members, and the curriculum committee will have four.
> Only one untenured professor may be on the budget committee.
> S and Y cannot be assigned to the same committee.
> U and W cannot be assigned to the same committee.
> V and X must be assigned to the same committee.
> If U and X are on the same committee, then Q must be on the other committee.

20. Which of the following could be the members of the budget committee?

(A) R, S, U, V, X
(B) Q, U, V, X, Y
(C) R, U, V, X, Y

(D) Q, T, V, X, Y
(E) S, T, V, X, Y

21. If Q and R are on the same committee, which of the following must be true?

(A)   U is on the curriculum committee.

(B)   V is on the curriculum committee.

(C)   Y is on the curriculum committee.

(D)   U is on the budget committee.

(E)   V is on the budget committee.

22. If Q and X are on the budget committee, which of the following is a pair of professors who must be on different committees?

(A)   U and V

(B)   V and Y

(C)   S and U

(D)   V and W

(E)   R and T

23. Which of the following CANNOT serve on the curriculum committee?

(A)   Q

(B)   R

(C)   U

(D)   W

(E)   X

Questions 24–28

On Saturdays, a college admissions office offers five campus tours for prospective students at 10:00, 11:00, 12:00, 1:00, and 2:00. Five students—Adam, Kit, Noah, Pete, and Rebecca—are available to lead the tours. The person in the admissions office who is in charge of scheduling the tours adheres to the following rules and preferences:

Each tour has exactly two leaders.

Each student must lead at least one tour.

No student can lead three consecutive tours.

Kit must be one of the leaders of the 10:00 tour.

Rebecca must lead both the 1:00 and 2:00 tours.

Kit and Pete cannot be assigned to lead the same tour.

24. If Pete leads three tours one Saturday, which of the following is a pair of tours he must lead?

(A)   10:00 and 12:00

(B)   11:00 and 12:00

(C)   11:00 and 1:00

(D)   11:00 and 2:00

(E)   12:00 and 2:00

25. If Kit is scheduled to give four tours one Saturday, which of the following could be the leaders of the 12:00 tour that day?

(A) Adam and Noah   (D) Kit and Rebecca

(B) Adam and Pete   (E) Adam and Kit

(C) Pete and Rebecca

26. If Pete and Rebecca are scheduled to lead the exact same tours, which of the following could be true?

(A) Adam and Noah lead two tours together.

(B) Kit leads a tour at 12:00.

(C) Pete leads a tour at 12:00.

(D) Noah leads a tour at 1:00.

(E) Adam leads a tour at 2:00.

27. In how many ways can an acceptable schedule be completed for a Saturday on which Adam leads four tours?

(A) 0   (D) 3

(B) 1   (E) 4

(C) 2

28. If on one Saturday, none of the students leads three tours, which of the following must be true?

(A) Adam and Noah must lead a tour together.

(B) Some pair of students must lead two tours together.

(C) Either Kit or Pete must lead a tour with Rebecca.

(D) Everyone leads two tours in a row.

(E) No one other than Rebecca leads two tours in a row.

Logical Reasoning

Questions 29 and 30

In a laboratory study, 160 rabbits in an experimental group were injected with Serum D, while 160 rabbits in a control group were injected with a harmless sugar solution. Within two weeks, 39% of the experimental group rabbits had contracted jungle fever, a highly contagious and usually fatal disease. Therefore, jungle fever must be caused by some substance similar to the substances found in Serum D.

29. The above argument would be most seriously weakened if it were shown that
    - (A) none of the substances in Serum D occurs naturally in the habitats of most species of rabbit
    - (B) the rabbits in the experimental group had been kept strictly isolated from one another
    - (C) jungle fever is usually found only among victims of the bite of the South American Lesser Hooded Viper
    - (D) the scientists administering the injections were unaware of the contents of the solutions they were using
    - (E) one of the rabbits in the experimental group had had jungle fever prior to the start of the experiment

30. The above argument would be most greatly strengthened if it were shown that
    - (A) the normal rate of jungle fever among rabbits is less than 1%
    - (B) 40% of the rabbits in the control group had also contracted jungle fever within two weeks
    - (C) Serum D contains substances extracted from the root of a certain poisonous jungle wildflower
    - (D) the blood of jungle fever victims invariably contains a high level of a certain toxic substance also found in Serum D
    - (E) nearly all the rabbits who contracted jungle fever died within two days of the appearance of the first symptoms

Analytical Reasoning

Questions 31–34

In a series of three assemblies for middle school students, six high school varsity athletes—J, K, L, M, N, and P—have been asked to speak about the sports that they play. Exactly four of the athletes will speak at each assembly—two about football and one each about basketball and tennis. J must speak during the first assembly; the other five athletes have no restrictions, except that no athlete will discuss the same sport in two consecutive assemblies. The sports that each of the athletes play is as follows:

   J, K, L, and M all play football.
   L and N play basketball.
   K, M, and P play tennis.

31. If J, K, L, and N speak at assembly 1, which of the following is a list of athletes who could speak at assembly 2?

- (A)   J, K, L, P
- (B)   J, L, M, P
- (C)   K, M, N, P
- (D)   L, M, N, P
- (E)   K, L, M, P

32. Which of the following is a complete list of the athletes for whom it is possible to create a schedule that would allow them to speak in each of the three assemblies?

- (A)   K, L
- (B)   K, M
- (C)   K, L, M
- (D)   J, K, L, M
- (E)   K, L, M, N, P

33. If L speaks about basketball in assembly 2, which of the following must be true?

- (A)   L does not speak in either assembly 1 or 3.
- (B)   J and L never speak in the same assembly.
- (C)   K and M speak about football in assembly 1.
- (D)   N speaks in exactly two of the three assemblies.
- (E)   P speaks about tennis in assembly 3.

34. If the high school athletic director needs one of the six students to attend a conference on the day of the assemblies, who could she send and still be able to run all three assemblies under the original conditions?

- (A)   K
- (B)   L
- (C)   M
- (D)   N
- (E)   P

Logical Reasoning

35. In recommending to the board of trustees a tuition increase of $500 per year, the president of the university said: "There were no student demonstrations over the previous increases of $300 last year and $200 the year before."

If the president's statement is accurate, which of the following can be validly inferred from the information given?

    I. Most students in previous years felt that the increases were justified because of increased operating costs.

    II. Student apathy was responsible for the failure of students to protest the previous tuition increases.

    III. Students are not likely to demonstrate over the new tuition increases.

(A) None

(B) I only

(C) II only

(D) III only

(E) I and III only

ANSWER KEY

Section 1—Verbal Ability

1.	D	6.	E	11.	B	16.	C	21.	B	26.	A
2.	B	7.	C	12.	A	17.	C	22.	E	27.	B
3.	B	8.	C	13.	A	18.	B	23.	E	28.	D
4.	C	9.	E	14.	D	19.	B	24.	C	29.	D
5.	B	10.	D	15.	C	20.	C	25.	E	30.	E

Section 2—Quantitative Ability

1.	D	6.	D	11.	A	16.	C	21.	D	26.	D
2.	C	7.	D	12.	C	17.	C	22.	D	27.	E
3.	B	8.	A	13.	B	18.	B	23.	A	28.	D
4.	B	9.	B	14.	E	19.	C	24.	C	
5.	B	10.	C	15.	C	20.	D	25.	C	

Section 3—Analytical Ability

1.	A	8.	B	15.	E	22.	A	29.	E
2.	E	9.	B	16.	D	23.	E	30.	D
3.	C	10.	D	17.	D	24.	D	31.	E
4.	D	11.	D	18.	D	25.	B	32.	C
5.	E	12.	A	19.	E	26.	B	33.	D
6.	C	13.	B	20.	C	27.	E	34.	E
7.	D	14.	D	21.	C	28.	C	35.	A

ANSWER EXPLANATIONS

Section 1—Verbal Ability

1. **D.** The opposite of a *prodigal* (spendthrift; extravagant person) is an *economical person*. Beware eye-catchers. Choice C is incorrect. A *prodigal* is not a *prodigy* (wonder; gifted person). Think of "a prodigal squandering his wealth."

2. **B.** The opposite of *artifice* (trickery; guile) is *sincerity*. Think of being "tricked by her skillful artifice."

3. **B.**   Given the ubiquity of light, it is *unsurprising* that creatures have *developed* the biologically helpful ability to make use of light energy. Note the use of *therefore* indicating that the omitted portion of the sentence supports or continues a thought developed elsewhere in the sentence.

4. **C.**   The politicians do not forsake center stage. However, if they did forsake center stage once in a while, the public might like them better for their *self-effacement* (withdrawal from attention).

5. **B.**   By definition, a *route* that is *circuitous* follows an indirect course. Likewise, an *argument* that is *devious* follows an indirect course.   (Defining Characteristic)

6. **E.**   To be *officious* (meddlesome) is to be *helpful* in an excessive, offensive manner. To be *sycophantic* (fawning, obsequious) is to be *deferential* (respectful) in an excessive, offensive manner.   (Manner)

7. **C.**   The author states that the later novels of James play down prominent action. Thus they lack *overtly dramatic incident*. However, the author goes on to state that James's novels do possess interest; they carry the reader through "a rich analysis of the mental adjustments of the characters to the realities of their personal situations." It is this implicitly dramatic psychological revelation that sustains the reader's interest.

   Question A is unanswerable on the basis of the passage. It is evident that James wrote psychological novels; it is nowhere stated that he originated the genre.

   Question B is unanswerable on the basis of the passage. Although conventional narrative technique relates "events in distinctly phased sequences," clearly separating them, it does not necessarily recount action in *strictly* chronological order.

   Question D is unanswerable on the basis of the passage. The passage does not deal with the general public's reaction to James.

Question E is unanswerable on the basis of the passage. The passage talks of qualities in James as a novelist in terms of their being *characteristic*, not in terms of their making him *unique*.

8. **C.** While the stories themselves grow simpler, their moral and psychological aspects become increasingly complex. Choice A is incorrect. The passage mentions the specific description of settings as characteristic of James's early, conventional novels, not of his later works.

    Choice B is incorrect. In his later novels James grew less concerned with plot and more concerned with psychological revelation.

    Choice D is incorrect. The "excitement of visible actions building up to a climactic event" (lines 26–27) is characteristic of the common novel, not of the Jamesian psychological novel.

    Choice E is incorrect. The later novels tend instead to subordinate dramatic effect to psychological exploration and revelation.

9. **E.** The author refers to novels of action as "overstuffed" and describes them as "crammed with *adventitious* events"— events that are not inherent in the situation, but that are added, possibly irrelevantly, to the general story. However, these comments are merely made in passing: the author is not launching an attack against the novel of action. Thus, his attitude is best described as one of *mild disapprobation* or disapproval.

    Choice A is incorrect. The author is not *pointedly indignant* or deeply resentful in tone. He is merely making mildly critical remarks in passing.

    Choice B is incorrect. The author does make passing comments that disparage the novel of action. He is not wholly *neutral* on the topic.

    Choice C is incorrect. While the author does disparage the novel of action, he does not ridicule or *deride* it sharply.

    Choice D is incorrect. The author is certainly not a *strong partisan* or advocate of the novel of action.

10. **D.** The opposite of to *equivocate* (avoid committing oneself in what one says) is to *pledge* (bind or commit oneself solemnly).
Think of politicians "hedging and equivocating."

11. **B.** The opposite of *opulence* (wealth; affluence) is *penury* or extreme poverty.
Think of "luxurious opulence."

12. **A.** Something *ephemeral* (fleeting; transient) lacks *permanence*. Something *erratic* (unpredictable) lacks *predictability*.
(Antonym Variant)

13. **A.** To be *nonplussed* (totally at a loss) is to exhibit *bafflement* (perplexity). To be *discomfited* (abashed; disconcerted) is to exhibit *embarrassment*.
Beware eye-catchers. Choice D is incorrect. To be *despicable* is to be worthy of *contempt*; it is not to *exhibit* contempt.
(Synonym Variant)

14. **D.** To *ogle* is to *observe* or look at someone provocatively (in an attention-getting manner). To *flaunt* is to *display* or show off something provocatively (in an attention-getting manner).
(Manner)

15. **C.** You are dealing with either similar or contradictory impulses. If the impulses are similar (that is, *analogous, comparable*, or *related*), the second missing word should be a synonym or near-synonym for *individualize*. If the impulses are contradictory (that is, *disparate* or *divergent*), the second missing word should be an antonym or near-antonym for *individualize*. In this case, the latter holds true. The impulses are *divergent*; they are the impulse to individualize and the contradictory impulse to *typify* (treat characters as representatives of a type).

16. **C.** In a case in which experts disagree, it is *incumbent* on responsible scholars (that is, falls upon them as a scholarly

duty or obligation) to *refrain from* making statements that are dogmatic or excessively assertive and arbitrary about the issue.

17. **C.**   The subduction zone is the site of the destruction or consumption of existing lithospheric material. In contrast, the mid-ocean ridge is the site of the creation or emergence of new lithospheric material.
Choice A is incorrect. Both mid-ocean ridges and subduction zones are boundaries between plates.
Choice B is incorrect. Both are located on the ocean floor.
Choice D is incorrect. It is unsupported by the passage.
Choice E is incorrect. The reverse is true.

18. **B.**   Choice B is correct. You are told that the new lithospheric material is injected into a mid-ocean ridge, a suboceanic mountain range. This new material does not disappear; it is added to the material already there. Thus, it is *incorporated into* the existing mid-ocean ridge.
Choice A is incorrect. "In general these plates move in relation to one another." Nothing suggests that they become immobilized; indeed, they are said to diverge from the ridge, sliding as they diverge.
Choice C is incorrect. The passage specifically denies it. ("The earth is not expanding to any appreciable degree.")
Choice D is incorrect. It is the earth itself whose magnetic field reverses. Nothing in the passage suggests the new lithospheric material has any such potential.
Choice E is incorrect. At a mid-ocean ridge, the site at which new lithospheric material is injected from below, the plates diverge; they do not sink. (They sink, one plate diving under another, at a subduction zone.)

19. **B.**   Lines 16–18 state that one plate is pushed under another and is reincorporated or absorbed into the mantle.
Choice A is incorrect. Lithospheric material rises at mid-ocean ridges, not at subduction zones.
Choice C is incorrect. New lithospheric material is injected at a mid-ocean ridge.

Choice D is incorrect. The injection of new lithospheric material causes sea-floor spreading around the mid-ocean ridge.

Choice E is incorrect. The lithospheric plates are described as diverging from a mid-ocean ridge, not from a subduction zone.

20. **C.**   The opposite of to *hone* or sharpen is to *dull* (make blunt).
Think of "honing a razor."

21. **B.**   The opposite of *phlegmatic* (stolid; undemonstrative) is *ardent* (passionate; eager).
Think of "phlegmatic and uncaring."

22. **E.**   The opposite of a *banality* (commonplace; trite or overused expression) is a *novel expression*.
Think of "the banality of a greeting card rhyme."

23. **E.**   *Thirst* is a specific example of a *drive* (state of instinctual need). *Smell* is a specific example of a *sense*.
(Class and Member)

24. **C.**   *Skulduggery* or dishonest, unscrupulous behavior is the mark of the *swindler*. *Chicanery* or trickery is the mark of the *trickster*.   (Defining Characteristic)

25. **E.**   After incubating the new functions, the next step would be to *nurture* or foster their growth until they were ready to be sent out into the world. Their departure, however, would not diminish the cities, for by continuing to breed fresh ideas the cities would *renew* themselves.
Note the metaphoric usage of *incubate* and *breed* that influences the writer's choice of words. Cities do not literally incubate businesses or breed ideas; they only do so figuratively.

26. **A.**   Man is *gregarious* or sociable. However, he is more in need of mental companionship than of physical compan-

ionship. The writer plays on words in his conceit that a man may like to go alone for a walk but hates to stand alone in his *opinions*.

27. **B.** The opposite of *erudite* (scholarly; learned) is *ignorant.* Think of "an erudite scholar."

28. **D.** The opposite of *effrontery* (shameless boldness) is diffidence (tentativeness; timidity). Think of "shocking effrontery."

29. **D.** The opening sentence describes the shattering of the Iroquois leadership's pro-British policy. The remainder of the passage describes how Iroquois policy changed to reflect changes in European military goals.
    Choice A is incorrect. The passage is expository, not accusatory.
    Choice B is incorrect. Nothing in the passage suggests that such charges were made against the Iroquois.
    Choice C is incorrect. It is unsupported by the passage.
    Choice E is incorrect. The passage demonstrates the Iroquois were able to play European power politics.
    Remember, when asked to find the main idea, be sure to check the opening and summary sentences of each paragraph.

30. **E.** Lines 15–28 indicate that in the early 1700s and through most of the eighteenth century the Iroquois did hold the balance of power. Therefore, Choice E is the correct answer.
    Choice A is incorrect. The raid on Lachine was an effective response to French aggression, as was the Iroquois-enforced policy of aggressive neutrality.
    Choice B is incorrect. James II's overthrow was followed by colonial uprisings.
    Choice C is incorrect. In response to the Iroquois leaders' supposed favoring of the British (lines 28–33), the French went to war.
    Choice D is incorrect. This sums up the policy of aggressive neutrality.

Section 2—Quantitative Ability

Two asterisks (**) indicate an alternative method of solving.

1. **D.** By the laws of exponents, Column A is $a^4a^5 = a^9$, and Column B is $(a^3)^2 = a^6$. If $a = 1$, the columns are equal; but if $a = 2$, Column A is much greater. Neither column is always greater, and the two columns are not always equal (D).

2. **C.** Since the measure of an exterior angle of a triangle is equal to the sum of the measures of the two opposite interior angles,
$c = a + b \Rightarrow a + b - c = 0$. The columns are equal (C).
**Plug in easy-to-use numbers. If $a = 60$ and $b = 70$, then $d = 50 \Rightarrow c = 130$, and $60 + 70 - 130 = 0$.

3. **B.**

	Column A	Column B
	$\sqrt{a + b}$	$\sqrt{a} + \sqrt{b}$
Since the quantities in each column are positive, we can square them.	$a + b$	$a + 2\sqrt{ab} + b$
Subtract $a + b$ from each column	0	$2\sqrt{ab}$

Since a and b are positive, $2\sqrt{ab}$ is positive. Column B is greater.

4. **B.** There are three primes between 40 and 50: 41, 43, and 47, but only two primes between 30 and 40: 31 and 37. *Note:* remember that other than 2 and 5 every prime ends in 1, 3, 7, or 9, so those are the only numbers you need to check.

5. **B.** Since vertical angles have the same measure, the unmarked angle opposite the 60° angle also measures 60°, and the sum of the measures of all six angles in the diagram is 360°.

$360 = a + b + c + 20 + 60 + 60$
$\quad\ = a + b + c + 140.$

Subtracting 140 from each side, we get that $a + b + c = 220$.

6. **D.** Draw a Venn diagram. Since 10 seniors are in *both* band and orchestra, 30 are in band only and 50 are in orchestra only. Therefore, $10 + 30 + 50 = 90$ seniors are in at least one group, and the remaining 110 are in neither.

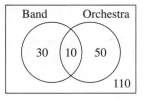

7. **D.** Let x be the amount in dollars that each of the 20 children were going to contribute; then $20x$ represents the cost of the present. When 4 children dropped out, the remaining 16 each had to pay $(x + 1.50)$ dollars. So, $16(x + 1.5) = 20x \Rightarrow 16x + 24 = 20x \Rightarrow 24 = 4x \Rightarrow x = 6$, and so the cost of the present was $20 \times 6 = 120$ dollars.

   **Since each of the 16 remaining children had to pay an extra $1.50, the extra payments totaled $16 \times \$1.50 = \$24$. This is the amount that each of the others would have paid, so each one would have paid $6. The cost of the gift was $20 \times \$6 = \$120$.

8. **A.**

	Column A	Column B
Rewrite 20^{10}.	10^{20}	$20^{10} = (2 \times 10)^{10}$
Use a law of exponents.	10^{20}	$2^{10} \times 10^{10}$
Divide each column by 10^{10}.	10^{10}	2^{10}

   Column A is *much* greater.

9. **B.** From the 124 people in front of Jill, remove Jack plus the 24 people in front of Jack: $124 - 25 = 99$. Column B is greater.

10. **C.** $3^{10} \times 27^2 = 3^{10} \times (3^3)^2 = 3^{10} \times 3^6 = 3^{16}$.
    Also, $9^2 \times 3^n = (3^2)^2 \times 3^n = 3^4 \times 3^n = 3^{4+n}$.
    So, $3^{16} = 3^{4+n}$ and $16 = 4 + n$. Then $n = 12$.

11. **A.** Since OA and OB are radii, they are each equal to 5. With no restrictions on x, chord AB could be any positive number

less than 10 (the length of a diameter), and the bigger x is, the bigger AB is. If x were 90, AB would be $\sqrt{50}$, but you are told that $x > 90$, so $AB > \sqrt{50} > 7$. Therefore, the perimeter of $\triangle AOB$ is greater than $5 + 5 + 7 = 17$. Column A is greater.

12. **C.** $\dfrac{a - b}{c - a} = 1 \Rightarrow a - b = c - a \Rightarrow 2a = b + c \Rightarrow a = \dfrac{b + c}{2}$. The columns are equal (C).

**Since you have an equation with three variables, choose values for two of them and find the third. Let $a = 2$ and $b = 1$. Then $\dfrac{2 - 1}{c - 2} = 1 \Rightarrow c = 3$. The average of b and c is 2, which equals a.

13. **B.**   If the side of a square is 10, its diagonal is $10\sqrt{2} \approx 14$. So the square in Column B is larger.
**The area of the square in Column A is $10^2 = 100$. The area of the square in Column B is $\dfrac{1}{2}(15^2) = \dfrac{1}{2}(225) = 112.5$.

14. **E.**   Exports to Eastern Europe from other Eastern European countries increased from \$9.8 billion (10% of \$98 billion) to \$20.88 billion (12% of \$174 billion)—an increase of slightly more than 100%.

15. **C.**   If France's exports to Eastern Europe were four times those of the United States, then France accounted for 8% of the total exports.
Since 8% is $\dfrac{1}{8}$ of 64%, France accounted for $\dfrac{1}{8}$ or 12.5% of the exports from the European Union.

16. **C.**   The average of the measures of the three angles of *any* triangle is $180° \div 3 = 60°$. The columns are equal (C).

17. **C.**   Ignore the x's and the y's. In any "staircase" the perimeter is just twice the sum of the height and the length. So the perimeter is $2(12 + 14) = 2(26) = 52$. The columns are equal (C).

18. **B.** We are given that

$$x^2 - y^2 = (x - y)^2$$

- Expand: $x^2 - y^2 = x^2 - 2xy + y^2$
- Subtract x^2 from each side: $-y^2 = -2xy + y^2$
- Add y^2 to each side: $0 = 2y^2 - 2xy = 2y(y - x)$

So, either $y = 0$ or $y - x = 0$. But, it is given that $x \neq y$, so $y - x \neq 0$.

Therefore, it *must* be that $y = 0$ (II is true). If we replace y by 0 in the original equation, we get $x^2 = x^2$ which is true for *any* value of x. Therefore, it is not true that x must equal 0 (I is false). Also, it is not true that $x = -y$ (III is also false). Then II only is true.

**Look at the choices. If $x = 0$, then $-y^2 = (-y)^2 = y^2$ which means that $y = 0$, which is impossible since $x \neq y$. So, I is false. Eliminate choices A, D, and E. If $y = 0$, then $(x)^2 = x^2$, which is always true *no matter what x is*. So, y *could be* 0. Don't eliminate B yet. If $x = -y$, $x^2 = y^2 \Rightarrow x^2 - y^2 = 0$; but $(x - y)^2 = (x + x)^2 = (2x)^2 = 4x^2$, which clearly does not have to be 0. Eliminate Choice C. The answer must be (B).

19. **C.** Set up the equation:

$$(x + 3) + (2x - 3) + (3x - 5) = 25$$

Collect like terms: $6x - 5 = 25$
Add 5 to each side: $6x = 30$
Divide each side by 6: $x = 5$

Plugging in 5 for x, we get that the lengths of the sides are 8, 7, and 10. The length of the shortest side is 7.

20. **D.** In each election with only two candidates, the candidate who received the greater number of votes, received more than 50% of them. In 1972 and 1980 the number of votes received by other major candidates was far less than and in 1996 that number was approximately equal to, the difference between the number of votes received by the Republican and the Democrat. Therefore, the percent of votes won by the winner was greater than or approximately equal to 50%. In 1992, however, the sum of the number of votes received by the Republican and the other major candidate greatly exceeded that of the Democratic winner. Consequently, the winner had fewer than 50% of the votes.

21. **D.** It is easy to see that 1992 was the only year in which the total number of votes cast for president exceeded 100 million.

22. **D.** Pick easy-to-use numbers. Assume that in 1990 there were 200 boys and 100 girls who earned varsity letters. Then in 2000, there were 150 boys and 125 girls. So, the ratio of girls to boys was 125:150 = 5:6 or $\frac{5}{6}$.

23. **A.** Pick a simple number for the radius of circle Q—say, 1. Then the radius of circle P is 2, and the radius of circle O is 4. The area of the large shaded region is the area of circle O minus the area of circle P: $16\pi - 4\pi = 12\pi$. The small shaded region is just circle Q, whose area is π. Then, the total shaded area is $12\pi + \pi = 13\pi$.
    The white area is the area of circle P minus the area of circle Q: $4\pi - \pi = 3\pi$. The area of the shaded region is more than 4 times the area of the white region. Column A is greater.

24. **C.** Let x = Adam's age in 1980. Then, in 1980, Judy's age was $3x$ and Elaine's age was $8x$. Since Elaine is 20 years older than Judy, $8x = 3x + 20 \Rightarrow 5x = 20 \Rightarrow x = 4$. Therefore, in 1988, Adam was $4 + 8 = 12$. The columns are equal (C).

25. **C.** The area of the shaded region is the area of the large circle, 25π, minus the area of the middle circle, 16π: $25\pi - 16\pi = 9\pi$. The striped region is just a circle of radius 3. Its area is also 9π. The columns are equal (C).

26. **D.** Since you need a ratio, the length of the side is irrelevant. The area of a square is s^2 and the area of an equilateral triangle is $\frac{s^2\sqrt{3}}{4}$. Then the ratio is

$$s^2 \div \frac{s^2\sqrt{3}}{4} = s^2 \times \frac{4}{s^2\sqrt{3}} = \frac{4}{\sqrt{3}} = \frac{4\sqrt{3}}{3}.$$

Of course, you could have used any number instead of s, and if you forgot the formula for the area of an equilateral triangle, you could have used $A = \frac{1}{2}bh$.

27. **E.**   Let $x = 2$ and $y = 1$. Then $xy = 2$, $a = 4$ and $b = 0$. Now, plug in 4 for a and 0 for b and see which of the five choices is equal to 2. Only (E) works: $\dfrac{a^2 - b^2}{8} = \dfrac{4^2 - 0^2}{8} = \dfrac{16}{8} = 2$.

**Here is the correct algebraic solution.

Add the two equations:

$$x + 2y = a$$
$$+\ x - 2y = b$$
$$2x = a + b$$

Divide by 2:
$$x = \frac{a + b}{2}$$

Multiply the second equation by −1 and add it to the first:
$$x + 2y = a$$
$$+\ -x + 2y = -b$$
$$4y = a - b$$

Divide by 4:
$$y = \frac{a - b}{4}$$

Then $xy = \dfrac{a + b}{2} \cdot \dfrac{a - b}{4} = \dfrac{a^2 - b^2}{8}$.

This is the type of algebra you want to avoid.

28. **D.**   Draw in segment $EXY \perp AB$. Then $XY = 10$ since it is the same length as a side of the square. EX is the height of

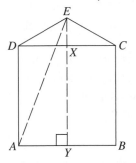

$\triangle ECD$, whose base is 10 and whose area is 10, so

$EX = 2\left[\dfrac{1}{2}bh = \dfrac{1}{2}(10)(2) = 10\right]$, and $EY = 12$.

Since $\triangle ECD$ is isosceles, $DX = 5$, so $AY = 5$. Finally, recognize $\triangle AYE$ as a 5-12-13 right triangle, or use the Pythagorean theorem to find the hypotenuse, AE, of the triangle:

$$(AE)^2 = 5^2 + 12^2 = 25 + 144 = 169,$$

so $AE = 13$.

Section 3—Analytical Ability

1. **A.** The statement in Choice A may not weaken the argument. Texas is a much bigger, more heavily populated state than Connecticut. Even though there are 35% more nurses in Texas than Connecticut, the lower salary in Texas may still cause fewer nurses to go there than would otherwise go. Each of the other choices does weaken the argument.

Solutions 2–5

courses: A, B, E, H $A < B$ $E < H$

2. **E.** None of Choices A through D violate either condition. Choice E violates the condition that Jillian must do her algebra homework before she does her biology homework.

3. **C.** When a question asks, "How many?" and the choices are small numbers, often the best approach is just to list the possibilities. There are 3 orders that begin with algebra and 3 that begin with English:

   A, B, E, H   A, E, B, H   A, E, H, B
   E, H, A, B   E, A, H, B   E, A, B, H

4. **D.** If Jillian does her history before her algebra, the only acceptable order for doing her homework would be: English, history, algebra, biology. None of the other choices yields a unique order.

5. **E.** The only possible order for Jillian to do her assignments which conforms to the given conditions is: English, algebra, book report, history, biology. Only Choice E violates this order.

6. **C.** It is easy to see that each of the choices except (C) could be true. For example, assume that in 1995 there were 100 students, 20 of whom participated in the community service program. If the number of students increased to 200 and 80 of them participated, then (A) would be true. If the

number of students decreased to 90 and 36 of them participated, then (B) would be true. If the number of students
decreased to 70 and 28 of them participated, that would be
a 40% increase in the number of participants; so Choice D
would be true. If the number of students decreased to 50,
and the number of participants remained at 20, then
Choice E would be true. If the number of students
increased to more than 100, and the number of participants decreased to fewer than 20, then the rate of participation could not be 40% in 2000: Choice C cannot be true.

7. **D.** The author's only basis for advocating the banning of the
internal combustion engine is that the oil it burns is needed for other purposes. If a synthetic oil were developed
that did everything natural oil does, the author's complaint
would lose its force. All the other choices describe events
which would ameliorate the problem without eliminating it.

8. **B.** The author claims that the oil we are burning is needed to
produce many important commodities. Choice B under-
scores both the value of some of those items and the
necessity of using oil to produce them. Choice A supports
the author's secondary point that other methods of transportation could be developed, but does not directly support
the main conclusion that the internal combustion engine
should be banned. Choice C emphasizes the urgency of the
problem, but the original argument makes no claims about
time. Choices D and E provide bases of other arguments
for the banning of gasoline-burning cars, but have no
effect on the original argument.

Solutions 9–13

teachers: F, G, H, I, J, K, L
times: before, lunch, after

before: at least 2   after: at least 3

I = lunch   J = after   H = before or lunch
G before → F before

9. **B.** Since at least two teachers are scheduled before school and at least three are scheduled after school, there can be at most two who are scheduled during lunch. Since I and L are scheduled during lunch, no one else can be; and since H cannot be scheduled after school, H must give help before school. Choice C is impossible; the other choices could be true, but none need be true.

10. **D.** Only Choice D does not violate any of the given conditions.
Choice A violates the condition that at least two teachers give help before school.
Choice B violates the condition that if G gives help before school, then F must, also.
Choice C violates the condition that I gives help during lunch.
Choice E is impossible: since at least three teachers give help after school, and at least one gives help during lunch, there can be at most three teachers who give help before school.

11. **D.** Since there are seven teachers at least two of whom must hold their extra help classes before school, at least three of whom must hold theirs after school, and at least one of whom (I) holds hers during lunch, there are only three possibilities for the number of teachers giving help at each time:

Before School	Lunch	After School
3	1	3
2	2	3
2	1	4

Looking at these possibilities, we see that only Choice D cannot occur.

12. **A.** If F can be scheduled into any of the time slots, the schedule so far must include two teachers before school, one at lunch, and three after school. If G gives help before school, then F must also. Since F is not required to give help before school, G cannot be scheduled then. In fact, G must give help after school, since I is the only one scheduled so far at lunch. Choice A must be true. (NOTE: Choice C is false; choices B, D, and E could be true, but do not have to be true.)

13. **B.**   The given condition completely determines the schedule. Since G is scheduled to give help before school, so is F. Therefore, three teachers—F, G, H—are scheduled before school, I is scheduled at lunch, and J, K, and L must be scheduled after school. Only Choice B is not true.

14. **D.**   The issue of the danger of pesticides is addressed by A, C, and E, while B calls into question the objectivity of the Food and Agriculture Department. But Choice D deals with a different issue: air pollution. And if air pollution is a cause of illness, pesticides may be less to blame.

Solutions 15–18

women: A, B, C, D   men: E, F, G, H

Draw a rectangle to represent the table and use the given conditions to place as many people as possible. Put the hostess in seat 1 and the host in seat 5. Then place Alice at the hostess's right, in seat 2, and Frank in seat 3.

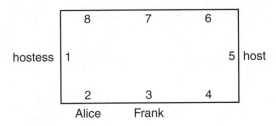

Harry and Diane are sitting opposite one another in seats 4 and 6. If Harry were in seat 4 he would be between two men, which is not allowed, so place Diane in seat 4 and Harry in seat 6. If George were the host, Harry would be at his right, not a woman, so Harry must be in seat 8.

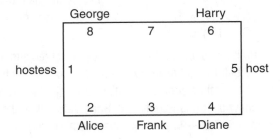

15. **E.**   Since Eric is the only man not yet in the diagram, he *must* be the host. (I is true.) Either Carol or Bette is the hostess, and the other is in seat 7. Bette *could be* the hostess. (II is true.) Since each man is sitting opposite a woman, it is possible that each man is opposite his wife. (III is true.)

16. **D.**   From the diagram of the table, we see that George and Alice are sitting opposite one another in seats 2 and 8. Since we are unsure of where Bette and Carol are sitting, some of the other couples listed *could be* married.

17. **D.**   Frank is sitting between two women: Alice and Diane. Diane is sitting between two men: Frank and Eric, who is the host. The woman in seat 7—Bette or Carol—is sitting between two men: Harry and George. There are 3 people who are sitting between two people of the opposite sex.

18. **D.**   Looking at the diagram, below, of the new seating arrange-ment, it is clear that I and III are true, and that II is not true.

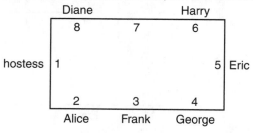

Bette or Carol is the hostess; the other is in seat 7.

19. **E.**   Represent "Rorie wakes up after 7:00" by W; "today is a school day" by S, and "Rorie has a granola bar for breakfast" by G. Then the logical structure of the first given statement is:

$(W \wedge S) \rightarrow G$ which is equivalent to
$\sim G \rightarrow \sim(W \wedge S)$ which is equivalent to
$\sim G \rightarrow (\sim W \vee \sim S)$.

So if Rorie did not have a granola bar, then either she woke up before 7:00 or today is not a school day (or both). None of the other choices must be true. (Note that we do not know anything about what Rorie eats when she wakes up before 7:00—on school days or otherwise.)

Solutions 20–23

untenured: Q, R, S   tenured: T, U, V, W, X, Y
budget: 5   curriculum: 5
of Q, R, S: 1 on budget, 2 on curriculum
$S \neq Y$ $U \neq W$ $V = X$ $(U = X) \rightarrow Q \neq X$

20. **C.** Only Choice C doesn't violate any of the conditions.
Choice A violates the condition that only one untenured professor can be on the budget committee.
Choice B violates the condition that if U and X are on a committee, then Q is not on that committee.
Choice D is not possible. Since neither U nor W is listed, they must both be on the curriculum committee, violating the condition that they not be on the same committee.
Choice E violates the condition that S and Y are not on the same committee.

21. **C.** If the two untenured professors Q and R are on the same committee, the committee must be the curriculum committee, and the third untenured professor, S, must be on the budget committee. Since Y cannot serve with S, Y is on the curriculum committee. None of the other choices must be true, although each of them could be true.

22. **A.** The condition that Q and X are on the budget committee completely determines the composition of both committees. V must be on the budget committee with X. R and S must be the two untenured professors on the curriculum committee. U must also be on the curriculum committee, since U, X, and Q cannot be on the same committee. Then, since U and W must be on different committees, W is on the budget committee. Similarly, S and Y must be on different committees, and so Y is on the budget committee. Finally, T is the fourth member of the curriculum committee. The committees are as follows: Budget—Q, V, W, X, Y—and Curriculum—R, S, T, U. Only Choice A lists two professors on different committees.

23. **E.** Suppose that X was on the curriculum committee. Then V must also be on the committee ($V = X$). This leaves room

for only two more members, both of whom must be untenured. Therefore, U and W must both be on the budget committee, which is impossible (U ≠ W). Each of the other choices is possible.

Solutions 24–28

students: A, K, N, P, R   times: 10, 11, 12, 1, 2

2 students/tour   each student at least 1 tour

not 3 in a row

K = 10   R = 1 and R = 2   K ≠ P

24. **D.**   Since Pete and Kit cannot be assigned to the same tour, and since Kit leads the 10:00 tour, Pete cannot lead the tour at 10:00. Therefore, he must lead three of the four tours between 11:00 and 2:00. To avoid leading three tours in a row, he must lead the tours at 11:00, 12:00, and 2:00 or the tours at 11:00, 1:00, and 2:00. Either way, he must lead tours at both 11:00 and 2:00.

25. **B.**   To avoid leading three tours in a row, Kit must be scheduled at 10:00, 11:00, 1:00 and 2:00. Since she cannot give the 12:00 tour, eliminate choices D and E. Since Pete cannot lead a tour with Kit, and since he must lead at least one tour, he must be scheduled at 12:00; eliminate Choice A. Since Rebecca gives the 1:00 and 2:00 tours, she cannot also give a tour at 12:00; eliminate Choice C.

26. **B.**   Since Pete and Rebecca must lead the 1:00 and 2:00 tours, no one else can lead a tour at those times, so eliminate choices D and E. Also, Pete cannot lead three tours in a row, so eliminate Choice C. The only times available for Adam and Noah to lead tours together would be 11:00 and 12:00 (since Kit leads the tour at 10:00); but if that occurred, no one would be available to lead the 10:00 tour with Kit, so eliminate Choice A. There are several ways to schedule Kit, Adam, and Noah with Kit leading a tour at 12:00.

27. **E.**   To avoid leading three tours in a row, Adam must lead the tours at 10:00, 11:00, 1:00, and 2:00. This means that so far the schedule is as follows:

A/K	A/–	–/–	A/R	A/R
10	11	12	1	2

Since Pete and Kit can't lead the same tour, Noah must be one of the leaders at 12:00 (since neither Adam nor Rebecca is eligible).

- If Noah leads that tour with Kit, then Pete must lead the 11:00 tour with Adam (otherwise Pete wouldn't be on the schedule), and there is only one possible schedule:

A/K	A/P	N/K	A/R	A/R
10	11	12	1	2

- If Noah leads the 12:00 tour with Pete, then any of Kit, Noah, or Pete could lead the 11:00 tour with Adam; so there are three more possibilities.
- There are a total of 4 possible ways to complete the schedule.

28. **C.**   If none of the students leads three tours, then each of them must lead two tours. Since Kit and Pete cannot lead a tour together, they must lead four separate tours; they cannot all be scheduled between 10:00 and 12:00, and so at least one of them must lead a tour with Rebecca at either 1:00 or 2:00. None of the other choices must be true.

29. **E.**   Since we are told that jungle fever is a "highly contagious" disease, Choice E suggests an alternative explanation for the high rate of jungle fever in the experimental group. Choice A is irrelevant, since we have no idea whether rabbits in general or any particular species of rabbits are frequent victims of jungle fever in the first place. Choice B would strengthen the argument, not weaken it.

30. **D.**   The conclusion that some substance found in Serum D causes jungle fever would be greatly strengthened if the

substance and the fever were invariably found together, as stated in Choice D. Choice A does not help to establish the cause of the high rate of jungle fever in the experimental group. Choice B would weaken the original argument, not strengthen it. Choices C and E would neither weaken nor strengthen the argument.

Solutions 31–34

athletes: J, K, L, M, N, P   assemblies: 1, 2, 3

football: J, K, L, M   basketball: L, N   tennis: K, M, P

J = 1   each assembly: 2 football, 1 basketball, 1 tennis

no one speaks about the same sport in assemblies 1 and 2 or 2 and 3

31. **E.** In assembly 1, K must speak about tennis, since he is the only one of the four who plays that sport. Therefore, the athletes who speak about football in assembly 1 are J and L, and since they can't speak about football in two assemblies in a row, K and M must be the football speakers in assembly 2. This leaves P as the only tennis player available for assembly 2. Finally, since N is speaking about basketball in assembly 1, L must be the basketball speaker in assembly 2.

32. **C.** Since no one is allowed to speak about the same sport in two consecutive assemblies, no one who plays only one sport can speak in all three assemblies. This rules out J, N, and P, so eliminate choices D and E. It is easy to create a schedule in which any of K, L, or M could be scheduled three times.

33. **D.** Since L and N are the only basketball players, and since L cannot speak about basketball in either the first or third assembly, N must speak in both of those assemblies. Further, N cannot speak in assembly 2, since his only sport is basketball, and L is speaking about basketball then. None of the other choices must be true.

34. **E.** Since two of the athletes have to speak about football during assembly 1, and two different athletes have to speak about football during assembly 2, all four football players must be present. Eliminate choices A, B, and C. Since L and N are the only basketball players, one of them must speak in assembly 1 and the other in assembly 2, so they both must be present. Eliminate Choice D. It is possible to make a complete schedule without P.

35. **A.** Statements I and II are plausible explanations for the students' passivity in previous years, but neither one can be inferred definitely; you cannot conclude that one of them must be true (some third explanation is possible). From the students' previous behavior, no valid inferences about their response to a new, larger tuition hike are possible.

Answer Sheet—Test 2

Section 1

1. Ⓐ Ⓑ Ⓒ Ⓓ Ⓔ	11. Ⓐ Ⓑ Ⓒ Ⓓ Ⓔ	21. Ⓐ Ⓑ Ⓒ Ⓓ Ⓔ
2. Ⓐ Ⓑ Ⓒ Ⓓ Ⓔ	12. Ⓐ Ⓑ Ⓒ Ⓓ Ⓔ	22. Ⓐ Ⓑ Ⓒ Ⓓ Ⓔ
3. Ⓐ Ⓑ Ⓒ Ⓓ Ⓔ	13. Ⓐ Ⓑ Ⓒ Ⓓ Ⓔ	23. Ⓐ Ⓑ Ⓒ Ⓓ Ⓔ
4. Ⓐ Ⓑ Ⓒ Ⓓ Ⓔ	14. Ⓐ Ⓑ Ⓒ Ⓓ Ⓔ	24. Ⓐ Ⓑ Ⓒ Ⓓ Ⓔ
5. Ⓐ Ⓑ Ⓒ Ⓓ Ⓔ	15. Ⓐ Ⓑ Ⓒ Ⓓ Ⓔ	25. Ⓐ Ⓑ Ⓒ Ⓓ Ⓔ
6. Ⓐ Ⓑ Ⓒ Ⓓ Ⓔ	16. Ⓐ Ⓑ Ⓒ Ⓓ Ⓔ	26. Ⓐ Ⓑ Ⓒ Ⓓ Ⓔ
7. Ⓐ Ⓑ Ⓒ Ⓓ Ⓔ	17. Ⓐ Ⓑ Ⓒ Ⓓ Ⓔ	27. Ⓐ Ⓑ Ⓒ Ⓓ Ⓔ
8. Ⓐ Ⓑ Ⓒ Ⓓ Ⓔ	18. Ⓐ Ⓑ Ⓒ Ⓓ Ⓔ	28. Ⓐ Ⓑ Ⓒ Ⓓ Ⓔ
9. Ⓐ Ⓑ Ⓒ Ⓓ Ⓔ	19. Ⓐ Ⓑ Ⓒ Ⓓ Ⓔ	29. Ⓐ Ⓑ Ⓒ Ⓓ Ⓔ
10. Ⓐ Ⓑ Ⓒ Ⓓ Ⓔ	20. Ⓐ Ⓑ Ⓒ Ⓓ Ⓔ	30. Ⓐ Ⓑ Ⓒ Ⓓ Ⓔ

Section 2

1. Ⓐ Ⓑ Ⓒ Ⓓ Ⓔ	11. Ⓐ Ⓑ Ⓒ Ⓓ Ⓔ	21. Ⓐ Ⓑ Ⓒ Ⓓ Ⓔ
2. Ⓐ Ⓑ Ⓒ Ⓓ Ⓔ	12. Ⓐ Ⓑ Ⓒ Ⓓ Ⓔ	22. Ⓐ Ⓑ Ⓒ Ⓓ Ⓔ
3. Ⓐ Ⓑ Ⓒ Ⓓ Ⓔ	13. Ⓐ Ⓑ Ⓒ Ⓓ Ⓔ	23. Ⓐ Ⓑ Ⓒ Ⓓ Ⓔ
4. Ⓐ Ⓑ Ⓒ Ⓓ Ⓔ	14. Ⓐ Ⓑ Ⓒ Ⓓ Ⓔ	24. Ⓐ Ⓑ Ⓒ Ⓓ Ⓔ
5. Ⓐ Ⓑ Ⓒ Ⓓ Ⓔ	15. Ⓐ Ⓑ Ⓒ Ⓓ Ⓔ	25. Ⓐ Ⓑ Ⓒ Ⓓ Ⓔ
6. Ⓐ Ⓑ Ⓒ Ⓓ Ⓔ	16. Ⓐ Ⓑ Ⓒ Ⓓ Ⓔ	26. Ⓐ Ⓑ Ⓒ Ⓓ Ⓔ
7. Ⓐ Ⓑ Ⓒ Ⓓ Ⓔ	17. Ⓐ Ⓑ Ⓒ Ⓓ Ⓔ	27. Ⓐ Ⓑ Ⓒ Ⓓ Ⓔ
8. Ⓐ Ⓑ Ⓒ Ⓓ Ⓔ	18. Ⓐ Ⓑ Ⓒ Ⓓ Ⓔ	28. Ⓐ Ⓑ Ⓒ Ⓓ Ⓔ
9. Ⓐ Ⓑ Ⓒ Ⓓ Ⓔ	19. Ⓐ Ⓑ Ⓒ Ⓓ Ⓔ	
10. Ⓐ Ⓑ Ⓒ Ⓓ Ⓔ	20. Ⓐ Ⓑ Ⓒ Ⓓ Ⓔ	

Section 3

1. Ⓐ Ⓑ Ⓒ Ⓓ Ⓔ	13. Ⓐ Ⓑ Ⓒ Ⓓ Ⓔ	25. Ⓐ Ⓑ Ⓒ Ⓓ Ⓔ
2. Ⓐ Ⓑ Ⓒ Ⓓ Ⓔ	14. Ⓐ Ⓑ Ⓒ Ⓓ Ⓔ	26. Ⓐ Ⓑ Ⓒ Ⓓ Ⓔ
3. Ⓐ Ⓑ Ⓒ Ⓓ Ⓔ	15. Ⓐ Ⓑ Ⓒ Ⓓ Ⓔ	27. Ⓐ Ⓑ Ⓒ Ⓓ Ⓔ
4. Ⓐ Ⓑ Ⓒ Ⓓ Ⓔ	16. Ⓐ Ⓑ Ⓒ Ⓓ Ⓔ	28. Ⓐ Ⓑ Ⓒ Ⓓ Ⓔ
5. Ⓐ Ⓑ Ⓒ Ⓓ Ⓔ	17. Ⓐ Ⓑ Ⓒ Ⓓ Ⓔ	29. Ⓐ Ⓑ Ⓒ Ⓓ Ⓔ
6. Ⓐ Ⓑ Ⓒ Ⓓ Ⓔ	18. Ⓐ Ⓑ Ⓒ Ⓓ Ⓔ	30. Ⓐ Ⓑ Ⓒ Ⓓ Ⓔ
7. Ⓐ Ⓑ Ⓒ Ⓓ Ⓔ	19. Ⓐ Ⓑ Ⓒ Ⓓ Ⓔ	31. Ⓐ Ⓑ Ⓒ Ⓓ Ⓔ
8. Ⓐ Ⓑ Ⓒ Ⓓ Ⓔ	20. Ⓐ Ⓑ Ⓒ Ⓓ Ⓔ	32. Ⓐ Ⓑ Ⓒ Ⓓ Ⓔ
9. Ⓐ Ⓑ Ⓒ Ⓓ Ⓔ	21. Ⓐ Ⓑ Ⓒ Ⓓ Ⓔ	33. Ⓐ Ⓑ Ⓒ Ⓓ Ⓔ
10. Ⓐ Ⓑ Ⓒ Ⓓ Ⓔ	22. Ⓐ Ⓑ Ⓒ Ⓓ Ⓔ	34. Ⓐ Ⓑ Ⓒ Ⓓ Ⓔ
11. Ⓐ Ⓑ Ⓒ Ⓓ Ⓔ	23. Ⓐ Ⓑ Ⓒ Ⓓ Ⓔ	35. Ⓐ Ⓑ Ⓒ Ⓓ Ⓔ
12. Ⓐ Ⓑ Ⓒ Ⓓ Ⓔ	24. Ⓐ Ⓑ Ⓒ Ⓓ Ⓔ	

Model Test 2
Section 1—Verbal Ability
30 Questions—30 Minutes

<u>Antonym Directions</u>: In each of the following antonym questions, a word printed in capital letters precedes five lettered words or phrases. From these five lettered words or phrases, pick the one most nearly *opposite* in meaning to the capitalized word.

1. ESTRANGE:
    - (A) reconcile
    - (B) feign
    - (C) perplex
    - (D) arbitrate
    - (E) commiserate

2. PROVIDENT:
    - (A) manifest
    - (B) prodigal
    - (C) thankful
    - (D) tidy
    - (E) refuted

<u>Sentence Completion Directions</u>: Each of the following sentence completion questions contains one or two blanks. These blanks signify that a word or set of words has been left out. Below each sentence are five words or sets of words. For each blank, pick the word or set of words that *best* reflects the sentence's overall meaning.

3. Like the theory of evolution, the big-bang model of the universe's formation has undergone modification and ----, but it has ---- all serious challenges.
    - (A) alteration...confirmed
    - (B) refinement...resisted
    - (C) transformation...ignored
    - (D) evaluation...acknowledged
    - (E) refutation...misdirected

4. A university training enables a graduate to see things as they are, to go right to the point, to disentangle a ---- of thought.
    - (A) line
    - (B) strand
    - (C) mass
    - (D) plethora
    - (E) skein

Analogy Directions: Each of the following analogy questions presents a related pair of words linked by a colon. Five lettered pairs of words follow the linked pair. Choose the lettered pair of words whose relationship is *most like* the relationship expressed in the original linked pair.

5. SONG : CYCLE ::
  (A) waltz : dance
  (B) tune : arrangement
  (C) sonnet : sequence
  (D) agenda : meeting
  (E) cadenza : aria

6. OBDURATE : FLEXIBILITY ::
  (A) accurate : perception
  (B) turbid : roughness
  (C) principled : fallibility
  (D) diaphanous : transparency
  (E) adamant : submissiveness

Reading Comprehension Directions: Each of the following reading comprehension questions is based on the content of the following passage. Read the passage and then determine the best answer choice for each question. Base your choice on what this passage *states directly* or *implies*, not on any information you may have gained elsewhere.

(This passage was written prior to 1950.)

In the long run a government will always encroach upon free-dom to the extent to which it has the power to do so; this is almost a natural law of politics, since, whatever the intentions of
Line the men who exercise political power, the sheer momentum of
(5) government leads to a constant pressure upon the liberties of the citizen. But in many countries society has responded by throwing up its own defenses in the shape of social classes or organized corporations which, enjoying economic power and popular support, have been able to set limits to the scope of
(10) action of the executive. Such, for example, in England was the origin of all our liberties—won from government by the stand first of the feudal nobility, then of churches and political parties,

and latterly of trade unions, commercial organizations, and the
societies for promoting various causes. Even in European lands
(15) which were arbitrarily ruled, the powers of the monarchy,
though absolute in theory, were in their exercise checked in a
similar fashion. Indeed, the fascist dictatorships of today are the
first truly tyrannical governments which western Europe has
known for centuries, and they have been rendered possible only
(20) because on coming to power they destroyed all forms of social
organization which were in any way rivals to the state.

7. According to the passage, the natural relationship between
    government and individual liberty is one of
    (A) marked indifference
    (B) secret collusion
    (C) inherent opposition
    (D) moderate complicity
    (E) fundamental interdependence

8. Fascist dictatorships differ from monarchies of recent times in
    (A) setting limits to their scope of action
    (B) effecting results by sheer momentum
    (C) rivaling the state in power
    (D) exerting constant pressure on liberties
    (E) eradicating people's organizations

9. The passage suggests which of the following about fascist dic-
    tatorships?
    (A) They represent a more efficient form of the executive.
    (B) Their rise to power came about through an accident of
        history.
    (C) They mark a regression to earlier despotic forms of gov-
        ernment.
    (D) Despite superficial dissimilarities, they are in essence like
        absolute monarchies.
    (E) They maintain their dominance by rechanneling opposing
        forces in new directions.

Sentence Completion

10. We have in America a ---- speech that is neither American, Oxford English, nor colloquial English, but ---- of all three.
    (A) motley...an enhancement
    (B) hybrid...a combination
    (C) nasal...a blend
    (D) mangled...a medley
    (E) formal...a patchwork

11. Rather than portraying Joseph II as a radical reformer whose reign was strikingly enlightened, the play Amadeus depicts him as ---- thinker, too wedded to orthodox theories of musical composition to appreciate an artist of Mozart's genius.
    (A) a revolutionary   (D) a doctrinaire
    (B) an idiosyncratic   (E) an iconoclastic
    (C) a politic

Antonyms

12. CAPITULATE:
    (A) initiate   (D) resist
    (B) defame   (E) repeat
    (C) exonerate

13. INDIGENOUS:
    (A) affluent   (D) serene
    (B) parochial   (E) inimical
    (C) alien

Analogies

14. SCURRY : MOVE ::
    (A) chant : sing   (D) sleep : drowse
    (B) chatter : talk   (E) limp : walk
    (C) carry : lift

15. CHAMELEON : HERPETOLOGIST ::
    (A) fungi : ecologist   (D) oriole : virologist
    (B) salmon : ichthyologist   (E) aphid : etymologist
    (C) mongoose : ornithologist

Reading Comprehension

As the works of dozens of women writers have been rescued from what E.P. Thompson calls "the enormous condescension of posterity," and considered in relation to each other, the lost
Line continent of the female tradition has risen like Atlantis from
(5) the sea of English literature. It is now becoming clear that, contrary to Mill's theory, women have had a literature of their own all along. The woman novelist, according to Vineta Colby, was "really neither single nor anomalous," but she was also more than a "register and spokesman for her age." She was
(10) part of a tradition that had its origins before her age, and has carried on through our own.

Many literary historians have begun to reinterpret and revise the study of women writers. Ellen Moers sees women's literature as an international movement, "apart from, but
(15) hardly subordinate to the mainstream: an undercurrent, rapid and powerful. This 'movement' began in the late eighteenth century, was multinational, and produced some of the greatest literary works of two centuries, as well as most of the lucrative pot-boilers." Patricia Meyer Spacks, in *The Female*
(20) *Imagination,* finds that "for readily discernible historical reasons women have characteristically concerned themselves with matters more or less peripheral to male concerns, or at least slightly skewed from them. The differences between traditional female preoccupations and roles and male ones make
(25) a difference in female writing." Many other critics are beginning to agree that when we look at women writers collectively we can see an imaginative continuum, the recurrence of certain patterns, themes, problems, and images from generation to generation.

16. In the second paragraph of the passage the author's attitude toward the literary critics cited can best be described as one of

(A) irony

(B) ambivalence

(C) disparagement

(D) receptiveness

(E) awe

17. The passage supplies information for answering which of the following questions?
    (A) Does the author believe the female literary tradition to be richer in depth than its masculine counterpart?
    (B) Are women psychological as well as sociological chameleons?
    (C) Does Moers share Mill's concern over the ephemeral nature of female literary renown?
    (D) What patterns, themes, images, and problems recur sufficiently in the work of women writers to belong to the female imaginative continuum?
    (E) Did Mill acknowledge the existence of a separate female literary tradition?

18. In the first paragraph, the author makes use of all the following techniques EXCEPT
    (A) extended metaphor
    (B) enumeration and classification
    (C) classical allusion
    (D) direct quotation
    (E) comparison and contrast

Antonyms

19. CHAGRIN:
    (A) frown
    (B) disguise
    (C) make indifferent
    (D) make aware
    (E) please

20. DISINGENUOUS:
    (A) naive
    (B) accurate
    (C) hostile
    (D) witty
    (E) polite

Sentence Completion

21. When those whom he had injured accused him of being a ----, he retorted curtly that he had never been a quack.

    (A) libertine   (D) plagiarist
    (B) sycophant   (E) reprobate
    (C) charlatan

22. There is an essential ---- in human gestures, and when someone raises the palms of his hands together, we do not know whether it is to bury himself in prayer or to throw himself into the sea.

    (A) economy   (D) reverence
    (B) dignity   (E) ambiguity
    (C) insincerity

Analogies

23. ASCETIC : SELF-DENIAL ::

    (A) nomad : dissipation   (D) renegade : loyalty
    (B) miser : affluence   (E) athlete : stamina
    (C) zealot : fanaticism

24. CAMOUFLAGE : DISCERN ::

    (A) encipher : comprehend   (D) renovate : construct
    (B) adorn : admire   (E) embroider : unravel
    (C) magnify : observe

25. SEER : PROPHECY ::

    (A) mentor : reward   (D) diplomat : flattery
    (B) sage : wisdom   (E) virtuoso : penance
    (C) pilgrim : diligence

Reading Comprehension

The physics of elementary particles is notorious for the fanci-
fulness of its terminology, abounding as it does in names such
as "quark," "flavor," "strangeness" and "charm." One term,
Line however, even to the nonscientist seems most apt: "gluon."
(5) Physicists conjecture that the gluon is the "glue" connecting

quarks into hadrons or strongly interacting particles (protons, neutrons, pions, etc.). Initially, physicists envisaged the gluon's adhesive strength to be so powerful that a quark could not be extracted from a hadron no matter how great the force brought
(10) to bear on it. Furthermore, the gluon itself also seemed to be permanently bound: just as no force seemed strong enough to pry apart the quarks, none appeared strong enough to squeeze out a single drop of the glue that bound them. Today, however, some physicists hypothesize the existence of pure glue: gluons
(15) without quarks, or gluonium, as they call it.

26. The author refers to charms and quarks (line 3) primarily in order to
    (A) demonstrate the similarity between these particles and the gluon
    (B) make a distinction between apposite and inapposite terminology
    (C) offer an objection to suggestions of similar frivolous names
    (D) provide illustrations of idiosyncratic nomenclature in contemporary physics
    (E) cite preliminary experimental evidence supporting the existence of gluons

27. The tone of the author's discussion of the neologisms coined by physicists is one of
    (A) scientific detachment
    (B) moderate indignation
    (C) marked derision
    (D) amused approbation
    (E) qualified skepticism

Antonyms

28. SPURIOUS:
    (A) cautious
    (B) fantastic
    (C) modest
    (D) genuine
    (E) pertinent

29. TANTAMOUNT:
    (A) not negotiable
    (B) not equivalent
    (C) not ambitious
    (D) not evident
    (E) not relevant

Sentence Completion

30. It has been Virginia Woolf's peculiar destiny to be declared annoyingly feminine by male critics at the same time that she has been ---- by women interested in the sexual revolution as not really eligible to be ---- their ranks.

    (A) lauded...enlisted in

    (B) emulated...counted among

    (C) neglected...helpful to

    (D) dismissed...drafted into

    (E) excoriated...discharged from

Section 2—Quantitative Ability

28 Questions—45 Minutes

<u>Quantitative Comparison Directions</u>: In the following type of question, two quantities appear, one in Column A and one in Column B. You must compare them. The correct answer to the question is

A if the quantity in Column A is greater
B if the quantity in Column B is greater
C if the two quantities are equal
D if it is impossible to determine which quantity is greater

<u>Notes</u>: Sometimes information about one or both of the quantities is centered above the two columns. If the same symbol appears in both columns, it represents the same thing each time.

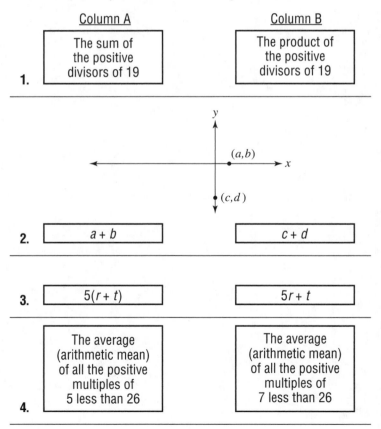

Column A	Column B
The sum of the positive divisors of 19	The product of the positive divisors of 19

1.

2. $a + b$ | $c + d$

3. $5(r + t)$ | $5r + t$

The average (arithmetic mean) of all the positive multiples of 5 less than 26	The average (arithmetic mean) of all the positive multiples of 7 less than 26

4.

<u>Discrete Quantitative and Data Interpretation Directions</u>: In the following questions, choose the best answer from the five choices listed.

5. If it is now June, what month will it be 400 months from now?

(A) January   (D) October

(B) April   (E) December

(C) June

6. If $\frac{5}{9}$ of the members of the school chorus are boys, what is the ratio of girls to boys in the chorus?

(A) $\frac{4}{9}$ (D) $\frac{9}{4}$

(B) $\frac{4}{5}$ (E) It cannot be determined from the information given.

(C) $\frac{5}{4}$

7. What is the volume of a cube whose surface area is 54?

(A) 9   (D) 81

(B) 27   (E) 729

(C) 54

Quantitative Comparison

	Column A	Column B
8.	$(a + b)(a - b)$	$a(b + a) - b(a + b)$

Dalia put exactly 75 cents worth of postage on an envelope using only 5-cent stamps and 7-cent stamps.

	The number of 5-cent stamps she used	The number of 7-cent stamps she used
9.		

Data Interpretation

10. If *A* is 25 kilometers east of *B*, which is 12 kilometers south of *C*, which is 9 kilometers west of *D*, how far is it, in kilometers, from *A* to *D*?

(A) 20

(D) $10\sqrt{13}$

(B) $5\sqrt{34}$

(E) 71

(C) $5\sqrt{41}$

Quantitative Comparison

Column A	Column B

A wooden cube whose edges are
4 inches is painted red.
The cube is then cut into 64 small
cubes whose edges are 1 inch.

11.

The number of small cubes that have exactly three red faces	The number of small cubes that have no red faces

c and *d* are positive

$$\frac{1}{c} = 1 + \frac{1}{d}$$

12.

c	*d*

A number is a *palindrome* if it reads exactly the same
from right to left as it does from left to right.
For example, 959 and 24742 are palindromes.

13.

The probability that a three-digit number chosen at random is a palindrome	$\frac{1}{10}$

Data Interpretation

Questions 14–15 refer to the following graphs.

Total enrollment in higher education institutions, by control and type of institution: Fall 1972–95

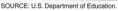

SOURCE: U.S. Department of Education.

14. In 1995 the number of students enrolled in public institutions of higher education was approximately how many times the number of students enrolled in private institutions of higher education?

(A) 2
(B) 2.5
(C) 3

(D) 3.5
(E) 4

15. If the total enrollment in institutions of higher education in 1972 was 5,000,000, approximately how many students were enrolled in private 4-year institutions in 1995?

(A) 1,000,000   (D) 1,500,000

(B) 1,100,000   (E) 1,650,000

(C) 1,250,000

Quantitative Comparison

<u>Column A</u>   <u>Column B</u>

Jack and Jill each bought the same TV set using a 10% off coupon. Jack's cashier took 10% off the price and then added 8.5% sales tax. Jill's cashier first added the tax and then took 10% off the total price.

16.

The amount Jack paid	The amount Jill paid

$$ABA$$
$$\times\ A$$
$$\overline{DCD}$$

In the multiplication problem above, each letter represents a different digit.

17.

B	5

Discrete Quantitative

18. If the lengths of two of the sides of a triangle are 9 and 10, which of the following could be the length of the third side?

 I. 1

 II. 11

 III. 21

(A) None   (D) I and II only

(B) I only   (E) I, II, and III

(C) II only

19. Which of the following is equal to $\left(\dfrac{1}{a}+a\right)^2-\left(\dfrac{1}{a}-a\right)^2$?

(A) 0

(D) $\dfrac{2}{a^2}-2a^2$

(B) 4

(E) $\dfrac{1}{a^2}-4-a^2$

(C) $\dfrac{1}{a^2}-a^2$

Data Interpretation

Questions 20–21 refer to the following graphs.

Percentage of students who reported spending time on homework and watching television

SOURCE: U.S. Department of Education.

20. In 1996, what percent of fourth-graders did between 1 and 2 hours of homework per day?

(A) 5%

(D) 40%

(B) 15%

(E) 55%

(C) 25%

21. If in 1984 there were 2,000,000 eleventh-graders, and if between 1984 and 1996 the number of eleventh-graders increased by 10%, then how many more eleventh-graders watched 4 or more hours of television in 1984 than in 1996?

(A) 25,000   (D) 100,000

(B) 50,000   (E) 150,000

(C) 75,000

Discrete Quantitative

22. Which of the following expresses the area of a circle in terms of C, its circumference?

(A) $\dfrac{C^2}{4\pi}$ (D) $\dfrac{C\pi}{4}$

(B) $\dfrac{C^2}{2\pi}$ (E) $\dfrac{C}{4\pi}$

(C) $\dfrac{\sqrt{C}}{2\pi}$

Quantitative Comparison

Column A   Column B

23. | The area of $\triangle ABC$ | | The area of $\triangle DEF$ |

A is the sum of the integers from 1 to 50, and
B is the sum of the integers from 51 to 100.

24. | $B - A$ | | 2500 |

Column A   Column B

Each small circle has radius r,
and the large circle has radius R.
The areas of the shaded region
and the white region are equal.

25.

| $\dfrac{R}{r}$ | 2 |

Discrete Quantitative

26. If p pencils cost c cents, how many can be bought for d dollars?

(A) cdp

(B) $100\,cdp$

(C) $\dfrac{dp}{100c}$

(D) $\dfrac{100\,cd}{p}$

(E) $\dfrac{100\,dp}{c}$

27. Because her test turned out to be more difficult than she intended it to be, a teacher decided to adjust the grades by deducting only half the number of points a student missed. For example, if a student missed 10 points, she received a 95 instead of a 90. Before the grades were adjusted the class average was A. What was the average after the adjustment?

(A) $50 + \dfrac{A}{2}$

(B) $\dfrac{1}{2}(100 - A)$

(C) $100 - \dfrac{A}{2}$

(D) $\dfrac{50 + A}{2}$

(E) $A + 25$

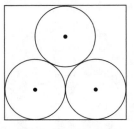

28. In the figure above, each circle is tangent to the other two circles and to the sides of the rectangle. If the diameter of each circle is 10, what is the area of the rectangle?

(A) 300

(B) 400

(C) $100 + 200\sqrt{3}$

(D) $200 + 100\sqrt{3}$

(E) $200 + 200\sqrt{3}$

Section 3—Analytical Ability

35 Questions—60 Minutes

Directions: In this section, each set of questions is based on a short passage or a set of conditions. Sometimes, in answering these questions, you might want to make a table or diagram. For each question, choose the best answer from the five choices listed.

Logical Reasoning

1. The gill-net is used to catch halibut and sea bass, but up to 72 percent of what it ensnares is not marketable and is thrown back dead. Gill-nets are often called "walls of death" because they entangle and painfully kill mammals such as dolphins, whales, and sea otters. To use the gill-net at sea is like strip mining or clear-cutting on land.

   Powerful lobbyists representing the commercial fishing industry have prevented the legislature from passing a ban on the use of gill-nets within the three-mile limit. They claim that the banning of gill-nets will raise the price of fish. They also charge that the law would benefit rich sport fishermen who want the ocean for their yachts.

   Which one of the following, if true, would support the argument in favor of a ban on gill-nets within the three-mile limit?
   (A) Less than one percent of the fish sold in this country is imported from abroad.
   (B) Gill-net users catch all but two percent of their fish within the three-mile limit.
   (C) The halibut population has fallen to a near extinction level.
   (D) There is a serious overpopulation of the coastal sea otter.
   (E) Coastal sea otters have nearly destroyed the abalone beds along the coast.

Analytical Reasoning

Questions 2–5

John purchased a toy for his young daughter. The toy included nine colorful plastic pieces in the shape of the numbers from 1 to 9. In examining these pieces he made the following observations:

> One piece is purple and two pieces each are red, green, yellow, and blue.
>
> The two red pieces are consecutive numbers.
>
> The number 4 is green.
>
> The two blue pieces are not consecutive numbers.
>
> Both the 1 and the 9 are yellow.
>
> The purple piece is not a number immediately greater than or less than either green piece.

2. If one of the red pieces is the number 3, what number is the other red piece?

(A) 2   (D) 6

(B) 4   (E) 7

(C) 5

3. If the number 5 is green, each of the following could be true EXCEPT

(A) The purple piece and one of the yellow pieces are consecutive numbers.

(B) The number 6 is purple.

(C) The two blue pieces and the purple piece are three consecutive numbers.

(D) The number 2 is red.

(E) The number 8 is red.

4. If the number 6 is green, which of the following could be true?

(A) The number 2 is blue.   (D) The number 5 is purple.

(B) The number 3 is purple.   (E) The number 7 is blue.

(C) The number 5 is red.

5. Which of the following, if true, would enable you to determine the color of every number?
   (A) The 2 is blue.   (D) The 7 is blue.
   (B) The 3 is blue.   (E) The 7 is green.
   (C) The 5 is red.

Logical Reasoning

Questions 6–7

Strict gun control laws cause a decrease in violent crime; in the six months since the city council passed a gun control law, armed robberies in City X have dropped by 18 percent.

6. All of the following, if true, are valid objections to the argument above EXCEPT
   (A) A decrease in crime in one city does not mean that such a decrease would occur anywhere a gun control law was enacted.
   (B) Other factors may have caused the drop in armed robberies.
   (C) Armed robbery is only one category of violent crime that might be affected by a gun control law.
   (D) The gun control law has made it more difficult for citizens to purchase guns for legitimate purposes of self-defense.
   (E) Since the law was passed, murders involving guns in City X have increased by 22 percent.

7. Which of the following statements, if true, would weaken the argument above?
   I.   In the six months since the law was passed, 40 percent more police have been hired.
   II. In the six months since the law was passed, accidental deaths by firearms have increased by 10 percent.
   III. Only 30 percent of those indicted under the new law have been convicted.
   (A) I only   (D) I and III only
   (B) III only   (E) II and III only
   (C) I and II only

8. Each week the forensics teams at Roslyn High School and Manhasset High School debate each other. Each team has several members, and each week three are selected to debate. Whenever Aviva debates for Roslyn, Roslyn wins; and whenever Zachary debates for Roslyn, Roslyn wins. Whenever Josh debates for Roslyn, Manhasset wins.

If one week Roslyn lost to Manhasset, which of the following must be true?

(A) Josh debated for Roslyn.
(B) Either Aviva or Zachary debated for Roslyn.
(C) Neither Aviva nor Zachary debated for Roslyn.
(D) Josh and either Aviva or Zachary debated for Roslyn.
(E) Josh and neither Aviva nor Zachary debated for Roslyn.

Analytical Reasoning

Questions 9–13

The Fairfield Foreign Film Festival plans to show six films—one each from Belgium, Canada, Denmark, England, France, and Germany. The festival will open on a Thursday and close three days later on a Sunday. Each film will be shown once during the four days of the festival. The order in which the films will be shown must adhere to the following conditions:

> At least one film will be shown each day.
> No more than three films will be shown on any two consecutive days.
> The Belgian film must be shown on Saturday.
> The Canadian film must be shown on the same day as another film.
> The French film must be shown on a day before the German film is shown.
> The Danish film must be shown on a day after the English film is shown.

9. If only one film is shown on Thursday, it could be the entry from which of the following countries?

(A) Belgium   (D) France
(B) Canada   (E) Germany
(C) Denmark

10. If the Belgian and French films are shown on the same day, which of the following must be true?

(A) The film from Denmark will be shown on Thursday.

(B) The film from Denmark will be shown on Friday.

(C) The film from Germany will be shown on Thursday.

(D) The film from Canada will be shown on Sunday.

(E) The film from England will be shown on Sunday.

11. If the director of the festival decides to show two films on Thursday and two on Sunday, how many films would be eligible to be shown on Friday?

(A) 1 (D) 4

(B) 2 (E) 5

(C) 3

12. If the English and German films are shown on the same day, which of the following must be true?

(A) The film from England will be shown on Thursday.

(B) The film from France will be shown on Friday.

(C) The film from Canada will be shown on Saturday.

(D) The film from Germany will be shown on Saturday.

(E) The film from Canada will be shown on Sunday.

13. If the film from England is shown on Saturday, which of the following films cannot be shown on the same day as any other film?

(A) The film from Belgium. (D) The film from France.

(B) The film from Canada. (E) The film from Germany.

(C) The film from England.

Logical Reasoning

14. Excessive amounts of mercury in drinking water, associated with certain types of industrial pollution, have been shown to cause Hobson's disease. Island R. has an economy based entirely on subsistence-level agriculture; modern industry of any kind is unknown. The inhabitants of Island R. have an unusually high incidence of Hobson's disease.

Which of the following can be validly inferred from the above statements?

    I. Mercury in drinking water is actually perfectly safe.

    II. Mercury in drinking water can have sources other than industrial pollution.

    III. Hobson's disease has causes other than mercury in drinking water.

(A) II only   (D) I and III only

(B) III only   (E) II and III only

(C) I and II only

Analytical Reasoning

Questions 15–18

A group of at least three townspeople is to be chosen by the mayor to accompany her on a trip to the state capital. There are seven people who are eligible to be chosen—one man, one woman, two boys, and three girls. In choosing the group, the mayor must adhere to the following conditions:

    At least one adult must be chosen.

    At least one male must be chosen.

    The group selected cannot include all three males.

    The group selected cannot include all four females.

    If the woman is chosen, at least one of the girls must be chosen.

15. If all three girls are chosen, who else must be in the group?

(A) No one else

(B) The man

(C) One of the boys

(D) The man and one of the boys

(E) The man, the woman, and one of the boys

16. Which of the following could be the complete make-up of the group?

(A) The three girls

(B) Both boys and two of the girls

(C) The woman and two of the girls

(D) The woman, a boy, and two of the girls

(E) The man, both boys, and one of the girls

17. If both adults are chosen, each of the following could be a complete list of the other members of the group EXCEPT

(A) One girl
(B) One boy
(C) One girl and one boy
(D) Two girls and one boy
(E) Two boys and one girl

18. Each of the following statements about the composition of the group could be true EXCEPT

(A) There are more males than females.
(B) There are more females than males.
(C) There are exactly four members.
(D) There are exactly five members.
(E) There are exactly six members.

Logical Reasoning

19. *Chariots of Fire* may have caught professional critics off guard in 1982 as the Motion Picture Academy's choice for an Oscar as the year's best film, but it won wide audience approval as superb entertainment.

This award-winning film has a theme that extols traditional religious values—without a shred of offensive sex, violence, or profanity.

Those who condemn the motion picture industry for producing many objectionable films can do their part by patronizing wholesome ones, thereby encouraging future Academy Award judges to recognize and reward decency.

Which one of the following is a basic assumption underlying the final sentence of the passage?

(A) Academy judges are not decent people.
(B) The popularity of a film influences academy judges.
(C) Future academy judges will be better than past ones.
(D) There are those who condemn the motion picture industry.
(E) *Chariots of Fire* is a patronizing film.

<u>**Analytical Reasoning**</u>

<u>Questions 20–23</u>

Each of the integers from 1 to 7, inclusive, is to be assigned to one of two sets—X and Y—such that:

> No integer is a member of both sets.
> Neither set has more than four members.
> 1 and 4 must be in the same set.
> If 2 is a member of set X, then so is 7.
> If 6 is a member of set Y, then 5 is not a member of Y.

20. Which of the following could be a complete list of the integers in set X?

(A) 1, 4
(B) 1, 2, 7
(C) 1, 4, 7

(D) 1, 2, 4
(E) 1, 4, 5, 7

21. Which of the following CANNOT be true?

(A) 4 and 7 are in X.
(B) 5 and 6 are in X.
(C) 1 and 2 are in Y.

(D) 1, 3, and 7 are in X.
(E) 2, 3, and 6 are in Y.

22. If 5 and 7 are both members of set Y, how many different ways are there to assign the other five numbers to the two sets?

(A) 1
(B) 2
(C) 3

(D) 5
(E) 6

23. If X has four members, none of which is 1, which of the following numbers must be in X?

(A) 2
(B) 3
(C) 5

(D) 6
(E) 7

<u>Questions 24–28</u>

A four-person congressional committee is to be formed consisting of two senators and two representatives. The senators are to be chosen from W, X, Y, and Z; the representatives are to be chosen from P, Q, R, and S. The committee will be chosen by the vice-president subject to the following conditions:

S will not serve on the committee unless X does.

Y will not serve on a committee with Q.

The vice-president has decided that Y or Z must be included, but neither Y nor Z is willing to serve with the other.

24. Which of the following could be the fourth member of a committee that already consists of R, W, and Y?

(A) P   (D) X

(B) Q   (E) Z

(C) S

25. If neither P nor R is assigned to the committee, which two senators must be on the committee?

(A) W and Y   (D) X and Z

(B) X and Y   (E) Y and Z

(C) W and Z

26. Which of the following could be the other three members of a committee that includes Y?

(A) P, R, Z   (D) R, S, X

(B) P, S, W   (E) S, W, X

(C) Q, R, X

27. If the vice-president chooses S to be on the committee, which of the following CANNOT be on the committee?

(A) P   (D) W

(B) Q   (E) X

(C) R

28. If Q is chosen to be on the committee and X is not chosen, how many different committees could be formed?

(A) 1   (D) 4

(B) 2   (E) 6

(C) 3

Logical Reasoning

29. Now Mesa Electronics brings tomorrow's technology to today's home stereo. The same space-age circuitry used by the Wanderer spacecraft to send images of the most distant planets back to earth has been incorporated in the new Mesa X-2700 stereo system. If your home entertainment is important to you, why settle for an old-fashioned stereo system when the Mesa X-2700 is priced at only a few dollars more?

   The most serious logical weakness of this argument is its failure to

   (A) provide technical data on the manufacturing specifications of the Mesa X-2700

   (B) show the relevance of space-age circuitry to the requirements of home stereo

   (C) specify the exact price difference between the Mesa X-2700 and old-fashioned stereo systems

   (D) acknowledge the contributions of scientists in the space program to the development of the advanced circuitry mentioned

   (E) explain the precise meaning of the technical terms used

30. There are 39 members on the Central High School student government council. When a vote took place on a certain proposal, all of the seniors and none of the freshmen voted for it. Some of the juniors and some of the sophomores voted for the proposal and some voted against it.

   If a simple majority of the votes cast is required for the proposal to be adopted, which of the following statements, if true, would enable you to determine whether the proposal was adopted?

   (A) There are more seniors than freshmen on the council.

   (B) A majority of the freshmen and a majority of the sophomores voted for the proposal.

   (C) There are 18 seniors on the council.

   (D) There are the same number of seniors and freshmen combined as there are sophomores and juniors combined.

   (E) There are more juniors than sophomores and freshmen combined, and more than 90% of the juniors voted against the proposal.

Analytical Reasoning

<u>Questions 31–34</u>

Seven applicants for a job—F, G, H, I, J, K, and L—are each to be interviewed on Monday or Tuesday. Each applicant is to be interviewed exactly once, and the interview schedule must conform to the following conditions:

> There must be at least two interviews each day.
>
> I cannot have the first interview on Monday.
>
> F must have the first or last interview on either Monday or Tuesday.
>
> H and L must interview on the same day, with no other applicant interviewing between them.
>
> I and K cannot interview on the same day.
>
> At least one interview must be scheduled between the interviews of G and L.

31. Which of the following is an acceptable schedule, in order, of interviews for the seven applicants?

	<u>Monday</u>	<u>Tuesday</u>
(A)	H, L	F, G, I, J, K
(B)	K, J, G	L, H, I, F
(C)	H, K, L, F	I, G, J
(D)	L, H, I, J	K, F, G
(E)	L, H, K, J	I, G, F

32. If G has the very first interview, and if exactly four people are interviewed on Tuesday, which of the following could be the schedule for the two interviews immediately following G's?
    (A) First H, then L
    (B) First L, then F
    (C) First I, then L
    (D) First F, then I
    (E) First H, then F

33. If the only applicants who have interviews on Monday are F, I, and J, and if H is the first applicant to be interviewed on Tuesday, which of the following statements must be true?

(A) K has the second interview on Tuesday.

(B) G has the third interview on Tuesday.

(C) L has the third interview on Tuesday.

(D) G has the last interview on Tuesday.

(E) K has the last interview on Tuesday.

34. If three interviews are scheduled for Monday, and if H and I have the first and last interviews, respectively, on Tuesday, which of the following must be true?

(A) F has the first interview on Monday.

(B) F has the third interview on Monday.

(C) G has an interview on Tuesday.

(D) J has the second interview on Tuesday.

(E) J has the third interview on Tuesday.

Logical Reasoning

35. Sales of new homes in Arizona fell almost 20 percent in the month of February, compared to last year. Analysts attribute the decline to several factors. Record rainfalls kept both builders and buyers indoors for most of the month. The rise in the interest rates has brought mortgage rates to a ten-month high. Both the sales of new homes and housing starts have reached new lows. With every indication that mortgage rates will remain high for the rest of the year, Arizona home-builders foresee a very grim year ahead.

Which one of the following would add support to the conclusion of this passage?

(A) Last year's sales increased in the second half of the year, despite some increase in interest rates.

(B) Last year's sales were accelerated by good weather in January and February.

(C) Widespread advertising and incentives to attract buyers this February were ineffective.

(D) Rain in Arizona usually ends late in February.

(E) Home sales and building starts throughout the country are about the same this year as last year.

ANSWER KEY

Section 1—Verbal Ability

1.	A	6.	E	11.	D	16.	D	21.	C	26.	D
2.	B	7.	C	12.	D	17.	E	22.	E	27.	D
3.	B	8.	E	13.	C	18.	B	23.	C	28.	D
4.	E	9.	C	14.	B	19.	E	24.	A	29.	B
5.	C	10.	B	15.	B	20.	A	25.	B	30.	D

Section 2—Quantitative Ability

1.	A	6.	B	11.	C	16.	C	21.	D	26.	E
2.	A	7.	B	12.	B	17.	B	22.	A	27.	A
3.	D	8.	C	13.	C	18.	C	23.	A	28.	D
4.	A	9.	D	14.	D	19.	B	24.	C		
5.	D	10.	A	15.	E	20.	B	25.	A		

Section 3—Analytical Ability

1.	C	8.	C	15.	B	22.	B	29.	B
2.	A	9.	D	16.	D	23.	E	30.	C
3.	B	10.	B	17.	E	24.	A	31.	E
4.	E	11.	D	18.	E	25.	D	32.	C
5.	E	12.	E	19.	B	26.	D	33.	D
6.	D	13.	E	20.	E	27.	D	34.	E
7.	A	14.	B	21.	D	28.	B	35.	C

ANSWER EXPLANATIONS

Section 1—Verbal Ability

1. **A.** The opposite of to *estrange* or to alienate is to *reconcile*. Think of "estranged couples" in a divorce.

2. **B.** The opposite of *provident* or frugal is *prodigal* or extravagant.
   Think of the fable of the prodigal grasshopper and the provident ant.

3. **B.** The author concedes that the big-bang theory has been changed somewhat: it has undergone *refinement* or polishing. However, he denies that its validity has been threatened seriously by any rival theories: it has *resisted* or defied all challenges.

   The use of the support signal *and* indicates that the first missing word is similar in meaning to "modification." The use of the contrast signal *but* indicates that the second missing word is contrary in meaning to "undergone modification."

4. **E.** One would have to disentangle a *skein* or coiled and twisted bundle of yarn.

   Note how the presence of the verb *disentangle*, which may be used both figuratively and literally, influences the writer's choice of words. In this case, while *line* and *strand* are possible choices, neither word possesses the connotations of twistings and tangled contortions that make *skein* the most suitable choice.

5. **C.** A *song* is part of a *cycle* or series of songs. A *sonnet* is part of a *sequence* or series of sonnets.

   (Group and Member)

6. **E.** Someone *obdurate* (unyielding, inflexible) is lacking in *flexibility*. Someone *adamant* (unshakable in opposition) is lacking in *submissiveness*. (Antonym Variant)

7. **C.** The author says that the tendency for a government to encroach upon individual liberty to the extent to which it has the power to do so is "almost a natural law" of politics. Thus, government and individual liberty are *inherently* by their very natures in *opposition* to one another.

8. **E.** The final sentence states that the fascist dictatorships "destroyed (*eradicated*) all forms of social organization that were in any way rivals to the state."

9. **C.** If the fascist dictatorships "are the first truly tyrannical governments which western Europe has known for cen-

turies," then it can be inferred that centuries ago there were tyrannical or *despotic* governments in western Europe. Thus, the fascist governments represent a regression or reversion to an earlier form of government.

10. **B.** Speech that is *hybrid* (made up of several elements) by definition combines these elements. The technical term *hybrid* best suits this context because it is a neutral term devoid of negative connotations (which *motley* and *mangled* possess).

11. **D.** A man too wedded to *orthodox* theories or doctrines can best be described as *doctrinaire* or dogmatic.

12. **D.** The opposite of to *capitulate* or yield is to *resist*. Think of "capitulating without a fight."

13. **C.** The opposite of *indigenous* or native is *alien* or foreign. Beware eye-catchers. Choice A is incorrect. Do not confuse *indigenous* or native with *indigent* or poor.

14. **B.** To *scurry* is to *move* in a brisk and rapid manner. To *chatter* is to *talk* in a brisk and rapid manner.   (Manner)

15. **B.** A *chameleon*, a kind of lizard, is studied by a *herpetologist* (scientist who studies reptiles and amphibians). A *salmon*, a kind of fish, is studied by an *ichthyologist*.
                                                        (Defining Characteristic)

16. **D.** The author opens the paragraph by stating that many literary critics have begun reinterpreting the study of women's literature. She then goes on to cite individual comments that support her assertion. Clearly, she is receptive or open to the ideas of these writers, for they and she share a common sense of the need to reinterpret their common field.
Choices A and B are incorrect. The author cites the literary critics straightforwardly, presenting their statements as evidence supporting her thesis.
Choice C is incorrect. The author does not *disparage* or belittle these critics. By quoting them respectfully she implicitly acknowledges their competence.

Choice E is incorrect. The author quotes the critics as acknowledged experts in the field. However, she is quite ready to disagree with their conclusions (as she disagrees with Moers' view of women's literature as an international movement). Clearly, she does not look on these critics with *awe*.

17. **E.**   Question E is answerable on the basis of the passage. According to lines 5–6, Mill disbelieved in the idea that women "have had a literature of their own all along."

18. **B.**   The writer neither lists (*enumerates*) nor sorts (*classifies*) anything in the opening paragraph.
Choice A is incorrect. The writer likens the female tradition to a lost continent and develops the metaphor by describing the continent "rising ... from the sea of English literature."
Choice C is incorrect. The author refers or *alludes* to the classical legend of Atlantis.
Choice D is incorrect. The author quotes Colby and Thompson.
Choice E is incorrect. The author contrasts the revised view of women's literature with Mill's view.

19. **E.**   The opposite of to *chagrin* (disappoint) is to *please*.
Beware eye-catchers. Choice A is incorrect. *Chagrin* is unrelated to grin.
Think of "being chagrined by a defeat."

20. **A.**   The opposite of *disingenuous* or guileful (giving a false impression of naiveté) is *naive* or unsophisticated.
Think of a "disingenuous appearance of candor."

21. **C.**   *Charlatan* is another term for a *quack* or pretender to medical knowledge.

22. **E.**   The statement that "we do not know" whether a gesture indicates devotion or despair suggests that gestures are by their nature *ambiguous* or unclear.

23. **C.**   By definition, an *ascetic* (one who practices severe self-discipline) is characterized by *self-denial*. A *zealot* (extreme enthusiast) is characterized by *fanaticism*.

Beware eye-catchers. A *miser* may hoard wealth, but he is not necessarily characterized by *affluence*. Even poor persons may be misers. (Defining Characteristic)

24. **A.** To *camouflage* something is to make it difficult to *discern* or perceive. To *encipher* or encode something is to make it difficult to *comprehend*. (Function)

25. **B.** A *seer* or prophet is by definition someone gifted in *prophecy*. A *sage* or wise person is by definition someone gifted in *wisdom*. (Defining Characteristic)

26. **D.** The author provides them as examples of what he means by the "fanciful ... terminology" or *idiosyncratic nomenclature* in modern particle physics.

27. **D.** Since the author considers the gluon to be *aptly* named, he clearly views this particular neologism or newly coined term with *approbation*. However, he tempers his approval with *amusement*, for he finds the terms fanciful (capricious, whimsical) as well as apt.

28. **D.** The opposite of *spurious* (false or fraudulent) is *genuine*. Think of forgers selling "a spurious work of art."

29. **B.** The opposite of *tantamount* or equivalent in value is *not equivalent*.
    Context Clue: "Failure to publish is tantamount to suppression."

30. **D.** The incongruity here is that one group finds Woolf too feminine for their tastes while another finds her not feminine (or perhaps feminist) enough for theirs.
    Note that the word *peculiar* signals that Woolf's destiny is an unexpected one.

Section 2—Quantitative Ability

Two asterisks (**) indicate an alternative method of solving.

1. **A.** The only positive divisors of 19 are 1 and 19.
   Column A: $1 + 19 = 20$.
   Column B: $1 \times 19 = 19$.

2. **A.** Since (a, b) is on the positive portion of the x-axis, a is positive and $b = 0$; so $a + b$ is positive. Also, since (c, d) is on the negative portion of the y-axis, c is negative and $d = 0$; so $c + d$ is negative. Column A is greater.

3. **D.** Column A: by the distributive law, $5(r + t) = 5r + 5t$. Subtract $5r$ from each column, and compare $5t$ and t. They are equal if $t = 0$ and unequal otherwise. Neither column is always greater, and the two columns are not always equal (D).

4. **A.** Column A: there are 5 positive multiples of 5 less than 26: 5, 10, 15, 20, 25; their average is 15, the middle one.
   Column B: there are 3 positive multiples of 7 less than 26: 7, 14, 21; their average is 14.
   Column A is greater.

5. **D.** Since $400 = 12 \times 33 + 4$, 100 months is 4 months more than 33 years. So 33 years from now it will again be June, and 4 months later it will be October.
   **Look for a pattern. Since there are 12 months in a year, after every 12 months it will again be June; i.e., it will be June after 12, 24, 36, 48,..., 120,..., 360 months. So, 396 (33×12) months from now, it will again be June. Count 4 more months to October.

6. **B.** Pick an easy-to-use number. Since $\frac{5}{9}$ of the members are boys, assume there are 9 members, 5 of whom are boys. Then the other 4 are girls, and the ratio of girls to boys is 4 to 5, or $\frac{4}{5}$.

7. **B.** Since the surface area is 54, each of the six faces of the cube is a square whose area is $54 \div 6 = 9$. Then each edge is 3, and the volume is $3^3 = 27$.

8. **C.** Column B: $a(b + a) - b(a + b) = ab + a^2 - ba - b^2 = a^2 - b^2$.
Column A: $(a + b)(a - b) = a^2 - b^2$.

9. **D.** If x and y represent the number of 5-cent stamps and 7-cent stamps, respectively, that Dalia used, then $5x + 7y = 75$. There are infinitely many solutions to this equation, but there are only two solutions in which x and y are both positive integers: $y = 10$ and $x = 1$ or $y = 5$ and $x = 8$. Neither column is always greater, and the two columns are not always equal (D).

10. **A.** Draw a diagram. In the figure below, form rectangle *BCDE* by drawing $DE \perp AB$. Then, $BE = 9$, $AE = 16$, and $DE = 12$. Finally, $DA = 20$, because right triangle *AED* is a 3-4-5 triangle in which each side is multiplied by 4. If you don't realize that, use the Pythagorean theorem to get *DA*:
$$(DA)^2 = (AE)^2 + (DE)^2 = 256 + 144 = 400 \Rightarrow DA = 20.$$

11. **C.** Draw a diagram, and on each small cube write the number of red faces it has. The cubes with three red faces are the eight corners. The cubes with no red faces are the "inside" ones that can't be seen. If you cut off the top and bottom rows, the front and back rows, and the left and right rows, you are left with a small 2-inch cube, none of whose faces is red. That 2-inch cube is made up of eight 1-inch cubes. The columns are equal (C).

12. **B.**   Since $\frac{1}{c} = 1 + \frac{1}{d}$, then $1 = \frac{1}{c} - \frac{1}{d} = \frac{d-c}{cd}$.

Therefore, $d - c = cd$, which is positive. Then, $d - c$ is positive, and so $d > c$. Column B is greater.

13. **C.**   The simplest solution is to realize that there is one palindrome between 100 and 109 (101), one between 390 and 399 (393), one between 880 and 889 (888), and in general, one out of every 10 numbers. So the probability is $\frac{1}{10}$. The answer is (C).

**The more direct solution is to count the number of palindromes. Either systematically make a list and notice that there are 10 of them between 100 and 199, and 10 in each of the hundreds from the 100s to the 900s, for a total of 90; or use the counting principle: the first digit can be chosen in any of 9 ways, the second in any of 10 ways, and the third, since it must match the first, can be chosen in only 1 way ($9 \times 10 \times 1 = 90$). Since there are 900 three-digit numbers, the probability is $\frac{90}{900} = \frac{1}{10}$.

14. **D.**   From the bottom graph, we can estimate the percentage distribution of total enrollment to be:

Public 4-year	41%	Private 4-year	21%
Public 2-year	37%	Private 2-year	1%
Total public	78%	Total private	22%

$78 \div 22 \approx 3.5$, so there were 3.5 times as many students enrolled in public institutions as private ones.

15. **E.**   In 1972, enrollment in private 4-year institutions was approximately 1,100,000 (22% of the total enrollment of 5,000,000). By 1995, the index for private 4-year institutions had increased from 80 to 120, a 50% increase. Therefore, the number of private 4-year students enrolled in 1995 was approximately 1,650,000 (50% more than the 1,100,000 students enrolled in 1972).

16. **C.**   Let P = the price of the TV set. Then Jack paid $1.085(.90P)$, whereas Jill paid $.90(1.085P)$. The columns are equal (C).

**Choose a convenient number: assume the TV cost $100. Jack paid $90 plus $7.65 tax (8.5% of $90) for a total of $97.65. Jill's cashier rang up $100 plus $8.50 tax and then deducted $10.85 (10% of $108.50) for a final cost of $97.65.

17. **B.** Since A times ABA is a three-digit number, A has to be less than 4; but 1 times ABA is ABA, so $A \neq 1$. Therefore, $A = 2$ or $A = 3$.

$$
\begin{array}{r} 2B2 \\ \times\ 2 \\ \hline 4C4 \end{array}
\quad \text{or} \quad
\begin{array}{r} 3B3 \\ \times\ 3 \\ \hline 9C9 \end{array}
$$

Since there is no carrying, either $2 \times B = C$, a one-digit number, and $B < 5$, or $3 \times B = C$, and $B < 3$. In either case, Column B is greater.

18. **C.** By the triangle inequality,
- The third side must be *less* than $9 + 10 = 19$. (III is false.)
- The third side must be *greater* than $10 - 9 = 1$. (I is false.)
- *Any* number between 1 and 19 could be the length of the third side. (II is true.)

The answer is (C).

19. **B.** Expand each square: $\left(\dfrac{1}{a} + a\right)^2 =$

$$
\frac{1}{a^2} + 2\left(\frac{1}{a}\right)(a) + a^2 = \frac{1}{a^2} + 2 + a^2
$$

Similarly, $\left(\dfrac{1}{a} - a\right)^2 = \dfrac{1}{a^2} - 2 + a^2$.

Now subtract: $\left(\dfrac{1}{a^2} + 2 + a^2\right) - \left(\dfrac{1}{a^2} - 2 + a^2\right) = 4$.

**Let $a = 1$. Then

$$
\left(\frac{1}{a} + a\right)^2 - \left(\frac{1}{a} - a\right)^2 = 2^2 - 0^2 = 4 - 0 = 4.
$$

20. **B.** From the top graph, we see that among fourth-graders in 1996:
- 25% did no homework;
- 55% did less than 1 hour;
- 5% did more than 2 hours.

This accounts for 85% of the fourth-graders; the other 15% did between 1 and 2 hours of homework per day.

21. **D.**   In 1984, approximately 500,000 eleventh-graders watched television 4 hours or more per day (25% of 2,000,000). By 1996, the number of eleventh-graders had increased by 10% to 2,200,000, but the percent of them who watched television for 4 hours or more per day decreased to about 18%: 18% of 2,200,000 is 396,000 or approximately 400,000, a decrease of 100,000.

22. **A.**   Since $C = 2\pi r$, then $r = \dfrac{C}{2\pi}$, and area of circle $= \pi r^2 =$

$$\pi\left(\frac{C}{2\pi}\right)^2 = \pi\left(\frac{C^2}{4\pi^2}\right) = \frac{C^2}{4\pi}$$

23. **A.**   Column A: Since the hypotenuse is 2, the length of each leg is $\dfrac{2}{\sqrt{2}} = \sqrt{2}$, and the area is $\dfrac{1}{2}\left(\sqrt{2}\right)\left(\sqrt{2}\right) = \dfrac{1}{2}(2) = 1.$

Column B: Since the hypotenuse is 2, the shorter leg is 1, the longer leg is $\sqrt{3}$, and the area is

$$\frac{1}{2}(1)\left(\sqrt{3}\right) = \frac{\sqrt{3}}{2} \approx 0.866.$$

Column A is greater.

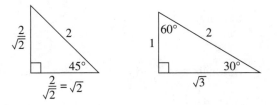

24. **C.** $B - A = (51 + 52 + 53 + \ldots + 99 + 100) - (1 + 2 + 3 + \ldots + 49 + 50)$
$= (51 - 1) + (52 - 2) + (53 - 3) + \ldots + (99 - 49) + (100 - 50)$
$= 50 + 50 + 50 + \ldots + 50 + 50 = 50 \times 50 = 2500.$

**If you know the formula, $\dfrac{n(n+1)}{2}$, for adding up the first

n positive integers, you can use it: $A = \dfrac{50(51)}{2} = 25(51) = 1275$. B is the sum of the integers from 1 to 100 minus the sum of the integers from 1 to 50:

$$B = \frac{100(101)}{2} - 1275 = 50(101) - 1275 = 5050 - 1275 = 3875.$$

Finally, $B - A = 3875 - 1275 = 2500$.
The columns are equal (C).

25. **A.** Since the area of each small circle is πr^2, the area of the white region is $3\pi r^2$. Also, since the area of the large circle is πR^2, the shaded area is $\pi R^2 - 3\pi r^2 = \pi(R^2 - 3r^2)$. Since the areas of the white region and the shaded region are equal:

$$3\pi r^2 = \pi(R^2 - 3r^2) \Rightarrow 3r^2 = R^2 - 3r^2 \Rightarrow$$
$$R^2 = 6r^2 \Rightarrow \frac{R^2}{r^2} = 6 \Rightarrow \frac{R}{r} = \sqrt{6},$$

which is greater than 2. Column A is greater.

26. **E.** Since p pencils cost c cents, each pencil costs $\dfrac{c}{p}$ cents.

By dividing the number of cents we have by $\dfrac{c}{p}$, we find

out how many pencils we can buy. Since d dollars equals

$100d$ cents, we divide $100d$ by $\dfrac{c}{p}$, which is equivalent to

multiplying $100d$ by $\dfrac{p}{c}$: $100d\left(\dfrac{p}{c}\right) = \dfrac{100dp}{c}$.

You will probably prefer the alternate solution below.
**Assume 2 pencils cost 10 cents. So, pencils cost 5 cents each or 20 for one dollar. So, for 3 dollars, we can buy 60 pencils. Which of the choices equals 60 when $p = 2$, $c = 10$, and $d = 3$? Only $\dfrac{100dp}{c}$.

27. **A.** If a student earned a grade of g, she missed $(100 - g)$ points. In adjusting the grades, the teacher decided to

deduct only half that number: $\frac{100-g}{2}$. So the student's new grade was

$$100 - \left(\frac{100-g}{2}\right) = 100 - 50 + \frac{g}{2} = 50 + \frac{g}{2}.$$

Since this was done to each student's grade, the effect on the average was exactly the same. The new average was $50 + \frac{A}{2}$.

28. **D.** The length of the rectangle is clearly 20, the length of two diameters. The width of the rectangle is 10 + h, where h is the height of the equilateral triangle formed by joining the centers of the three circles. Since the sides of that triangle are 10, the height is $5\sqrt{3}$. Then the width is 10 + $5\sqrt{3}$ and the area is 20(10 + $5\sqrt{3}$) = 200 + $100\sqrt{3}$.

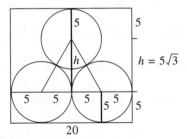

**Trust the diagram. Clearly, the length is 20, and the width is much more than 10, but less than 20. You should even see that the width must be more than 15, so the area is between 300 and 400.

Section 3—Analytical Ability

1. **C.** If the halibut population is endangered, the banning of gill-nets would improve the fish's chance for survival. If Choices A and B are true, the fisheries' argument about the price rise has more merit. If Choices D and E are true, the reduction of the sea otter population would be more defensible.

Solutions 2–5

$$P, R, R, G, G, Y, Y, B, B$$
$$R \ll R \quad 4 = G \quad B \ll B$$
$$1 = Y \quad 9 = Y \quad P \ll G \quad G \ll P$$

2. **A.** Since the red numbers are consecutive, the other red piece must be the 2 or the 4. However, it is given that the number 4 is green; so the other red piece must be the 2.

3. **B.** If the number 6 were purple, then the purple piece and one of the green pieces would be consecutive numbers, which violates one of the given conditions. It is easy to show that each of the other choices is possible.

4. **E.** The following list shows that Choice E does not violate any of the given conditions, and so could be true:

$$\underline{Y} \quad \underline{R} \quad \underline{R} \quad \underline{G} \quad \underline{B} \quad \underline{G} \quad \underline{B} \quad \underline{P} \quad \underline{Y}$$
$$1 \quad 2 \quad 3 \quad 4 \quad 5 \quad 6 \quad 7 \quad 8 \quad 9$$

Each of the other choices violates at least one of the conditions.

Choice A is impossible because if 2 is blue, then the red pieces must be 7 and 8, and then the purple piece would be consecutive with one of the green pieces:

$$\underline{Y} \quad \underline{B} \quad \_ \quad \underline{G} \quad \_ \quad \underline{G} \quad \underline{R} \quad \underline{R} \quad \underline{Y}$$
$$1 \quad 2 \quad 3 \quad 4 \quad 5 \quad 6 \quad 7 \quad 8 \quad 9$$

Choices B and D are impossible because a purple and green piece cannot be consecutive numbers.

Choice C violates the condition that the two red pieces must be consecutive numbers.

5. **E.** Only Choice E completely determines the colors of each number. If the 7 is green, then since the purple number cannot be consecutive with either green number, the purple number must be 2. Then the red pieces must be 5 and 6 (the only consecutive numbers available), and the blue pieces must be 3 and 8.

$$\underline{Y} \quad \underline{P} \quad \underline{B} \quad \underline{G} \quad \underline{R} \quad \underline{R} \quad \underline{G} \quad \underline{B} \quad \underline{Y}$$
$$1 \quad 2 \quad 3 \quad 4 \quad 5 \quad 6 \quad 7 \quad 8 \quad 9$$

None of the other choices completely determines the colors of each number.

6. **D.** The argument states that gun control laws reduce violent crime; the evidence is a drop in armed robberies in one city. This involves unwarranted generalizations (choices A and C), a failure to consider alternative explanations (Choice B), and a possible failure to consider contrary evidence (Choice E). Choice D, however, raises an objection to gun control laws unrelated to either the validity of the evidence or the validity of the conclusion in the argument.

7. **A.** Statement I weakens the argument by suggesting an alternative explanation for the drop in the crime rate. Statement II has nothing to do with the crime rate. Statement III does not, in itself, suggest that the gun control law is an ineffective *deterrent*.

8. **C.** Since Manhasset won, neither Aviva nor Zachary could have debated, since if either of them had debated, then Roslyn would have won. None of the other choices must be true, although some could be true.

Solutions 9–13

Films: B, C, D, E, F, G   Days: Th, Fri, Sat, Sun
Each day: 1 or 2 films   2 consecutive days: 2 or 3 films
B = Sat   C—x   F < G   E < D

9. **D.** Only Choice D does not violate any of the given conditions.
(A) violates the condition that the Belgian film will be shown on Saturday (B = Sat).
(B) violates the condition that the Canadian film cannot be the only film shown on a particular day (C—x).
(C) and (E) are impossible. Since the Danish film must be shown on a day after the English film is shown (E < D) and the German film must be shown on a day after the French film is shown (F < G), neither can be shown on Thursday, the first day of the festival.

10. **B.** The condition that the Belgian and French films are shown on the same day completely determines the schedule. They must be shown on Saturday (B = Sat). To avoid having more than three films being shown on two consecutive

days, there can be only one film shown on Friday and one on Sunday, which means there will be two on Thursday. Since (F < G), the German film will be shown on Sunday. Since (E < D), the English film will be shown on Thursday and the Danish film on Friday. Finally, the Canadian film will be the second film shown on Thursday.

C/E	D	B/F	G
Th.	Fri.	Sat.	Sun.

Only Choice B is consistent with this schedule.

11. **D.** Since only one film can be shown on Friday, it cannot be the Canadian one (C—x); and, of course, it cannot be the Belgian one (B = Sat.). Any of the other four films could be shown on Friday as indicated on the following schedules:

E/F	D	B	C/G
Th.	Fri.	Sat.	Sun.
C/F	E	B	D/G
Th.	Fri.	Sat.	Sun.
C/E	F	B	D/G
Th.	Fri.	Sat.	Sun.
E/F	G	B	C/D
Th.	Fri.	Sat.	Sun.

12. **E.** The condition that the English and German films are shown on the same day completely determines the schedule. They cannot be shown on Saturday (B = Sat); they cannot be shown on Sunday since the Danish film must be shown after the English film (E < D); and they cannot be shown on Thursday since the French film must precede the German film (F < G). So the English and German films must be shown on Friday. To avoid having more than three films being shown on two consecutive days, there can be only one film shown on Thursday and one on Saturday, which means there will be two on Sunday. The complete schedule is as follows:

F	E/G	B	C/D
Th.	Fri.	Sat.	Sun.

Only Choice E is consistent with this schedule.

13. **E.** Since the films from England and Belgium are both being shown on Saturday, eliminate choices A and C. Since the Canadian film may not be shown alone, eliminate Choice B. Finally, since the Danish film must be shown on Sunday (E < D), the French film must be shown on Thursday and the German film on Friday (F < G). Eliminate Choice D. The complete schedule is:

C/F	G	B/E	D
Th.	Fri.	Sat.	Sun.

14. **B.** I is denied by the statement that some forms of mercury cause Hobson's disease. II may be true, but it cannot be inferred from the given statement. III alludes to the fact that this island has no industrial wastes and yet has a high incidence of this disease.

Solutions 15–18

M, W, B, B, G, G, G: at least 3

M ∨ W   M ∨ B   not M, B, B

not W, G, G, G   W → G

15. **B.** The man must be chosen, because at least one adult must be chosen, and choosing the woman would violate the condition that the group cannot contain four females. Although one of the boys could also be chosen, it is not required.

16. **D.** Only Choice D does not violate any of the conditions. Since an adult must be chosen, eliminate choices A and B; since at least one male must be chosen, eliminate Choice C; since the group cannot include all three males, eliminate Choice E.

17. **E.** Choice E violates the condition that the group cannot include all three males. None of the other choices violates a given condition.

18. **E.** Only Choice E is impossible. The mayor could choose two males and three females, but the sixth member would either be a third male or a fourth female, each of which would violate one of the given conditions. Each of the other choices is possible.

19. **B.**   By urging moviegoers to patronize films *in order to* influence academy judges, the author reveals his assumption that the academy will be influenced by the number of people paying to see a movie.

Solutions 20–23

X and Y: no # in common

Each set: at most 4 #   hence, each set: at least 3 #

$1 \leftrightarrow 4$ $2 \in X \Rightarrow 7 \in X$ $6 \in Y \Rightarrow 5 \notin Y$

20. **E.**   Only Choice E does not violate any of the given conditions.

(A) violates the condition that each set has at least three members.

(B) violates the condition that 1 and 4 must be in the same set.

(C) violates the condition that 5 and 6 cannot both be members of set Y ($6 \in Y \Rightarrow 5 \notin Y$).

(D) violates the condition that if 2 is in X, then 7 is also in X ($2 \in X \Rightarrow 7 \in X$). Note that in E, 7 is in X, even though 2 is not in X; this does not violate the condition: $2 \in X \Rightarrow 7 \in X$.

21. **D.**   Only Choice D *cannot* be true. If 1, 3, and 7 were in X, then so would 4 ($1 \leftrightarrow 4$); then Y would contain 2, 5, and 6. This, however, violates the condition: $6 \in Y \Rightarrow 5 \notin Y$. Each of the other choices could be true.

22. **B.**   Since, $2 \in X \Rightarrow 7 \in X$, and since $7 \in Y$, 2 must also be in Y. Since 1 and 4 have to be in the same set ($1 \leftrightarrow 4$), and Y can't have five members, then 1 and 4 are in set X. Also, since $6 \in Y \Rightarrow 5 \notin Y$ and $5 \in Y$, then $6 \in X$. The only number whose position is not determined is 3, which could be in either set without violating any conditions. There are two possibilities:

$X = \{1, 3, 4, 6\}$ and $Y = \{2, 5, 7\}$
$X = \{1, 4, 6\}$ and $Y = \{2, 3, 5, 7\}$

23. **E.**   Since 1 is in Y, 4 must also be in Y ($1 \leftrightarrow 4$). If 7 were the third member of Y, then the four members of X would be 2, 3, 5, and 6. This, however, is impossible, because $2 \in X \Rightarrow 7$

∈ X. Therefore, 7 cannot be in Y, and so 7 must be in X. Each of the other choices could be the third member of Y, and hence do not have to be in X.

Solutions 24–28

Senators: W, X, Y, Z — 2
Representatives: P, Q, R, S — 2
$S \Rightarrow X$ $Y \Rightarrow \sim Q$ (and equivalently $Q \Rightarrow \sim Y$)
$Y \vee Z$ $\sim(Y \wedge Z)$

24. **A.** Only Choice A doesn't violate any of the given conditions.
Since Y will not serve with Q ($Y \Rightarrow \sim Q$), eliminate Choice B.
Since S will not serve unless X does ($S \Rightarrow X$), eliminate Choice C.
Since the fourth member of the committee must be a second representative, eliminate Choice D.
Since Y and Z cannot both serve [$\sim(Y \wedge Z)$], eliminate Choice E.

25. **D.** Since neither P nor R is on the committee, the two representatives on the committee are Q and S. Since S won't serve unless X does ($S \Rightarrow X$), X must also be on the committee. Also, Y cannot serve on the committee ($Y \Rightarrow \sim Q$). Finally, since either Y or Z must be chosen, Z is on the committee.

26. **D.** Only Choice D doesn't violate any of the given conditions.
Since Y is not willing to serve with Q or Z, eliminate choices A and C.
Since S will not serve on the committee unless X does, eliminate Choice B.
Finally, eliminate Choice E, since it includes three senators and only one representative.

27. **D.** Since S is on the committee, so is X ($S \Rightarrow X$). Then the other senator has to be Y or Z ($Y \vee Z$), so it *cannot* be W.

28. **B.** Since Q is on the committee, Y is not on the committee ($Y \Rightarrow \sim Q$). Then neither X nor Y is on the committee, so the two senators on the committee are W and Z. Also, S cannot

be on the committee since X isn't ($S \Rightarrow X$). The only people we don't know about are P and R, either of whom could serve. So there are two possibilities: P, Q, W, Z and Q, R, W, Z.

29. **B.**   The force of the argument presented in this advertisement lies in the attractiveness of the promise of "space-age circuitry" in the X-2700 stereo system. Choice B effectively points out the fundamental weakness of this appeal. All the other choices present features of the advertisement which might be regarded as flaws, but which are very minor in comparison to the flaw indicated in Choice B.

30. **C.**   At least one junior and at least one sophomore voted for the proposal, so if there are 18 seniors on the council, all of whom voted for the proposal, then there were at least 20 votes cast in favor of the proposal, and it was adopted. None of the other choices provides enough information to answer the question.

Solutions 31–34

$$\text{Mon — at least 2   Tues — at least 2}$$
$$I \neq \text{1st on Mon}$$
$$F = \text{1st or last on Mon or Tues}$$
$$(I = \text{Mon}) \Rightarrow (K = \text{Tues})$$
$$(I = \text{Tues}) \Rightarrow (K = \text{Mon})$$
$$H \ll L \text{ or } L \ll H$$
$$G < x < L \text{ or } L < x < G$$

31. **E.**   Only Choice E does not violate any of the given conditions. Choice A violates the condition that I and K cannot interview on the same day.
Choice B violates the condition that there be at least one interview scheduled between those of G and L.
Choice C violates the condition that there be no interview scheduled between those of H and L.
Choice D violates the condition that F have the first or last interview of the day.

32. **C.**   Only Choice C does not violate any of the conditions.
Choice A is incorrect, because if Monday's schedule is G,

H, L, then I and K both have interviews scheduled on Tuesday, which is not allowed.

Choice B violates the condition that there be an interview scheduled between those of G and L.

Choice D violates the condition that F be the first or last interview of the day.

Choice E violates the condition that H and L interview on the same day.

33. **D.** Since F, I, and J have interviews on Monday, G, H, K, and L have their interviews on Tuesday. Since it is given that H has the first interview and no interview can be scheduled between those of H and L, then L must have the second interview. It is also required that there be at least one interview between that of G and L, so K is third and G is last. The complete Tuesday schedule is H, L, K, G, and only Choice D is true.

34. **E.** Since F does not have either the first or last interview on Tuesday, F must have the first or last interview on Monday. So either Choice A or Choice B is true, but neither one *must* be true. On Tuesday, since H is first, L must be second; but G cannot immediately follow L, so G must have an interview on Monday: eliminate Choice C. Since I has an interview on Tuesday, K must have a Monday interview. This leaves J for the last applicant to be interviewed on Tuesday. The Tuesday schedule is H, L, J, I; Choice E is true.

35. **C.** The conclusion is the prediction of a grim year for home-builders. Choices A, B, D, and E do not point to continued bad sales, but Choice C, revealing that sales fell even with advertising and incentives, supports the prediction of a bad year ahead.

Answer Sheet—Test 3

Section 1

1. Ⓐ Ⓑ Ⓒ Ⓓ Ⓔ	11. Ⓐ Ⓑ Ⓒ Ⓓ Ⓔ	21. Ⓐ Ⓑ Ⓒ Ⓓ Ⓔ
2. Ⓐ Ⓑ Ⓒ Ⓓ Ⓔ	12. Ⓐ Ⓑ Ⓒ Ⓓ Ⓔ	22. Ⓐ Ⓑ Ⓒ Ⓓ Ⓔ
3. Ⓐ Ⓑ Ⓒ Ⓓ Ⓔ	13. Ⓐ Ⓑ Ⓒ Ⓓ Ⓔ	23. Ⓐ Ⓑ Ⓒ Ⓓ Ⓔ
4. Ⓐ Ⓑ Ⓒ Ⓓ Ⓔ	14. Ⓐ Ⓑ Ⓒ Ⓓ Ⓔ	24. Ⓐ Ⓑ Ⓒ Ⓓ Ⓔ
5. Ⓐ Ⓑ Ⓒ Ⓓ Ⓔ	15. Ⓐ Ⓑ Ⓒ Ⓓ Ⓔ	25. Ⓐ Ⓑ Ⓒ Ⓓ Ⓔ
6. Ⓐ Ⓑ Ⓒ Ⓓ Ⓔ	16. Ⓐ Ⓑ Ⓒ Ⓓ Ⓔ	26. Ⓐ Ⓑ Ⓒ Ⓓ Ⓔ
7. Ⓐ Ⓑ Ⓒ Ⓓ Ⓔ	17. Ⓐ Ⓑ Ⓒ Ⓓ Ⓔ	27. Ⓐ Ⓑ Ⓒ Ⓓ Ⓔ
8. Ⓐ Ⓑ Ⓒ Ⓓ Ⓔ	18. Ⓐ Ⓑ Ⓒ Ⓓ Ⓔ	28. Ⓐ Ⓑ Ⓒ Ⓓ Ⓔ
9. Ⓐ Ⓑ Ⓒ Ⓓ Ⓔ	19. Ⓐ Ⓑ Ⓒ Ⓓ Ⓔ	29. Ⓐ Ⓑ Ⓒ Ⓓ Ⓔ
10. Ⓐ Ⓑ Ⓒ Ⓓ Ⓔ	20. Ⓐ Ⓑ Ⓒ Ⓓ Ⓔ	30. Ⓐ Ⓑ Ⓒ Ⓓ Ⓔ

Section 2

1. Ⓐ Ⓑ Ⓒ Ⓓ Ⓔ	11. Ⓐ Ⓑ Ⓒ Ⓓ Ⓔ	21. Ⓐ Ⓑ Ⓒ Ⓓ Ⓔ
2. Ⓐ Ⓑ Ⓒ Ⓓ Ⓔ	12. Ⓐ Ⓑ Ⓒ Ⓓ Ⓔ	22. Ⓐ Ⓑ Ⓒ Ⓓ Ⓔ
3. Ⓐ Ⓑ Ⓒ Ⓓ Ⓔ	13. Ⓐ Ⓑ Ⓒ Ⓓ Ⓔ	23. Ⓐ Ⓑ Ⓒ Ⓓ Ⓔ
4. Ⓐ Ⓑ Ⓒ Ⓓ Ⓔ	14. Ⓐ Ⓑ Ⓒ Ⓓ Ⓔ	24. Ⓐ Ⓑ Ⓒ Ⓓ Ⓔ
5. Ⓐ Ⓑ Ⓒ Ⓓ Ⓔ	15. Ⓐ Ⓑ Ⓒ Ⓓ Ⓔ	25. Ⓐ Ⓑ Ⓒ Ⓓ Ⓔ
6. Ⓐ Ⓑ Ⓒ Ⓓ Ⓔ	16. Ⓐ Ⓑ Ⓒ Ⓓ Ⓔ	26. Ⓐ Ⓑ Ⓒ Ⓓ Ⓔ
7. Ⓐ Ⓑ Ⓒ Ⓓ Ⓔ	17. Ⓐ Ⓑ Ⓒ Ⓓ Ⓔ	27. Ⓐ Ⓑ Ⓒ Ⓓ Ⓔ
8. Ⓐ Ⓑ Ⓒ Ⓓ Ⓔ	18. Ⓐ Ⓑ Ⓒ Ⓓ Ⓔ	28. Ⓐ Ⓑ Ⓒ Ⓓ Ⓔ
9. Ⓐ Ⓑ Ⓒ Ⓓ Ⓔ	19. Ⓐ Ⓑ Ⓒ Ⓓ Ⓔ	
10. Ⓐ Ⓑ Ⓒ Ⓓ Ⓔ	20. Ⓐ Ⓑ Ⓒ Ⓓ Ⓔ	

Section 3

1. Ⓐ Ⓑ Ⓒ Ⓓ Ⓔ	13. Ⓐ Ⓑ Ⓒ Ⓓ Ⓔ	25. Ⓐ Ⓑ Ⓒ Ⓓ Ⓔ
2. Ⓐ Ⓑ Ⓒ Ⓓ Ⓔ	14. Ⓐ Ⓑ Ⓒ Ⓓ Ⓔ	26. Ⓐ Ⓑ Ⓒ Ⓓ Ⓔ
3. Ⓐ Ⓑ Ⓒ Ⓓ Ⓔ	15. Ⓐ Ⓑ Ⓒ Ⓓ Ⓔ	27. Ⓐ Ⓑ Ⓒ Ⓓ Ⓔ
4. Ⓐ Ⓑ Ⓒ Ⓓ Ⓔ	16. Ⓐ Ⓑ Ⓒ Ⓓ Ⓔ	28. Ⓐ Ⓑ Ⓒ Ⓓ Ⓔ
5. Ⓐ Ⓑ Ⓒ Ⓓ Ⓔ	17. Ⓐ Ⓑ Ⓒ Ⓓ Ⓔ	29. Ⓐ Ⓑ Ⓒ Ⓓ Ⓔ
6. Ⓐ Ⓑ Ⓒ Ⓓ Ⓔ	18. Ⓐ Ⓑ Ⓒ Ⓓ Ⓔ	30. Ⓐ Ⓑ Ⓒ Ⓓ Ⓔ
7. Ⓐ Ⓑ Ⓒ Ⓓ Ⓔ	19. Ⓐ Ⓑ Ⓒ Ⓓ Ⓔ	31. Ⓐ Ⓑ Ⓒ Ⓓ Ⓔ
8. Ⓐ Ⓑ Ⓒ Ⓓ Ⓔ	20. Ⓐ Ⓑ Ⓒ Ⓓ Ⓔ	32. Ⓐ Ⓑ Ⓒ Ⓓ Ⓔ
9. Ⓐ Ⓑ Ⓒ Ⓓ Ⓔ	21. Ⓐ Ⓑ Ⓒ Ⓓ Ⓔ	33. Ⓐ Ⓑ Ⓒ Ⓓ Ⓔ
10. Ⓐ Ⓑ Ⓒ Ⓓ Ⓔ	22. Ⓐ Ⓑ Ⓒ Ⓓ Ⓔ	34. Ⓐ Ⓑ Ⓒ Ⓓ Ⓔ
11. Ⓐ Ⓑ Ⓒ Ⓓ Ⓔ	23. Ⓐ Ⓑ Ⓒ Ⓓ Ⓔ	35. Ⓐ Ⓑ Ⓒ Ⓓ Ⓔ
12. Ⓐ Ⓑ Ⓒ Ⓓ Ⓔ	24. Ⓐ Ⓑ Ⓒ Ⓓ Ⓔ	

Model Test 3
Section 1—Verbal Ability

30 Questions—30 Minutes

<u>Antonym Directions</u>: In each of the following antonym questions, a word printed in capital letters precedes five lettered words or phrases. From these five lettered words or phrases, pick the one most nearly *opposite* in meaning to the capitalized word.

1. ELATED:
   - (A) crestfallen
   - (B) inebriated
   - (C) punctual
   - (D) insulted
   - (E) lamented

2. RETICENCE:
   - (A) irascibility
   - (B) loquaciousness
   - (C) quiescence
   - (D) patience
   - (E) surrender

<u>Sentence Completion Directions</u>: Each of the following sentence completion questions contains one or two blanks. These blanks signify that a word or set of words has been left out. Below each sentence are five words or sets of words. For each blank, pick the word or set of words that *best* reflects the sentence's overall meaning.

3. You may wonder how the expert on fossil remains is able to trace descent through teeth, which seem ---- pegs upon which to hang whole ancestries.
   - (A) novel
   - (B) reliable
   - (C) specious
   - (D) inadequate
   - (E) academic

4. An essential purpose of the criminal justice system is to enable purgation to take place; that is, to provide a ---- by which a community expresses its collective ---- the transgression of the criminal.

    (A) catharsis...outrage at
    (B) disclaimer...forgiveness of
    (C) means...empathy with
    (D) procedure...distaste for
    (E) document...disapprobation of

Analogy Directions: Each of the following analogy questions presents a related pair of words linked by a colon. Five lettered pairs of words follow the linked pair. Choose the lettered pair of words whose relationship is *most like* the relationship expressed in the original linked pair.

5. VINDICTIVE : MERCY ::

    (A) avaricious : greed
    (B) insightful : hope
    (C) modest : dignity
    (D) skeptical : trustfulness
    (E) pathetic : sympathy

6. RUFFLE : COMPOSURE ::

    (A) flounce : turmoil
    (B) flourish : prosperity
    (C) provoke : discussion
    (D) adjust : balance
    (E) upset : equilibrium

Reading Comprehension Directions: Each of the following reading comprehension questions is based on the content of the following passage. Read the passage and then determine the best answer choice for each question. Base your choice on what this passage *states directly* or *implies,* not on any information you may have gained elsewhere.

Given the persistent and intransigent nature of the American race system, which proved quite impervious to black attacks, Du Bois in his speeches and writings moved from one pro-

Line posed solution to another, and the salience of various parts of

(5)   his philosophy changed as his perceptions of the needs and strategies of black America shifted over time. Aloof and

autonomous in his personality, Du Bois did not hesitate to depart markedly from whatever was the current mainstream of black thinking when he perceived that the conventional wis-
(10) dom being enunciated by black spokesmen was proving inadequate to the task of advancing the race. His willingness to seek different solutions often placed him well in advance of his contemporaries, and this, combined with a strong-willed, even arrogant personality made his career as a black leader essen-
(15) tially a series of stormy conflicts.

Thus Du Bois first achieved his role as a major black leader in the controversy that arose over the program of Booker T. Washington, the most prominent and influential black leader at the opening of the twentieth century. Amidst the wave of
(20) lynchings, disfranchisement, and segregation laws, Washington, seeking the good will of powerful whites, taught blacks not to protest against discrimination, but to elevate themselves through industrial education, hard work, and property accumulation; then, they would ultimately obtain recogni-
(25) tion of their citizenship rights. At first Du Bois agreed with this gradualist strategy, but in 1903 with the publication of his most influential book, *Souls of Black Folk,* he became the chief leader of the onslaught against Washington that polarized the black community into two wings—the "conservative" support-
(30) ers of Washington and his "radical" critics.

7. Which of the following statements about W.E.B. Du Bois does the passage best support?
   (A) He sacrificed the proven strategies of earlier black leaders to his craving for political novelty.
   (B) Preferring conflict to harmony, he followed a disruptive course that alienated him from the bulk of his followers.
   (C) He proved unable to change with the times in mounting fresh attacks against white racism.
   (D) He relied on the fundamental benevolence of the white population for the eventual success of his movement.
   (E) Once an adherent of Washington's policies, he ultimately lost patience with them for their inefficacy.

8. It can be inferred that Booker T. Washington in comparison with W.E.B. Du Bois could be described as all of the following EXCEPT
   - (A) submissive to the majority
   - (B) concerned with financial success
   - (C) versatile in adopting strategies
   - (D) traditional in preaching industry
   - (E) respectful of authority

9. The author's attitude toward Du Bois' departure from conventional black policies can best be described as
   - (A) skeptical
   - (B) derisive
   - (C) shocked
   - (D) approving
   - (E) resigned

Antonyms

10. REVILE:
    - (A) compose
    - (B) awake
    - (C) deaden
    - (D) praise
    - (E) secrete

11. PROPITIOUS:
    - (A) adjacent
    - (B) clandestine
    - (C) contentious
    - (D) unfavorable
    - (E) coy

Analogies

12. OFFHAND : PREMEDITATION ::
    - (A) upright : integrity
    - (B) aboveboard : guile
    - (C) cutthroat : competition
    - (D) backward : direction
    - (E) underlying : foundation

13. LARVAL : INSECT ::
    - (A) serpentine : snake
    - (B) floral : plant
    - (C) amphibian : reptile
    - (D) embryonic : mammal
    - (E) alate : bird

Sentence Completion

14. When facts are ---- and data hard to come by, even scientists occasionally throw aside the professional pretense of ---- and tear into each other with shameless appeals to authority and arguments that are unabashedly ad hominem.

(A) elusive...objectivity

(B) established...courtesy

(C) demonstrable...neutrality

(D) ineluctable...cooperation

(E) hypothetical...scholarship

15. In the tradition of scholarly ----, the poet and scholar A.E. Housman once assailed a German rival for relying on manuscripts "as a drunkard relies on lampposts, for ---- rather than illumination."

(A) animosity...current

(B) discourse...stability

(C) erudition...shadow

(D) invective...support

(E) competition...assistance

Reading Comprehension

At night, schools of prey and predators are almost always spectacularly illuminated by the bioluminescence produced by the microscopic and larger plankton. The reason for the ubiquitous
Line production of light by the microorganisms of the sea remains
(5) obscure, and suggested explanations are controversial. It has been suggested that light is a kind of inadvertent by-product of life in transparent organisms. It has also been hypothesized that the emission of light on disturbance is advantageous to the plankton in making the predators of the plankton conspicuous
(10) to their predators! Unquestionably, it does act this way. Indeed, some fisheries base the detection of their prey on the bioluminescence that the fish excite. It is difficult, however, to defend the thesis that this effect was the direct factor in the original development of bioluminescence, since the effect was of no
(15) advantage to the individual microorganism that first developed

it. Perhaps the luminescence of a microorganism also discourages attack by light-avoiding predators and is of initial survival benefit to the individual. As it then becomes general in the population, the effect of revealing plankton predators to their preda-
(20) tors would also become important.

16. The primary topic of the passage is which of the following?
  (A) The origin of bioluminescence in plankton predators
  (B) The disadvantages of bioluminescence in microorganisms
  (C) The varieties of marine bioluminescent life forms
  (D) Symbiotic relationships between predators and their prey
  (E) Hypotheses on the causes of bioluminescence in plankton

17. The author mentions the activities of fisheries in order to provide an example of
  (A) how ubiquitous the phenomenon of bioluminescence is coastally
  (B) how predators make use of bioluminescence in locating their prey
  (C) how human intervention imperils bioluminescent microorganisms
  (D) how nocturnal fishing expeditions are becoming more and more widespread
  (E) how limited bioluminescence is as a source of light for human use

18. The passage provides an answer to which of the following questions?
  (A) What is the explanation for the phenomenon of bioluminescence in marine life?
  (B) Does the phenomenon of plankton bioluminescence have any practical applications?
  (C) Why do only certain specimens of marine life exhibit the phenomenon of bioluminescence?
  (D) How does underwater bioluminescence differ from atmospheric bioluminescence?
  (E) What are the steps that take place as an individual microorganism becomes bioluminescent?

Antonyms

19. INCONGRUOUS:
    (A) geometric
    (B) prudent
    (C) legitimate
    (D) harmonious
    (E) efficacious

20. APOSTATE:
    (A) laggard
    (B) loyalist
    (C) martinet
    (D) predecessor
    (E) skeptic

Analogies

21. SEXTANT : NAUTICAL ::
    (A) octet : musical
    (B) therapy : physical
    (C) forceps : surgical
    (D) comet : astronomical
    (E) blueprint : mechanical

22. REFRACTORY : MANAGE ::
    (A) redoubtable : impress
    (B) lethargic : stimulate
    (C) pedantic : convince
    (D) officious : arrange
    (E) aggrieved : distress

Antonyms

23. ENSUE:
    (A) litigate
    (B) precede
    (C) arbitrate
    (D) accentuate
    (E) delay

Sentence Completion

24. While the disease is in ---- state it is almost impossible to deter-
    mine its existence by ----.
    (A) a dormant...postulate
    (B) a critical...examination
    (C) an acute...analysis
    (D) a suspended...estimate
    (E) a latent...observation

25.   Virginia Woolf ---- conventional notions of truth: in her words, one cannot receive from any lecture "a nugget of pure truth" to wrap up between the pages of one's notebook and keep on the mantelpiece forever.

(A) anticipates   (D) mocks

(B) articulates   (E) rationalizes

(C) neglects

Reading Comprehension

The curtain rises; the Cardinal and Daniel de Bosola enter from the right. In appearance, the Cardinal is something between an El Greco cardinal and a Van Dyke noble lord. He has the tall,
Line spare form—the elongated hands and features—of the for-
(5) mer; the trim pointed beard, the imperial repose, the commanding authority of the latter. But the El Greco features are not really those of asceticism or inner mystic spirituality. They are the index to a cold, refined but ruthless cruelty in a highly civilized controlled form. Neither is the imperial repose an
(10) aloof mood of proud detachment. It is a refined expression of satanic pride of place and talent.

To a degree, the Cardinal's coldness is artificially cultivated. He has defined himself against his younger brother Duke Ferdinand and is the opposite to the overwrought emotionality of
(15) the latter. But the Cardinal's aloof mood is not one of bland detachment. It is the deliberate detachment of a methodical man who collects his thoughts and emotions into the most compact and formidable shape—that when he strikes, he may strike with the more efficient and devastating force. His easy movements are
(20) those of the slowly circling eagle just before the swift descent with the exposed talons. Above all else, he is a man who never for a moment doubts his destined authority as a governor. He derisively and sharply rebukes his brother the Duke as easily and readily as he mocks his mistress Julia. If he has betrayed his
(25) hireling Bosola, he uses his brother as the tool to win back his "familiar." His court dress is a long brilliant scarlet cardinal's gown with white cuffs and a white collar turned back over the red, both collar and cuffs being elaborately scalloped and embroidered. He wears a small cape, reaching only to the elbows. His

(30) cassock is buttoned to the ground, giving a heightened effect to his already tall presence. Richelieu would have adored his neatly trimmed beard. A richly jeweled and ornamented cross lies on his breast, suspended from his neck by a gold chain.

26. In lines 19–20 the author most likely compares the movements of the Cardinal to those of a circling eagle in order to emphasize his
   (A) flightiness
   (B) love of freedom
   (C) eminence
   (D) sense of spirituality
   (E) mercilessness

27. Which of the following best characterizes the author's attitude toward the Cardinal?
   (A) He deprecates his inability to sustain warm familial relationships.
   (B) He esteems him for his spiritual and emotional control.
   (C) He admires his grace in movement and sure sense of personal authority.
   (D) He finds him formidable both as an opponent and as a dramatic character.
   (E) He is perturbed by his inconsistencies in behavior.

Analogies

28. AUSTERE : STYLE ::
   (A) controlled : movement
   (B) affluent : wealth
   (C) subservient : demeanor
   (D) inspirational : faith
   (E) pragmatic : speech

Antonyms

29. RETROSPECTION:
   (A) introversion
   (B) deliberation
   (C) anticipation
   (D) gregariousness
   (E) equivocation

30. TOPICAL:
   (A) general
   (B) disinterested
   (C) chronological
   (D) fallacious
   (E) imperceptible

Section 2—Quantitative Ability

28 Questions—45 Minutes

<u>Quantitative Comparison Directions</u>: In the following type of question, two quantities appear, one in Column A and one in Column B. You must compare them. The correct answer to the question is

A if the quantity in Column A is greater
B if the quantity in Column B is greater
C if the two quantities are equal
D if it is impossible to determine which quantity is greater

<u>Notes</u>: Sometimes information about one or both of the quantities is centered above the two columns. If the same symbol appears in both columns, it represents the same thing each time.

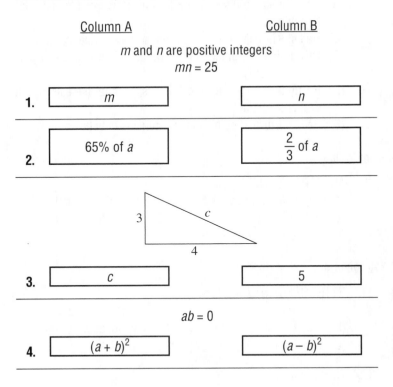

<u>Column A</u>   <u>Column B</u>

m and *n* are positive integers
$mn = 25$

1. m n

2. 65% of a $\frac{2}{3}$ of a

3. c 5

$ab = 0$

4. $(a + b)^2$ $(a - b)^2$

<u>Discrete Quantitative and Data Interpretation Directions</u>: In the following questions, choose the best answer from the five choices listed.

5. The Center City Little League is divided into d divisions. Each division has t teams, and each team has p players. How many players are there in the entire league?

(A) $d + t + p$

(B) dtp

(C) $\dfrac{pt}{d}$

(D) $\dfrac{dt}{p}$

(E) $\dfrac{d}{pt}$

6. A number x is chosen at random from the set of positive integers less than 10. What is the probability that $\dfrac{9}{x} > x$?

(A) $\dfrac{1}{5}$

(B) $\dfrac{2}{9}$

(C) $\dfrac{1}{3}$

(D) $\dfrac{2}{3}$

(E) $\dfrac{7}{9}$

7. If $\dfrac{1}{a} + \dfrac{1}{a} + \dfrac{1}{a} = 12$, then $a =$

(A) $\dfrac{1}{12}$

(B) $\dfrac{1}{4}$

(C) $\dfrac{1}{3}$

(D) 3

(E) 4

Quantitative Comparison

Column A	Column B
8. y	20

Column A   Column B

$$a + b = 24$$
$$a - b = 25$$

9. | b | | 0 |

Data Interpretation

10. In 1980, the cost of p pounds of potatoes was d dollars. In 1990, the cost of $2p$ pounds of potatoes was $\frac{1}{2}d$ dollars. By what percent did the price of potatoes decrease from 1980 to 1990?
(A) 25%   (D) 100%
(B) 50%   (E) 400%
(C) 75%

Quantitative Comparison

Column A   Column B

$$a + 2b = 6d$$
$$c - b = 5d$$

11. | The average (arithmetic mean) of a, b, c, and d | | $3d$ |

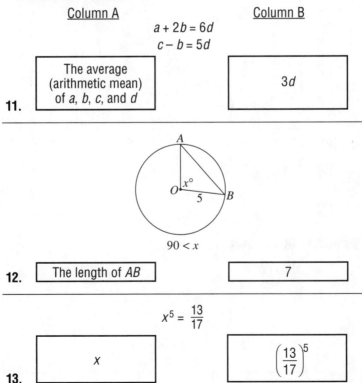

$$90 < x$$

12. | The length of AB | | 7 |

$$x^5 = \frac{13}{17}$$

13. | x | | $\left(\frac{13}{17}\right)^5$ |

Data Interpretation

Questions 14–15 refer to the following graphs.

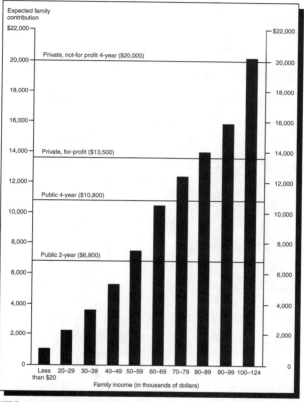

Average expected family contribution (EFC) for dependent students, by family income: Academic year 1995–96

NOTE: The horizontal lines on the figure represent the average student budgets for full-time, full-year students at the indicated type of institution.

SOURCE: U.S. Department of Education.

14. A family's *unmet need* (which must be covered by a financial aid package) is defined to be the total cost of attending an institution of higher education minus the expected family contribution. What is the unmet need of a family whose income is $55,000 and who has a child attending a 4-year public university?

(A) $700
(B) $3300
(C) $6800
(D) $7500
(E) $12,500

15. If family A has an income of $95,000 per year, and family B has an income of $35,000 per year, and each has a child attending a 4-year public university, to the nearest $1000, how much more would family A be expected to pay than family B?

(A) $4000

(B) $7000

(C) $10,000

(D) $12,000

(E) $15,000

Quantitative Comparison

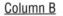

Column A	Column B

a and b are positive integers with a < b.

16.

The remainder when a is divided by b	The remainder when b is divided by a

Figure 1 Figure 2

ABCD and EFGH are squares, and all the circles are tangent to one another and to the sides of the squares.

17.

The area of the shaded region in Figure 1	The area of the shaded region in Figure 2

Discrete Quantitative

18. A bag contains 3 red, 4 white, and 5 blue marbles. Jason begins removing marbles from the bag at random, one at a time. What is the least number of marbles he must remove to be sure that he has at least one of each color?

(A) 3   (D) 10

(B) 6   (E) 12

(C) 8

19. Jordan has taken 5 math tests so far this semester. If he gets a 70 on his next test, it will lower the average (arithmetic mean) of his test scores by 4 points. What is his average now?

(A) 74   (D) 90

(B) 85   (E) 94

(C) 86

Data Interpretation

Questions 20–21 refer to the following graphs.

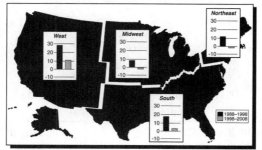

20. To the nearest million, how many more students were enrolled in school—both public and private, preK–12—in 1970 than in 1988?

(A) 3,000,000   (D) 44,000,000

(B) 6,000,000   (E) 51,000,000

(C) 10,000,000

21. In 1988 there were 40,000,000 public school students in the United States, of whom 22% lived in the West. Approximately, how many public school students are projected to be living in the West in 2008?

(A) 9,000,000   (D) 24,000,000

(B) 12,000,000   (E) 66,000,000

(C) 15,000,000

Discrete Quantitative

22. If a and b are the lengths of the legs of a right triangle whose hypotenuse is 10 and whose area is 20, what is the value of $(a + b)^2$?

(A) 100   (D) 180

(B) 120   (E) 200

(C) 140

Quantitative Comparison

<u>Column A</u>   <u>Column B</u>

The circumference of a circle is $a\pi$ inches.

The area of the same circle is $b\pi$ square inches.

23. | a | b |

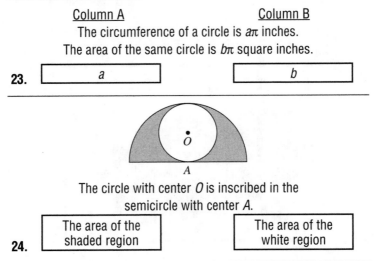

The circle with center O is inscribed in the semicircle with center A.

24. | The area of the shaded region | The area of the white region |

Column A   Column B

A school group charters three identical buses and

occupies $\frac{4}{5}$ of the seats. After $\frac{1}{4}$ of the passengers leave,

the remaining passengers use only two of the buses.

25.

| The fraction of the seats on the two buses that are now occupied | $\dfrac{9}{10}$ |

Discrete Quantitative

26. What is the average (arithmetic mean) of 3^{30}, 3^{60}, and 3^{90}?

(A) 3^{60} (D) $3^{27} + 3^{57} + 3^{87}$

(B) 3^{177} (E) $3^{29} + 3^{59} + 3^{89}$

(C) $3^{10} + 3^{20} + 3^{30}$

27. The figure at the right consists of four semicircles in a large semi-circle. If the small semicircles have radii of 1, 2, 3, and 4, what is the perimeter of the shaded region?

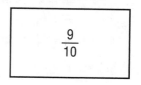

(A) 10π (D) 60π

(B) 20π (E) 100π

(C) 40π

28. If the sum of all the positive even integers less than 1000 is A, what is the sum of all the positive odd integers less than 1000?

(A) $A - 998$ (D) $A + 500$

(B) $A - 499$ (E) $\dfrac{A}{2} + 999$

(C) $A + 1$

Section 3—Analytical Ability

35 Questions—60 Minutes

Directions: In this section, each set of questions is based on a short passage or a set of conditions. Sometimes, in answering these questions, you might want to make a table or diagram. For each question, choose the best answer from the five choices listed.

Logical Reasoning

1. The Census Bureau's family portrait of America may remind us of the problems we face as a nation, but it also gives us reason to take heart in our ability to solve them in an enlightened way. The 1980 census was the first in history to show that the majority of the population in every state has completed high school. And the percentage of our people with at least 4 years of college rose from 11 percent in 1970 to 16.3 percent in 1980. That's progress—where it really counts.

   Which one of the following assumptions underlies the author's conclusion in the above passage?
   (A) Greater numbers of high school and college degrees coincide with other firsts in the 1980 census.
   (B) Greater numbers of high school and college degrees coincide with greater numbers of well-educated people.
   (C) Greater numbers of high school and college degrees coincide with a great commitment to social progress.
   (D) Greater numbers of high school and college degrees coincide with a better chance to avoid national catastrophe.
   (E) Greater numbers of high school and college degrees coincide with the 1980 census.

Analytical Reasoning

Questions 2–5
Seven students—F, G, H, I, J, K, and L—are being considered for a university fellowship. In evaluating these students, the dean has received from the registrar's office their official transcripts, including their cumulative grade point averages (GPAs). In analyzing this information, the dean made the following observations:

None of the students has exactly the same GPA as any other student.

K's GPA is higher than L's, but lower than H's.

I has a higher GPA than J.

Both F and G have higher GPAs than H.

2. Each of the following could be true EXCEPT
    (A) F has the highest GPA.
    (B) G has the highest GPA.
    (C) I has the highest GPA.
    (D) More than three students have higher GPAs than K.
    (E) More than three students have lower GPAs than K.

3. Which of the following, if true, would be sufficient to determine who has the lowest GPA?
    (A) I has the highest GPA.
    (B) I has a lower GPA than K.
    (C) K has a higher GPA than J.
    (D) J has a higher GPA than K.
    (E) Exactly five students have lower GPAs than F.

4. If J has a higher GPA than F, how many different rankings, by GPA, of the students are possible?
    (A) 1   (D) 6
    (B) 2   (E) 8
    (C) 4

5. If H has a higher GPA than I, which of the following CANNOT be true?
    (A) I's GPA is equal to the average of F's and G's.
    (B) I's GPA is equal to the average of K's and L's.
    (C) J's GPA is equal to the average of K's and L's.
    (D) J has the second lowest GPA.
    (E) J has the lowest GPA.

Logical Reasoning

Questions 6–7

By passing more and more regulations allegedly to protect the environment, the state is driving the manufacturing industry away. And when the employers leave, the workers will follow. The number of new no-growth or environmental rules passed each year is increasing by leaps and bounds. Rich environmentalists who think they are sympathetic to workers have no real sympathy for the blue-collar employees who are injured by their activities. One major manufacturer has been fined for failing to establish a car-pool plan. Another is accused of polluting the air with industrial emissions, although everyone knows that two thirds of the pollutants come from cars and trucks. No wonder the large manufacturers are moving to states with fewer restrictive laws. And as the manufacturers go, unemployment and the number of workers leaving the state will rise more rapidly than ever before.

6. The author's argument that strict environmental laws will eventually lead to loss of workers in the state will be most weakened if it can be shown that
   (A) so far, the number of manufacturers who have left the state is small
   (B) the unemployment rate has climbed steadily in the last three years
   (C) most workers who leave the state give as their reason for leaving the poor environmental quality
   (D) several other manufacturing states have strict environmental laws
   (E) rich environmentalists are more powerful in many other states

7. Which one of the following is NOT an argument of this passage?
   (A) Environmentalists are responsible for depriving workers of their jobs.
   (B) When workers leave a state, it is a sign that manufacturers will follow.
   (C) A car-pool law should not be enforced, as cars and trucks are responsible for most air pollution.
   (D) Large manufacturers prefer states with fewer restrictions.
   (E) A rise in unemployment will lead to an increase in workers leaving the state.

8. Grades on the midterm test in Mr. Walsh's chemistry class ranged from 68 to 97. Any student who received a grade below 75 or did not hand in all of the required lab reports must complete an extra-credit project.

   If the above statements are true, which of the following statements must also be true?
   (A) A student who earned an 83 on the midterm and who handed in all her labs, may not do the extra-credit project.
   (B) Most of the students in the class will not have to do the extra-credit project.
   (C) Any student may, but is not required to, do the extra-credit project.
   (D) If John's grade on the midterm was higher than the class average, and he handed in all of his labs, then he will not be required to do the extra-credit project.
   (E) If John did all of his labs and earned a 72 on the midterm, he will have to do the extra-credit project.

Analytical Reasoning

Questions 9–13

The personnel director of a large computer company is scheduling interviews for six candidates for the position of Director of Marketing. The applicants—F, G, H, I, J, and K—will all be interviewed on the same day. The interviews will be scheduled at 9:00, 10:00, 11:00, 1:00, 2:00, and 3:00, with a lunch break for the interviewers at noon. In scheduling the interviews, the personnel director must adhere to the following conditions:

J must have the first interview after the lunch break.

No one can be interviewed between G and I.

H must be interviewed earlier in the day than F.

9. Which of the following candidates for the position CANNOT be scheduled for the 3:00 interview?

(A) F

(B) G

(C) H

(D) I

(E) J

10. Which of the following would be an acceptable order for the interviews?

(A) G, I, H, F, J, K

(B) G, H, F, J, K, I

(C) F, G, I, J, K, H

(D) H, I, F, J, K, G

(E) H, K, F, J, I, G

11. If H and K are both interviewed before lunch, each of the following could be true EXCEPT

(A) H has the first interview of the day.

(B) K has the first interview of the day.

(C) F has the last interview of the day.

(D) G has the last interview of the day.

(E) I has the last interview of the day.

12. If F's interview is scheduled for 2:00, which of the following must be true?

(A) H has the first interview of the day.

(B) G has the first interview of the day.

(C) I has the first interview of the day.

(D) H has the third interview of the day.

(E) K has the last interview of the day.

13. If I has the first interview of the day, which of the following must be true?

(A) J's interview is earlier in the day than F's interview.

(B) J's interview is earlier in the day than H's interview.

(C) H has an interview in the morning.

(D) K has an interview in the morning.

(E) F has the last interview of the day.

Logical Reasoning

14. Since it is possible that substances contained in certain tree roots may provide a cure for cancer, the government must provide sufficient funds to allow thorough testing of this possibility.

The argument above assumes that

(A) substances contained in certain tree roots will probably cure cancer

(B) the line of research mentioned offers at present the most promising possibility for finding a cure for cancer

(C) the possibility of finding a cure is sufficient reason for funding research into possible cancer cures

(D) a cure for cancer would be extremely valuable to society

(E) the government is the only possible source of funds for the research described

Analytical Reasoning

Questions 15–18

A committee of four Republicans—Ash, Berg, Cox, and Day—and three Democrats—Ray, Sack, and Tyler—is conducting a hearing that will take place over five days, Monday through Friday. Because several committee members have other commitments and cannot attend each session, they agreed to the following guidelines:

Each day there will be the same number of Republicans and Democrats in attendance.

The three Democrats cannot all attend on the same day.

No committee member can attend on two consecutive days.

Ash and Ray will both attend at the final session on Friday.

Ray and Sack will never attend on the same day.

Neither Berg nor Tyler will attend a session unless the other does.

15. If Ash and Ray are not the only committee members in attendance on Friday, who else must be present?

(A) Berg and Tyler

(B) Berg and Sack

(C) Cox and Tyler

(D) Cox and Day

(E) Day and Tyler

16. If Ash and Ray are not the only committee members in attendance on Friday, who must be in attendance on Thursday?
    (A) Berg
    (B) Cox
    (C) Day
    (D) Sack
    (E) Tyler

17. If exactly six people in total attended the sessions on Wednesday, Thursday, and Friday, and none of them attended more than one session, for which of the following could the session on Tuesday be the only one he attended all week?
    (A) Tyler
    (B) Sack
    (C) Ray
    (D) Cox
    (E) Berg

18. If Ash and Berg attended Tuesday's session, who among the following could not have attended Monday's session?
    (A) Cox
    (B) Day
    (C) Ray
    (D) Sack
    (E) Tyler

Logical Reasoning

19. The Superintendent of Education complains that the share of the total state budget for education has decreased in each of the last four years; he blames the fall-off on the steady rise in the cost of law enforcement. Organizations opposing increased spending on education point out that the amount of money the state has spent on education has increased by at least three million dollars in each of the last four years.

    Which one of the following, if true, best resolves the apparent contradiction in the passage above?
    (A) The total state budget has increased more rapidly than the expenditure for education.
    (B) Both the pro- and con-educational-spending spokesmen have failed to take inflation into account.
    (C) Law-enforcement costs have not risen as rapidly as the superintendent claims.
    (D) Some educational expenses are not included in the state budget, but are paid by local taxes.
    (E) School construction is paid for by funds from bonds, not by funds from the state budget.

Analytical Reasoning

At Carlo's Continental Cafe, five wines—Beaujolais, Chablis, Merlot, Pinot Grigio, and Syrah—are served by the glass on weekdays (Monday through Friday), although not each wine is available every day. In selecting the wines that will be served on a given day, Carlo adheres to the following conditions:

> Exactly three wines will be served each day.
>
> No wine can be served on three consecutive days.
>
> On any two consecutive days, each wine must be available at least once.
>
> Between Monday and Friday of any week, each of the wines must be available the same number of times.

20. If Merlot, Syrah, and Pinot Grigio are available on a Wednesday, which of the following could be the three wines available on Thursday of the same week?
(A) Merlot, Syrah, Pinot Grigio
(B) Chablis, Merlot, Syrah
(C) Chablis, Pinot Grigio, Syrah
(D) Beaujolais, Merlot, Pinot Grigio
(E) Beaujolais, Chablis, Pinot Grigio

21. If Beaujolais, Chablis, and Merlot are served on Monday, and if Merlot and Pinot Grigio are served on Thursday, then each of the following could be served on Wednesday EXCEPT
(A) Beaujolais
(B) Chablis
(C) Merlot
(D) Pinot Grigio
(E) Syrah

22. Which of the following could be true?
(A) The same three wines are available on Tuesday and Thursday.
(B) Merlot and Syrah are both served on Monday and Tuesday.
(C) Merlot and Syrah are both served on Monday and Thursday.
(D) Chablis and Beaujolais are never available on the same night.
(E) Neither Chablis nor Beaujolais is available on Wednesday or Friday.

23.   In any week for how many of the wines is it true that that wine is available on two consecutive days?

(A) 1   (D) 4
(B) 2   (E) 5
(C) 3

Questions 24–28

A family group consisting of two men, three women, and four children have front-row seats for a Broadway show, where they will all sit next to one another in seats 101 through 109. The decision as to who sits in which seats must conform to the following two conditions:

> The four children must sit next to one another, in four consecutive seats.
>
> The two men must sit next to each other.

24.   If a man is sitting in seat 107 and a woman is sitting in seat 108, which of the following could be the seat that another woman is sitting in?

(A) 101   (D) 104
(B) 102   (E) 106
(C) 103

25.   All three women will be sitting next to one another if a man is in which of the following seats?

(A) 101   (D) 107
(B) 104   (E) 109
(C) 105

26.   If women are sitting in seats 103 and 109, which of the following seats could be occupied by the third woman?

(A) 101   (D) 106
(B) 102   (E) 107
(C) 104

27.   If a child is in seat 101 and a woman is in seat 105, which of the following pairs of seats must be occupied by people not of the same sex?

(A) 105 and 106   (D) 106 and 108
(B) 105 and 107   (E) 108 and 109
(C) 106 and 107

28. If no woman is sitting next to another woman, which of the following must be true?

(A) A man is in seat 102.

(D) A woman is in seat 106.

(B) A woman is in seat 104.

(E) A man is in seat 108.

(C) A child is in seat 105.

Logical Reasoning

29. Josh's GPA is higher than Sam's, but is lower than Dalia's. Erin's GPA is lower than Dalia's and lower than Anne's. Blayke's GPA is higher than Anne's.

Which of the following statements, if true, is sufficient to determine which of the students has the highest GPA?

(A) Erin's GPA is lower than Sam's.

(B) Dalia's GPA is higher than Anne's.

(C) Blayke's GPA is higher than Josh's.

(D) The average of Blayke's and Anne's GPAs is higher than Dalia's GPA.

(E) The average of Dalia's and Anne's GPAs is lower than Josh's GPA.

30. The traffic on the Imperial Highway has always been slowed by the dangerous curves in the road. It was built when cars were much smaller and less powerful, and very few drivers traveled between Imperial City and Fremont. All this has changed. The cost of widening and straightening the road would now be many times greater than building the proposed new toll road on the borders of the Imperial Wetlands reserve. Environmentalists fear the construction noise and waste will harm the wildlife in the reserve, and have urged that the toll road not be constructed.

Which one of the following, if true, would most strengthen the case of the environmentalists?

(A) None of the animals living in the Imperial Wetlands is on the list of endangered species.

(B) The traffic congestion on the Imperial Highway increases each year.

(C) The cost of building the new road will be amortized in ten years by the tolls collected.

(D) There are several less direct routes the toll road could take between Fremont and Imperial City.

(E) The environmentalists threaten to bring a lawsuit in federal court to halt construction of the road.

Analytical Reasoning

Questions 31–34

A high school principal periodically creates committees to work on special projects. Each such committee consists of three faculty members drawn from the following five departments: English, Foreign Language, Mathematics, Science, and Social Studies. The composition of a committee must conform to the following conditions:

> No committee can consist entirely of teachers from the same department.
>
> A social studies teacher can serve on a particular committee if and only if a mathematics teacher is also on the committee.
>
> If a foreign language teacher is on a committee, an English teacher must also be on that committee.
>
> No committee can have teachers from both the English and the science departments.

31. Which of the following would have to be the third teacher on a committee that already has assigned to it a social studies and a science teacher?

(A) Another social studies teacher

(B) Another science teacher

(C) A mathematics teacher

(D) An English teacher

(E) A foreign language teacher

32. Which of the following would be an acceptable committee?

(A) Three foreign language teachers

(B) One teacher each from the Social Studies, Foreign Language, and English departments

(C) One teacher each from the Science, Foreign Language, and English departments

    (D) Two foreign language teachers and one English teacher

    (E) Two mathematics teachers and one foreign language teacher

33. Which is the only department that CANNOT have two of its teachers on a committee?

    (A) Social Studies

    (B) English

    (C) Science

    (D) Mathematics

    (E) Foreign Language

34. Which of the following could be the two other teachers serving on a committee with a teacher from the Foreign Language department?

    (A) Another teacher from Foreign Languages and one from Mathematics

    (B) One teacher each from the Social Studies and Mathematics departments

    (C) One teacher each from the Science and English departments

    (D) Two mathematics teachers

    (E) Two English teachers

Logical Reasoning

35. So many arrogant and ill-tempered young men have dominated the tennis courts of late that we had begun to fear those characteristics were prerequisites for championship tennis.

    Tennis used to be a gentleman's game. What is sad is not just that the game has changed. With so much importance placed on success, it may be that something has gone out of the American character—such things as gentleness and graciousness.

Which one of the following statements, if true, would most weaken the above argument?

    (A) The American character is a result of American goals.

    (B) Tennis has only recently become a professional sport.

    (C) Some ill-tempered tennis players are unsuccessful.

    (D) The "gentlemen" of early tennis were often arrogant and nasty off the court.

    (E) Some even-tempered tennis players are successful.

ANSWER KEY

Section 1—Verbal Ability

1.	A	6.	E	11.	D	16.	E	21.	C	26.	E
2.	B	7.	E	12.	B	17.	B	22.	B	27.	D
3.	D	8.	C	13.	D	18.	B	23.	B	28.	A
4.	A	9.	D	14.	A	19.	D	24.	E	29.	C
5.	D	10.	D	15.	D	20.	B	25.	D	30.	A

Section 2—Quantitative Ability

1.	D	6.	B	11.	C	16.	A	21.	B	26.	E
2.	D	7.	B	12.	A	17.	C	22.	D	27.	B
3.	D	8.	D	13.	A	18.	D	23.	D	28.	D
4.	C	9.	B	14.	B	19.	E	24.	C		
5.	B	10.	C	15.	B	20.	B	25.	C		

Section 3—Analytical Ability

1.	B	8.	E	15.	A	22.	C	29.	D
2.	E	9.	C	16.	D	23.	D	30.	D
3.	D	10.	E	17.	D	24.	A	31.	C
4.	C	11.	C	18.	E	25.	C	32.	D
5.	A	12.	E	19.	A	26.	C	33.	C
6.	C	13.	A	20.	E	27.	D	34.	E
7.	B	14.	C	21.	D	28.	C	35.	D

ANSWER EXPLANATIONS

Section 1—Verbal Ability

1. **A.**   *Elated* (joyful, in high spirits) is the opposite of *crestfallen* (dejected).
   Think of "elated by her success."

2. **B.**   The opposite of *reticence* (uncommunicativeness; restraint in speech) is *loquaciousness* (talkativeness).
   Think of "speaking without reticence."

3. **D.** If "you may wonder" how the expert reaches his conclusions, it appears that it is questionable to rely on teeth for guidance in interpreting fossils. Choice D, *inadequate*, creates the element of doubt that the clause tries to develop. Choice C, *specious*, also creates an element of doubt; however, nothing in the context justifies the idea that the reasoning is specious or false.

   Note that here you are dealing with an extended metaphor. Picture yourself hanging a heavy winter coat on a slim wooden peg. Wouldn't you worry that the peg might prove inadequate or flimsy?

4. **A.** Here the task is to determine the communal reaction to crime. The writer maintains that the criminal justice system of punishments allows the community to purge itself of its anger, its sense of *outrage* at the criminal's acts. Thus, it provides a *catharsis* or purgation for the community.

   Remember, in double-blank sentences, go through the answers, testing the first word in each choice and eliminating those that don't fit. In this case, you can readily eliminate choices B and E: it is unlikely that an *essential* purpose of the criminal justice system would be the provision of either a *disclaimer* (denial or disavowal, as in disavowing responsibility for a legal claim) or a *document*.

5. **D.** Someone *vindictive* or vengeful is lacking in *mercy*. Someone *skeptical* or suspicious is lacking in *trustfulness*.
   (Antonym Variant)

6. **E.** To *ruffle* someone's *composure* is to disturb or trouble his self-possession. To *upset* someone's *equilibrium* is to disturb or trouble his balance. (Function)

7. **E.** The last sentence points out that Du Bois originally agreed with Washington's program.

   Choice A is incorrect. Nothing in the passage suggests that Du Bois sacrificed effective strategies out of a desire to try something new.

Choice B is incorrect. Du Bois gained in influence, effectively winning away large numbers of blacks from Washington's policies.

Choice C is incorrect. Du Bois' quickness to depart from conventional black wisdom when it proved inadequate to the task of advancing the race shows him to be well able to change with the times.

Choice D is incorrect. Washington, not Du Bois, is described as seeking the good will of powerful whites.

8. **C.**   The author does *not* portray Washington as versatile. Instead, he portrays Du Bois as versatile.

Choice A is incorrect. The author portrays Washington as submissive to the majority; he shows him teaching blacks not to protest.

Choice B is incorrect. The author portrays Washington as concerned with financial success; he shows him advocating property accumulation.

Choice D is incorrect. The author portrays Washington as traditional in preaching industry; he shows him advocating hard work.

Choice E is incorrect. The author portrays Washington as respectful of authority; he shows him deferring to powerful whites.

9. **D.**   Although the author points out that Du Bois' methods led him into conflicts, he describes Du Bois as "often...well in advance of his contemporaries" and stresses that his motives for departing from the mainstream were admirable. Thus, his attitude can best be described as *approving*.

10. **D.**   To *revile* (verbally abuse) something is the opposite of *praising* it.

Think of "reviled as a traitor."

11. **D.**   The opposite of *propitious* (favorable, advantageous) is *unfavorable*.

Think of being pleased by "propitious omens."

12. **B.** An *offhand* remark is made without forethought or *premeditation*. An *aboveboard* (open) deed is done without trickery or *guile*. (Antonym Variant)

13. **D.** The *larval* (immature) stage of an *insect* best corresponds to the *embryonic* stage of a *mammal*.
(Defining Characteristic)

14. **A.** Under certain circumstances scientists attack each other with *ad hominem* arguments (personal attacks) and shameless appeals. When is this likely to occur? When facts are *established* or *demonstrable* or *ineluctable* (unavoidable)? Hardly. Under such circumstances they would rely on facts to establish their case. It is when facts prove *elusive* that they lose control and, in doing so, abandon their pretense of *objectivity*.

15. **D.** The key word here is *assailed*. Housman is attacking his rival. Thus he is in the tradition of scholarly *invective* (vehement verbal attack), criticizing his foe for turning to manuscripts merely for confirmation or *support* of old theories and not for enlightenment or illumination.
Again, note the use of figurative language, in this case the simile of the drunkard.

16. **E.** The author first states that the reasons for bioluminescence in underwater microorganisms is obscure and then proceeds to enumerate various hypotheses.

17. **B.** The author does not deny that predators make use of bioluminescence in locating their prey. Instead, he gives an example of human predators who are drawn to their prey (the fish that prey on plankton) by the luminescence of the plankton.

18. **B.** As the previous answer makes clear, the phenomenon of plankton bioluminescence does have practical applications. It is a valuable tool for fisheries interested in increasing their catch of fish that prey on plankton.

19. **D.**   The opposite of *incongruous* (inconsistent, not fitting) is *harmonious*.
Think of being startled by "incongruous behavior."

20. **B.**   An *apostate* (renegade; person faithless to an allegiance) is the opposite of a *loyalist*.
Beware eye-catchers. Do not confuse *apostate* (renegade) with *apostle* (missionary; reformer).
Think of "a faithless apostate."

21. **C.**   By definition, a *sextant* is a piece of equipment that is *nautical*. Similarly, a *forceps* is a piece of equipment that is *surgical*.   (Defining Characteristic)

22. **B.**   Someone *refractory* (stubborn; unmanageable) by definition is hard to *manage*. Likewise, someone *lethargic* (sluggish; drowsy) by definition is hard to *stimulate*.   (Definition)

23. **B.**   The opposite of to *ensue* (happen later, follow) is to *precede*.
Think of "the wedding that ensued."

24. **E.**   A disease in a *latent* state has yet to manifest itself and emerge into view. Therefore it is impossible to *observe*.
Remember, in double-blank sentences, go through the answers, testing the *first* word in each choice and eliminating those that don't fit. When a disease is in a *critical* or *acute* state, its existence is obvious. Therefore, you can eliminate choices B and C.

25. **D.**   The second clause presents an example of literary *mockery*. The abstract idea of preserving a nugget of pure truth is appealing; the concrete example of setting it up on the mantel makes fun of the whole idea.

26. **E.**   The eagle is poised to strike "with exposed talons." It, like the Cardinal, collects itself to strike with greater force. The imagery accentuates the Cardinal's *mercilessness*.
Choice A is incorrect. The Cardinal is not *flighty* (light-headed and irresponsible); he is cold and calculating.
Choice B is incorrect. He loves power, not freedom.

Choice C is incorrect. An eagle poised to strike with bare claws suggests violence, not *eminence* (fame and high position).

Choice D is incorrect. Nothing in the passage suggests he is spiritual.

Beware eye-catchers. "Eminence" is a title of honor applied to cardinals in the Roman Catholic church. Choice D may attract you for this reason.

27. **D.** The author's depiction of the Cardinal stresses his redoubtable qualities as a foe (calculation, duplicity, merci-lessness) and as a challenge to an actor ("imperial repose," a commanding presence, smooth movements suggesting latent danger).

Choice A is incorrect. The author portrays the Cardinal's relations with his brother and mistress as cold, but he never apologizes for the Cardinal's lack of warmth. Indeed, the author somewhat savors it.

Choices B and C are incorrect. Neither esteem for a nonex-istent spirituality nor admiration for a villainous autocracy enters into the author's depiction of the Cardinal.

Choice E is incorrect. A cause of perturbation to others, the Cardinal is never perturbed.

28. **A.** An *austere style* is severely simple and restrained. *Controlled movement* is restrained as well.

(Defining Characteristic)

29. **C.** *Retrospection* (looking backward; the act of surveying the past) is the opposite of *anticipation* (looking forward).

Word Parts Clue: *Retro-* means backward; *spect-* means look. *Retrospection* means looking backward.

Think of "an old man lost in retrospection."

30. **A.** *Topical* (local, temporary) is the opposite of *general*.

Remember that words may be used in several different ways. Here *topical* does not mean arranged according to topics (as in a topical index).

Think of "a topical anesthetic," one applied locally, not generally.

Section 2—Quantitative Ability

Two asterisks (**) indicate an alternative method of solving.

1. **D.** Could m and n be equal? Sure, if each is 5. Eliminate choices A and B. Must they be equal? No, not if $m = 1$ and $n = 25$. Eliminate Choice C, as well. Neither column is always greater, and the two columns are not always equal (D).

2. **D.** Since $\frac{2}{3} = 66\frac{2}{3}\%$, which is clearly more than 65%, it *appears* that Column B is greater. *Be careful!* That would be true if a were positive, but no restrictions are placed on a. If $a = 0$, the columns are equal; if a is negative, Column A is greater. Neither column is always greater, and the two columns are not always equal (D).
   **Just let $a = 0$, and then let $a = 1$.

3. **D.** Could the columns be equal? Could $c = 5$? Sure, if this is a 3-4-5 right triangle. Must $c = 5$? No; if the triangle is not a right triangle, c could be less than or more than 5. Neither column is always greater, and the columns are not always equal (D). (Note: Since the figure may not be drawn to scale, do not assume that the triangle has a right angle.)

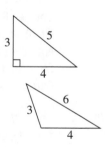

4. **C.** Column A: $(a + b)^2 = a^2 + 2ab + b^2 = a^2 + b^2$ (since $ab = 0$). Column B: $(a - b)^2 = a^2 - 2ab + b^2 = a^2 + b^2$ (since $ab = 0$). The columns are equal (C).
   **Let $a = 0$ and $b = 1$. Then $(a + b)^2 = (0 + 1)^2 = 1$ and $(a - b)^2 = (0 - 1)^2 = 1$. Eliminate (A) and (B) and try other values where either a or b is 0 (since $ab = 0$). The two expressions are always equal.

5. **B.** Since d divisions each have t teams, multiply to get dt teams; and since each team has p players, multiply the number of teams (dt) by p to get the total number of players: dtp.

**Pick three easy-to-use numbers for t, d, and p. Assume that there are 2 divisions, each consisting of 4 teams, so, there are $2 \times 4 = 8$ teams. Then assume that each team has 10 players, for a total of $8 \times 10 = 80$ players. Now check the choices. Which one is equal to 80 when $d = 2$, $t = 4$, and $p = 10$? Only dtp.

6. **B.** There are nine positive integers less than 10:

1, 2, ... , 9. For which of them is $\frac{9}{x} > x$? Only 1 and 2: $\frac{9}{1} > 1$

and $\frac{9}{2} > 2$. When $x = 3$, $\frac{9}{x} = x$, and for all the others $\frac{9}{x} < x$.

The probability is $\frac{2}{9}$.

7. **B.** Solve the given equation: $\qquad\qquad \frac{1}{a} + \frac{1}{a} + \frac{1}{a} = 12$

Add the fractions: $\qquad\qquad\qquad\qquad\qquad \frac{3}{a} = 12$

Multiply both sides by a: $\qquad\qquad\qquad 3 = 12a$

Divide both sides by 12: $\qquad\qquad a = \frac{3}{12} = \frac{1}{4}$

**Backsolve: try Choice C. If $a = \frac{1}{3}$, then $\frac{1}{a} = 3$, so the left-hand side equals 9. That's too small. Now, be careful: a fraction gets bigger when its denominator gets *smaller*. Eliminate choices C, D, and E, and try a smaller value for a: $\frac{1}{4}$ works.

8. **D.** Could $y = 20$? Yes, if the large triangle were equilateral, x would be 30 and y would be 20. Must $y = 20$? No, if $x = 45$, $y = 10$. (Note: Since the figure may not be drawn to scale, the triangle could be any triangle with a 60° angle.) Neither column is always larger, and the columns are not always equal (D).

9. **B.**   You don't *have* to solve for a and b. If $a - b > a + b$, then b is negative and Column B is greater.
**You *could* solve. Adding the two equations yields
$$2a = 49 \Rightarrow a = 24.5 \Rightarrow b = -.5.$$

10. **C.**   Since, in 1990, $2p$ pounds of potatoes cost $\frac{1}{2}d$ dollars, p pounds cost half as much: $\frac{1}{2}\left(\frac{1}{2}d\right) = \frac{1}{4}d$. This is $\frac{1}{4}$, or 25%, as much as the cost in 1980, which represents a decrease of 75%.
**In this type of problem it is *often* easier to use numbers. Assume that 1 pound of potatoes cost $100 in 1980. Then in 1990, 2 pounds cost $50, so 1 pound cost $25. This is a decrease of $75 in the cost of 1 pound of potatoes, and
$$\text{percent decrease} = \frac{\text{decrease}}{\text{original}}(100\%)$$
$$= \frac{75}{100}(100\%) = 75\%.$$

11. **C.**   Adding the two given equations, we get $a + b + c = 11d$. Then $a + b + c + d = 11d + d = 12d \Rightarrow \dfrac{a + b + c + d}{4} = \dfrac{12d}{4} = 3d$.
The columns are equal (C).

12. **A.**   Since in the given figure OA and OB are radii, each is equal to 5. With no restrictions on x, AB could be any positive number less than 10; and the larger x is, the larger AB is. If x were 90, AB would be $5\sqrt{2}$, but we are told that $x > 90$, so $AB > 5\sqrt{2} > 7$.

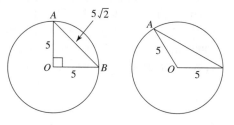

13. **A.**   Column B = $\left(\dfrac{13}{17}\right)^5 = (x^5)^5 = x^{25}$. Since $0 < x < 1$, $x^{25} < x$.

14. **B.** The average expected family contribution of a family with an income between $50,000 and $59,000 is about $7,500. Since the average cost of attending a 4-year public university is $10,800, there is an unmet need of $10,800 − $7,500 = $3,300.

15. **B.** Family A would be expected to pay $10,800, the full annual cost for a 4-year public university. Family B would be expected to pay approximately $3,500. Therefore, family A would pay $10,800 − $3,500 = $7,300 more.

16. **A.** Since $a < b$, when a is divided by b, the quotient is 0 and the remainder is a: $a = 0 \times b + a$. When any integer is divided by a, the remainder must be less than a. Column A is greater.

17. **C.** In Figure 1, since the radius of each circle is 3, the area of each circle is 9π, and the total area of the four circles is 36π. In Figure 2, the radius of each circle is 2, and so the area of each circle is 4π, and the total area of the nine circles is 36π. In the two figures, the white areas are equal, as are the shaded areas. The columns are equal (C).

18. **D.** If Jason were really unlucky, what could go wrong in his attempt to get one marble of each color? Well, his first nine picks *might* yield five blue marbles and four white ones. But then the tenth marble would be red, and now he would have at least one of each color. The answer is 10.

19. **E.** If a represents Jordan's average after 5 tests, then he has earned a total of $5a$ points. A grade of 70 on the sixth test will lower his average 4 points to $a − 4$. Therefore,

$$a - 4 = \frac{5a + 70}{6} \Rightarrow 6(a - 4) = 5a + 70 \Rightarrow$$
$$6a - 24 = 5a + 70 \Rightarrow 6a = 5a + 94 \Rightarrow a = 94.$$

**Assume Jordan's average is a because he earned a on each of his first 5 tests. Since after getting a 70 on his sixth test his average will be $a − 4$, the deviation on each of the first 5 tests is 4, for a total deviation above the average

of 20 points. So, the total deviation below must also be 20. Therefore, 70 is 20 less than the new average of $a - 4$:
$$70 = (a - 4) - 20 \Rightarrow a = 94.$$
**Backsolve. Start with Choice C, 86. If his 5-test average was 90, he had 450 points and a 70 on the sixth test would give him a total of 520 points, and an average of $520 \div 6 = 86.666$. So, the 70 lowered his average 3.333 points. That's not enough. Eliminate choices A, B, and C. Try choices D or E. Choice E, 94, works.

20. **B.** Reading from the top graph, we get the following enrollment figures:

	1970	1988
Public PreK–8	33,000,000	28,000,000
Public 9–12	13,000,000	12,000,000
Private PreK–8	4,000,000	4,000,000
Private 9–12	1,000,000	1,000,000
Total	51,000,000	45,000,000

$51,000,000 - 45,000,000 = 6,000,000$.

21. **B.** In 1988, 8,800,000 (22% of 40,000,000) students lived in the West. From 1988–1998 this figure increased by 27%—for simplicity use 25%: an additional 2,200,000 students; so the total was then 11,000,000. The projected increase from 1998–2008 is about 10%, so the number will grow by 1,100,000 to 12,100,000.

22. **D.** Expand:
$$(a + b)^2 = a^2 + 2ab + b^2 = (a^2 + b^2) + 2ab.$$
By the Pythagorean theorem, $a^2 + b^2 = 10^2 = 100$; and since the area is 20, $\frac{1}{2}ab = 20 \Rightarrow ab = 40$, and $2ab = 80$. Then
$$(a^2 + b^2) + 2ab = 100 + 80 = 180.$$

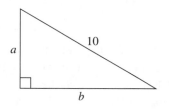

23. **D.**   Let r, C, and A represent the radius, circumference, and area of the circle.

$$C = 2\pi r = a\pi \Rightarrow a = \frac{2\pi r}{\pi} = 2r.$$

Similarly,

$$A = \pi r^2 = b\pi \Rightarrow b = \frac{\pi r^2}{\pi} = r^2.$$

The value of Column A is $2r$, and the value of Column B is r^2. Which is greater? Dividing each by r, yields 2 in Column A and r in Column B. Since there are no restrictions, r could be greater than, less than, or equal to r. Neither column is always greater, and the two columns are not always equal (D).
**Let $r = 1$. Then, $C = 2\pi$ and $A = \pi$; so $a = 2$ and $b = 1$. Column B is greater: eliminate (A) and (C). Try $r = 2$. Now, $C = 4\pi$ and $A = 4\pi$; $a = b$ and the columns are equal. Eliminate Choice B. The answer is (D).

24. **C.**   If r is the radius of the white circle, $2r$ is the radius of the shaded semicircle. The area of the white circle is πr^2. The area of the semicircle is $\frac{1}{2}\pi(2r)^2 = \frac{1}{2}\pi(4r^2) = 2\pi r^2$, so the area of the shaded region is $2\pi r^2 - \pi r^2 = \pi r^2$. The columns are equal (C).

**The solution is even easier if you let the radius of the circle be 1 instead of r, and proceed as above. The area of each region is π.

25. **C.**   If there are x seats on each bus, then the group is using $\frac{4}{5}(3x) = \frac{12}{5}x$ seats. After $\frac{1}{4}$ of them get off, $\frac{3}{4}$ of them, or $\frac{3}{4}\left(\frac{12}{5}x\right) = \frac{9}{5}x$ remain.

What fraction of the $2x$ seats on the two buses are now being used? $\dfrac{\frac{9}{5}x}{2x} = \dfrac{\frac{9}{5}}{2} = \dfrac{9}{10}$.

**To avoid the algebra, assume there are 20 seats on each bus. At the beginning, the group is using 48 of the 60 seats on the three buses $\left[\frac{4}{5}(60) = 48\right]$. When 12 people left $\left[\frac{1}{4}(48) = 12\right]$, the 36 remaining people used $\frac{36}{40} = \frac{9}{10}$ of the 40 seats on two buses.

26. **E.** To find the average of three numbers, divide their sum by 3: $\frac{3^{30} + 3^{60} + 3^{90}}{3}$. Now use the distributive law and divide each term in the numerator by 3: $\frac{3^{30}}{3} + \frac{3^{60}}{3} + \frac{3^{90}}{3} = 3^{29} + 3^{59} + 3^{89}$.

27. **B.** In the given figure, the diameters of the four small semi-circles are 2, 4, 6, and 8, so the diameter of the large semicircle is 2 + 4 + 6 + 8 = 20, and its radius is 10. The perimeter of the shaded region is the sum of the circumferences of all five semicircles. Since the circumference of a semicircle is π times its radius, the perimeter is $\pi + 2\pi + 3\pi + 4\pi + 10\pi = 20\pi$.

28. **D.** Let B be the sum of all the positive odd intergers less than 1000.
$A = 2 + 4 + 6 + 8 + \ldots + 996 + 998$
$\quad \downarrow \ \downarrow \ \downarrow \ \downarrow \qquad \ \ \downarrow \qquad \downarrow$
$B = (1 + 3 + 5 + 7 + \ldots + 995 + 997) + 999$
A is the sum of 499 even integers, each of which is 1 more than the corresponding odd integer in B. Then $(1 + 3 + 5 + \ldots + 997) = A - 499$, and $B = (A - 499) + 999 = A + 500$.

Section 3—Analytical Ability

1. **B.** To speak in positive terms about the increase in school degrees, the author must assume that the degrees indicate what they are supposed to indicate, that is, well-educated individuals. Choices A and E are empty statements; choices C and D are altogether unsubstantiated by either expressed or implied information.

Solutions 2–5

$$L < K < H \qquad I > J \qquad F > H \qquad G > H$$

Exhibiting this information on a line, we see:

lowest GPA _____ L   K   H   F _____ highest GPA
—G→
←J———I→

2. **E.** From the line we drew based on the given conditions, we see that any of F, G, or I could have the highest GPA, so any one of choices A, B, and C could be true. F, G, and H all have GPAs higher than K's, and I (and even J) could have a higher GPA, so Choice D could be true. At most there are three students (L, J, and I) who could have a lower GPA than K, so Choice E cannot be true.

3. **D.** From the line we drew based on the given conditions, we know that either J or L has the lowest GPA. Clearly, if J has a higher GPA than K (Choice D), then J's GPA cannot be lowest; so L's is. None of the other choices permits us to distinguish definitively between J and L.

4. **C.** From the line we drew based on the given conditions, we know that the correct order of F, G, H, K, L is either:

   L K H G F   or   L K H F G

   • Since J > F and it is given that I > J, in the first case, there is only one possibility: L K H G F J I.
   In the second case, there are three possibilities:
   • J and I could both be between F and G: L K H F J I G;
   • J and I could both be greater than G: L K H F G J I;
   • J could be between F and G, and I greater than G: L K H F J G I

   In all, there are four possible rankings.

5. **A.** Since both F and G have higher GPAs than H, the average of their GPAs is higher than H's, which is higher than I's. Choice A, therefore cannot be true. None of the other choices must be true, but each of them could be true.

6. **C.** The passage argues that environmental restrictions will lead to losses of jobs and hence workers, but if workers are already leaving because the environmental quality is poor, the argument is seriously weakened.

7. **B.** The passage makes no comment on workers leaving before a manufacturer. It argues that the loss of manufacturers leads to a loss of workers (E).

8. **E.** We know who *must* do the extra-credit project; we do not know if Mr. Walsh will permit other students to do the extra-credit project, as well. Eliminate choices A and C. Despite the fact that at least one student earned a 97, the class average could be below 75, and most of the students in the class will have to do the extra-credit project. Eliminate choices B and D. Choice E is true: even though John did all his labs, his test grade was below 75, and so he must do the extra-credit project.

Solutions 9–13

9, 10, 11, Lunch, 1, 2, 3

$J = 1{:}00$ $G \ll I$ or $I \ll G$ $H < F$

9. **C.** Since H must be interviewed earlier in the day than F ($H < F$), H cannot have the last interview of the day.

10. **E.** Only Choice E doesn't violate any of the given conditions.
Choice A violates the condition that J have the fourth interview ($J = 1{:}00$).
Choices B and D violate the condition that no one be interviewed between G and I ($G \ll I$ or $I \ll G$).
Choice C violates the condition that H be interviewed earlier in the day than F ($H < F$).

11. **C.** Since J has the 1:00 interview, and H and K both have morning interviews, the slots remaining for F, G, and I are the remaining morning slot and 2:00 and 3:00. Since G and I have interviews one after the other, they must have the last two interviews of the day. F cannot have the last interview; Choice C cannot be true.

12. **E.** Given that J and F are being interviewed at 1:00 and 2:00, respectively, H cannot have the 3:00 interview (H < F). Also, since G and I must have consecutive interviews, neither of them can be interviewed at 3:00. Therefore, K must have the 3:00 interview. Each of the other choices is possible, but none *must* be true.

13. **A.** Since I has the 9:00 interview, G has an interview at 10:00 (I << G). Since H's interview must precede F's interview (H < F), F cannot have the 11:00 interview, and so must have an interview at either 2:00 or 3:00, after J's 1:00 interview.

14. **C.** Examine the structure of the argument: the only reason given for funding the research is that the possibility exists that the substances cure cancer. The unstated assumption is that this is a sufficient reason for providing funds. No probability is mentioned (Choice A), and no comparison with other lines of research is made (Choice B). Choice D, while probably true, does not provide logical support for the argument about researching this specific possibility. The argument simply says that the government should provide the funds, not that they are definitely unavailable elsewhere (Choice E).

Solutions 15–18

Rep: A, B, C, D   Dem: R, S, T   Days: M, T, W, Th, F
each day: 1 Rep & 1 Dem or 2 Rep & 2 Dem
no one on 2 consec. days
Fri $\rightarrow (A \wedge R)$ R $\rightarrow$ ~S   B $\leftrightarrow$ T

15. **A.** Only Choice A doesn't violate any of the conditions.
Since neither Berg nor Tyler will attend a session unless the other does (B $\leftrightarrow$ T), eliminate choices B, C, and E. Since there can't be three Republicans and one Democrat, eliminate Choice D.

16. **D.** In the solution to question 15, we saw that Berg and Tyler also had to be in attendance on Friday. No one attending on Friday can attend on Thursday. The only Democrat not attending Friday's session is Sack, who, therefore, must attend on Thursday.

17. **D.** The three Democrats—Ray, Sack, and Tyler—each had to attend one of the sessions from Wednesday to Friday. Ash attended on Friday, and Berg attended with Tyler on either Wednesday or Thursday. Either Cox or Day attended with Sack, and the other attended on Tuesday. Day isn't one of the choices, so the answer is Choice D: Cox

18. **E.** Since Berg attended on Tuesday, so did Tyler (B ↔ T). Therefore, Tyler could not have attended on Monday.

19. **A.** The apparent contradiction disappears if the total state budget has increased enough so that the *expenditure* on education has been raised by three million each year while at the same time the *percentage* spent on education is a smaller part of the whole budget.

Solutions 20–23

Wines: B, C, M, P, S   Days: M, T, W, Th, F
each day: 3 wines   no wine on 3 consec. days
no wine can skip 2 days in a row
each wine: 3 times/week

20. **E.** Since neither Beaujolais nor Chablis were available on Wednesday, both must be available on Thursday. Only Choice E includes both Beaujolais and Chablis.

21. **D.** Since Beaujolais, Chablis, and Merlot are served on Monday, Pinot Grigio must be served on Tuesday; and since it is given that Pinot Grigio is served on Thursday, it *cannot* be served on Wednesday, since no wine can be served on three consecutive days.

22. **C.** Only Choice C doesn't violate any of the conditions.
   • If the same three wines are available on Tuesday and Thursday, none of them could be available on Wednesday (since no wine is served on three consecutive days), which would mean that only two wines (not three) would be available on Wednesday. Eliminate Choice A.

- If Merlot and Syrah are both served on Monday and Tuesday, then of the three other wines, one could be served on Monday and one on Tuesday, but the third would could not be served on either day. Eliminate Choice B.
- Since Chablis and Beaujolais are each available three times a week, there must be at least one day that both are available. Eliminate Choice D.
- If neither Chablis nor Beaujolais is available on Wednesday or Friday, then the other three wines are available on both of those days. This is the same situation as in Choice A. Eliminate Choice E.

23. **D.**   There are only four pairs of consecutive days: Monday-Tuesday, Tuesday-Wednesday, Wednesday-Thursday, and Thursday-Friday. Since there are only five wines, and on any pair of days there are six wines available, on each pair of days there must be one wine which is available on both days. So there must be at least four wines that are available consecutively. If two different wines were available on the same two consecutive days, only two of the other three wines would be available on either of those days, which is impossible. Therefore, at most four of the wines can be available on two consecutive days. The answer is 4 (D).

Solutions 24–28

M, M, W, W, W, C, C, C, C

C << C << C << C   M << M

24. **A.**   Since the two men must sit next to each other, a man is sitting in seat 106. Eliminate Choice E. Since the four children must sit in consecutive seats, they must be in seats 101–104 or 102–105; in either case, they occupy seats 102, 103, and 104. Eliminate choices B, C, and D.

	C	C	C		M	M	W	
101	102	103	104	105	106	107	108	109

25. **C.**   If a man is in seat 105, then there are four seats on either side of him. On one side, the four seats must be used by the four children. On the other side, the seat next to the

first man is reserved for the second man, and the next three seats would be for the women.

C C C C M M W W W or W W W M M C C C C
      105   105

26. **C.** The four children must be in seats 104–107 or 105–108; so they must occupy seats 105, 106, and 107:

W			C	C	C		W
101	102	103	104	105	106	107	108	109

Since the two men must sit next to each other, they occupy seats 101 and 102. The third woman could sit in either 104 or 108, with the fourth child in the other one.

27. **B.** The children occupy seats 101–104 and the adults occupy seats 105–109. The two men must be in seats 106–107, 107–108, or 108–109. In the first case, a man is in seat 106, and a woman is in seat 108; in the second and third cases, a man is in seat 108 and a woman is in seat 106.

28. **C.** If no woman is next to another woman, the women must be separated by the groups of children and men. Therefore, they must be in seats 101, 109, and either 104 or 106:

W	C	C	C	C	W	M	M	W
101	102	103	104	105	106	107	108	109

or

W	M	M	W	C	C	C	C	W
101	102	103	104	105	106	107	108	109

In either case, a child is in seat 105.

29. **D.** From the given statements we see that:

$$S < J < D \quad E < D \quad E < A < B$$

Therefore, either Dalia or Blayke has the highest GPA. If the average of Blayke's and Anne's GPAs is higher than Dalia's GPA, then either Blayke or Anne has a GPA which is higher than Dalia's and the other has a GPA which is lower than Dalia's. Since Blayke's GPA is higher than Anne's, it must be Blayke who has the highest GPA. None of the other choices allows us to determine whose GPA is the highest.

30. **D.**   Choices A, B, and C strengthen the case for building the toll road. The environmentalists may be able to make their case for one of the other possible routes that, if less direct, would not disturb the reserve. With the information we have, the value of Choice E is indeterminable.

Solutions 31–34

each committee <u>exactly 3</u> from E, F, M, S, SS
2 teachers from the same department OK—but <u>not</u> 3
SS $\leftrightarrow$ M   F $\rightarrow$ E   E $\rightarrow$ ~S (equivalently: S $\rightarrow$ ~E)

31. **C.**   Any committee containing a social studies teacher, must also have a mathematics teacher [SS $\leftrightarrow$ M].

32. **D.**   Only Choice D does not violate any of the given conditions.
Choice A includes three teachers from the same department.
Choice B includes a social studies teacher, but not a mathematics teacher [SS $\leftrightarrow$ M].
Choice C includes teachers from both the Science and English departments [E $\rightarrow$ ~S].
Choice E includes a mathematics teacher but not a social studies teacher [SS $\leftrightarrow$ M].

33. **C.**   Assume that there were two science teachers:
   - The third teacher could not be another science teacher, since all three teachers cannot be from the same department.
   - The third teacher could not be an English teacher [S $\rightarrow$ ~E].
   - Since any committee with a social studies teacher or a mathematics teacher must have teachers from both departments [SS $\leftrightarrow$ M], and since there is room for only one more teacher, that teacher could not be from either department.
   - The third teacher could not be from the Foreign Language department since then there would have to be a teacher from the English department [F $\rightarrow$ E].

- Each of the other departments could have two of its members on a committee.

34. **E.** Only Choice E does not violate any of the given conditions.
    - Since any committee with a foreign language teacher must also have an English teacher [F → E], eliminate choices A, B, and D.
    - Since no committee can have teachers from both the Science and the English departments [S → ~E], eliminate Choice C.

35. **D.** The choice repudiates the suggestion that gentleness and graciousness were once part of the American character. B, another choice worth considering, is not best because it does not address the temperament of tennis players as directly as does Choice D.

Majortests.com

Number2.com

www.nosh.com

www.testpractice.net

www.my-gre.com/GRE Online Verbal Test.html

www.testfever.com/viewtopic.php?t=272.

↳ free downloads.

www.mnemonicdictionary.com

gre-spot-blogspot.com/2009/08/gre-verbal-words